I0788269

Agent-Based Modelling
in Economics

Agent-Based Modelling
in Economics

Lynne Hamill and Nigel Gilbert

Centre for Research in Social Simulation (CRESS),
University of Surrey, UK

This edition first published 2016
© 2016 John Wiley & Sons, Ltd.

Registered Office
John Wiley & Sons, Ltd, The Atrium, Southern Gate, Chichester, West Sussex, PO19 8SQ, United Kingdom

For details of our global editorial offices, for customer services and for information about how to apply for permission to reuse the copyright material in this book please see our website at www.wiley.com.

The right of the author to be identified as the author of this work has been asserted in accordance with the Copyright, Designs and Patents Act 1988.

All rights reserved. No part of this publication may be reproduced, stored in a retrieval system, or transmitted, in any form or by any means, electronic, mechanical, photocopying, recording or otherwise, except as permitted by the UK Copyright, Designs and Patents Act 1988, without the prior permission of the publisher.

Wiley also publishes its books in a variety of electronic formats. Some content that appears in print may not be available in electronic books.

Designations used by companies to distinguish their products are often claimed as trademarks. All brand names and product names used in this book are trade names, service marks, trademarks or registered trademarks of their respective owners. The publisher is not associated with any product or vendor mentioned in this book.

Limit of Liability/Disclaimer of Warranty: While the publisher and author have used their best efforts in preparing this book, they make no representations or warranties with respect to the accuracy or completeness of the contents of this book and specifically disclaim any implied warranties of merchantability or fitness for a particular purpose. It is sold on the understanding that the publisher is not engaged in rendering professional services and neither the publisher nor the author shall be liable for damages arising herefrom. If professional advice or other expert assistance is required, the services of a competent professional should be sought.

Library of Congress Cataloging-in-Publication data applied for

ISBN: 9781118456071

A catalogue record for this book is available from the British Library.

Set in 9/11pt Times by SPi Global, Pondicherry, India
Printed and bound in Singapore by Markono Print Media Pte Ltd

1   2016

Contents

Preface

This book is an introduction to the power of using agent-based modelling (ABM) in economics. This is sometimes referred to as multi-agent modelling and in the context of economics, ACE, standing for Agent-based Computational Economics.

The book takes some of the usual topics covered in an undergraduate economics textbook and demonstrates how ABM can complement more traditional approaches to economic modelling and better link the micro and the macro.

This book is designed to appeal to:

- Trained economists who want an introduction to ABM

- Masters and doctoral students and researchers considering using ABM in their research

- Students in their third year of undergraduate study, either as the primary reading for a self-contained module on simulation approaches or as a starting point for an undergraduate dissertation.

We expect that most readers will be familiar with the basics of standard economics, up to the equivalent of a second-year undergraduate, but throughout, we give pointers to where more background can be found.

Thanks to colleagues in CRESS – Jen Badham, Tina Balke and Peter Johnson – and to Paul Levine and Creighton Redman.

Copyright notices

Data adapted from the Office for National Statistics is licensed under the Open Government Licence v.3.0.

Some of the material on social circles presented in Chapter 4 was previously published in 2010 in the journal *Emergence: Complexity and Emergence* by Institute for the Study of Coherence and Emergence and remains their copyright.

1

Why agent-based modelling is useful for economists

1.1 Introduction

This book provides an introduction to the power of using agent-based modelling (ABM) in economics. (ABM is sometimes referred to as multi-agent modelling and, in the context of economics, agent-based computational economics (ACE)). It takes some of the usual topics covered in undergraduate economics and demonstrates how ABM can complement more traditional approaches to economic modelling and better link the micro and the macro.

This chapter starts with a brief review of the history of economic modelling to set the context. There follows an outline of ABM: how it works and its strengths. Finally, we set out the plan for the rest of the book.

1.2 A very brief history of economic modelling

> The Method I take to do this, is not yet very usual; for instead of using only compar-
> ative and superlative Words, and intellectual Arguments, I have taken the course
> (as a Specimen of the Political Arithmetick I have long aimed at) to express my self
> in Terms of Number, Weight, or Measure; to use only Arguments of Sense, and to
> consider only such Causes, as have visible Foundations in Nature.
>
> Sir William Petty (1690)

Whether Sir William Petty was the first economic modeller is arguable. Was Quesnay's *Tableau Economique* dated 1767 the first macroeconomic model? Or Ricardo's 1821 model of a farm the first microeconomic model? (Those interested in these early models should read Morgan,

---

Agent-Based Modelling in Economics, First Edition. Lynne Hamill and Nigel Gilbert.
© 2016 John Wiley & Sons, Ltd. Published 2016 by John Wiley & Sons, Ltd.

2012, pp.3–8.) Nevertheless, books of political economy such as Smith's *Wealth of Nations* (1776) or Marshall's *Principles of Economics* (1920) had no modelling or mathematics. There is almost none in Keynes's *General Theory of Employment, Interest and Money* (1936).

Traditional macroeconomic models

For our purposes, we shall start with the macroeconomic models produced in the 1930s by Frisch and Tinbergen (Morgan, 2012, p.10). These models comprised a set of equations relying on correlations between time series generated from the national accounts. There was no formal link between these macroeconomic models and microeconomic analysis despite the traditional view that 'the laws of the aggregate depend of course upon the laws applying to individual cases' (Jevons, 1888, Chapter 3, para 20). Not all saw benefit in these new models. For example, Hayek (1931, p.5) wrote:

> …neither aggregates nor averages do act upon each other, and it will never be possible to establish necessary connections of cause and effect between them as we can between individual phenomena, individual prices, etc. I would even go as far as to assert that, from the very nature of economic theory, averages can never form a link in its reasoning.

Nevertheless, macroeconomics became identified as separate field from microeconomics with the publication of Samuelson's *Economics* in 1948 (Colander, 2006, p.52).

Dynamic stochastic general equilibrium models

The separation of macro- and microeconomics continued until the economic crisis of the mid-1970s prompted what is now known as the Lucas critique. In essence, Lucas (1976) pointed out that policy changes would change the way people behaved and thus the structure being modelled, and this meant that existing models could not be used to evaluate policy. The result was dynamic stochastic general equilibrium (DSGE) models that attempt 'to integrate macroeconomics with microeconomics by providing microeconomic foundations for macroeconomics' (Wickens, 2008, p.xiii). This integration is achieved by including 'a single individual who produces a good that can either be consumed or invested to increase future output and consumption' (Wickens, 2008, p.2). They are known as either the Ramsey (1928 and 1927) models or as the representative agent models. In effect, the representative agent represents an average person. And this average person bases their decision on optimisation. The limitations of using representative agents have been long recognised (e.g. by Kirman, 1992). But they have continued to be used because they make the analysis more tractable (Wickens, 2008, p.10). However, this is changing. Wickens noted in 2008 (2008, p.10) that 'more advanced treatments of macroeconomic problems often allow for heterogeneity', and the technical problems of using heterogeneous agents in DSGE models are now (in 2014) being addressed in cutting-edge research projects.

Complexity economics

Not all economists think that the DSGE models are the right way to proceed. For example, in 2006, Colander published *Post Walrasian Macroeconomics: Beyond the Dynamic Stochastic General Equilibrium Model*, a collection of papers that set out the agenda for an alternative approach to macroeconomics that did not make the restrictive assumptions found in DSGE models and in particular did not assume that people operated in an information-rich environment.

The DSGE approach assumes that the economy is capable of reaching and sustaining an equilibrium, although there is much debate about how equilibrium is defined. Others take the view that the economy is a non-linear, complex dynamic system which rarely, if ever, reaches equilibrium (see, e.g. Arthur, 2014). While in a linear system, macro level activity amounts to a simple adding up of the micro actions, in a non-linear system, something new may emerge. Arthur (1999) concluded:

> After two centuries of studying equilibria – static patterns that call for no further behavioral adjustments – economists are beginning to study the general emergence of structures and the unfolding of patterns in the economy. When viewed in out-of-equilibrium formation, economic patterns sometimes simplify into the simple static equilibria of standard economics. More often they are ever changing, showing perpetually novel behavior and emergent phenomena.

Furthermore, 'Complex dynamical systems full of non-linearities and sundry time lags have been completely beyond the state of the arts until rather recently', but 'agent-based simulations make it possible to investigate problems that Marshall and Keynes could only "talk" about' (Leijonhufvud, 2006). More recently, Stiglitz and Gallegati (2011) have pointed out that use of the representative agent 'rules out the possibility of the analysis of complex interactions'; and they 'advocate a bottom-up approach, where high-level (macroeconomic) systems may possess new and different properties than the low-level (microeconomic) systems on which they are based'. ABM is therefore seen by many as offering a way forward.

The impact of the 2008 economic crisis

Once again, it has taken an economic crisis to prompt a re-evaluation of economic modelling. Indeed, the 2008 economic crisis caused a crisis for economics as a discipline. It is now widely recognised that a new direction is needed and that ABM may provide that. Farmer and Foley (2009) argued in *Nature* that 'Agent-based models potentially present a way to model the financial economy as a complex system, as Keynes attempted to do, while taking human adaptation and learning into account, as Lucas advocated'. A year later, *The Economist* (2010) was asking if ABM can do better than 'conventional' models. Jean-Claude Trichet (2010), then president of the European Central Bank, spelt out what was needed:

> First, we have to think about how to characterise the *homo economicus* at the heart of any model. The atomistic, optimising agents underlying existing models do not capture behaviour during a crisis period. We need to deal better with heterogeneity across agents and the interaction among those heterogeneous agents. We need to entertain alternative motivations for economic choices. Behavioural economics draws on psychology to explain decisions made in crisis circumstances. Agent-based modelling dispenses with the optimisation assumption and allows for more complex interactions between agents. Such approaches are worthy of our attention.

The Review of the Monetary Policy Committee's Forecasting Capability for the Bank of England concluded that 'The financial crisis exposed virtually all major macro models as being woefully ill-equipped to understand the implications of this type of event' (Stockton, 2012, p.6). In early 2014, the United Kingdom's Economic and Social Research Council (ESRC) sponsored a conference on *Diversity in Macroeconomics*, subtitled *New Perspectives from Agent-Based Computational, Complexity and Behavioural Economics*, to bring together practitioners of the new approaches, mainstream academic economists and policymakers (Markose, 2014).

Furthermore, by 2013, the call for change had spread to the teaching of economics (*Economist*, 2013), and in 2014, *Curriculum Open-Access Resources in Economics* (CORE) was launched, providing an interactive online resource for a first course in economics, and it is planned to include agent-based simulations in this new way of teaching economics (CORE, 2014; Royal Economic Society, 2014).

So, what is ABM? We give an overview in the next section.

1.3   What is ABM?

The development of computational social simulation modelling started in the early 1960s with microsimulation (Gilbert & Troitzsch, 2005, p.6; Morgan, 2012, pp.301–315). Microsimulation takes a set of data about a population – of people, households or firms – and applies rules to reflect changes, enabling the modeller to look at the overall impact (Gilbert & Troitzsch, 2005, p.8). Such an approach is particularly useful for modelling policy changes, for example, to see who is made better or worse off by tax changes. However, although allowing for heterogeneity, microsimulation does not allow interaction. Only with the arrival of ABM did modelling interaction between agents become possible.

ABM grew out of research on non-linear dynamics and artificial intelligence and was facilitated by the arrival of personal computers in the 1980s and early 1990s. An agent-based model is a computer program that creates an artificial world of heterogeneous agents and enables investigation into how interactions between these agents, and between agents and other factors such as time and space, add up to form the patterns seen in the real world. The program creates agents located with different characteristics and tells them what they can do under different circumstances. Early work such as Epstein and Axtell's (1996) *Sugarscape* model demonstrated the potential power of this approach, and Squazzoni (2010) described what has been achieved since the mid-1990s.

Usually, an agent represents a person, but it can represent a household, a firm or even a nation, as we shall illustrate. Heterogeneity of agents is a key feature: each agent may have a unique set of characteristics and behaviour rules (Epstein, 2006, p.51). The agents are distributed across a space envisaged by the modeller which may represent a landscape or a social network or more abstract 'spaces' (Epstein, 2006, p.52). They may be distributed randomly across the whole space or according to some other principle. The space is typically two-dimensional and may have boundaries or be continuous.

The behaviour rules specify how agents interact with neighbours or their local landscape. Modellers can draw on a range of sources, from national statistics to information provided by small, ethnographic studies to explore the underlying mechanisms. While they can draw on standard economic theories, they can also use other theories such as those based on behavioural economics. The computer model can then be used to generate possible future scenarios and to study the effects of economic policies. ABM enables the testing of the validity of assumptions gleaned from different sources to see whether or not they generate the observed patterns.

Agent-based models can range from simple, abstract models to very complicated real-world case studies. They may have just two agents or millions of agents. And within a model, agents can represent different kinds of entities: people, households, firms, governments or countries or even animals.

Agents' characteristics fall under four possible headings:

• Perception: agents can see other agents in their neighbourhood and their environment.

• Performance: agents can act, such as moving and communicating.

• Memory: agents can recall their past states and actions.

• Policy: agents can have rules that determine what they do next.

Chapter 2 provides an introduction to doing ABM. For more background, see Gilbert and Troitzsch (2005) and Gilbert (2007).

1.4   The three themes of this book

Howitt (2012) suggested that agent-based economic models are 'the polar opposite to that of DSGE'. DSGE models in effect assume that 'people have an incredibly sophisticated ability to solve a computationally challenging intertemporal planning problem in an incredibly simple environment', while agent-based models assume that 'people have very simple rules of behavior for coping with an environment that is too complex for anyone fully to understand'. In short, Howitt argued that agent-based economic models can portray an economic system in which orderly behaviour can emerge as a result of interaction between heterogeneous agents, none of whom has any understanding of how the overall system functions.

In agent-based models, agents follow rules and react and interact over time. They may well be optimising, but it is within their perceived constraints, and they may not have full information. In contrast, neoclassical economics assumes people can optimise using full information (see, e.g. Axtell, 2007). In particular, in agent-based models, agents cannot foresee the future because it is determined by stochastic processes. And they may correct their behaviour following a mistake or not, depending on the learning algorithm used. DSGE models assume mistakes are not repeated.

The book focuses on using agent-based models to provide:

• The possibility of modelling heterogeneity

• An easy way to address dynamics

• The opportunity to model interactions between people and between people and their environment

We now take a brief look at each of these.

Heterogeneity

Traditional approaches to economics have long been criticised for 'lumping' things together. Think, for example, of a Cobb–Douglas production function in which two variables, labour and capital, are combined to produce output. Clearly, there are different types of labour and different types of capital, and one kind cannot replace another overnight: a bricklayer cannot just become a software designer, nor vice versa, and a factory producing cars cannot produce computer chips. Nor are all consumers the same: a rich household will have a very different spending pattern to a poor household. Some must save so that others can borrow. Indeed, without heterogeneity, there would be no scope for trading. ABM allows for such heterogeneity to be represented explicitly and without causing insuperable complications.

Dynamics

By dynamics, we here refer to adaptive processes, which, according to Leijonhufvud (2006), is the sense in which it was originally used in economics. Most economic textbooks only use comparative statics, that is, compare equilibrium situations. Yet as long ago as 1941, Samuelson pointed out that comparative statics were inadequate for the analysis of a range of economic problems (Samuelson, 1941). But as the examination of any basic economics textbook will show, comparative statics still dominates teaching. The question of how the economy moves from one equilibrium to another is not addressed. This is only now starting to change under the auspices of CORE, which gives prominence to dynamics (CORE, 2014). However, modelling dynamics by traditional methods is difficult as the mathematics quickly become unmanageable. Using ABM, simple rules can be applied and tested through simulation.

Interactions

People influence each other's behaviour. Herd behaviour is common in economics; people copy fashion, and markets take flight. Indeed, markets are based on interactions: sellers and buyers trade. The traditional economic models do not allow for this kind of interaction, but it is easily modelled using agents. ABM can also model in a simple manner how people can interact with the environment, for example, using up scarce resources.

1.5   Details of chapters

It is clearly impossible to cover everything presented in standard economics textbooks, which typically run to hundreds of pages (e.g. the British Begg *et al.*'s *Economics* (2011) and, from the United States, Varian's *Intermediate Economics* (2010)). So we have chosen topics within areas that seem to be particularly suitable for ABM, that is, where heterogeneity, interaction and dynamics are important.

Markets are a key theme of this book. We start with consumer choice in Chapter 3 and include fashion dynamics in Chapter 4 before introducing markets, through barter, in Chapter 5 with a fuller development in Chapter 6. The later chapters cover markets in the contexts of labour in Chapter 7 and international trade in Chapter 8. We have deliberately avoided discussion of financial markets as the usefulness of ABM has already been well established in this area by LeBaron (2006) and others. But Chapter 9 demonstrates the potentially explosive dynamics of the fractional reserve banking system. Chapter 10 shows how ABM can be used to model not only the interaction between economic agents but the interaction between agents and their natural environment.

Chapter 2: Starting agent-based modelling

Chapter 2 shows how to create a simple agent-based model and introduces the programming environment, NetLogo, that will be used for the models described in the rest of the book. The model simulates consumers shopping for fruit and vegetables in a produce market. The consumer agents are initially programmed to choose a market stall to purchase from at random, and then successive enhancements are made to record the cost of purchases, to stop them revisiting a stall they have previously been to and to try to find the cheapest stalls to buy from. Many of the basic building blocks of NetLogo programming are described.

Chapter 3: Heterogeneous demand

Chapter 3 introduces ABM by showing how it can be used to create heterogeneous agents whose characteristics and behaviour can be summed to generate observed macro patterns. Three models are presented in which agents represent households. The first model generates a budget distribution to replicate the observed distribution of income in the United Kingdom. The second adds a

Cobb–Douglas utility function to draw both individual and aggregate demand curves and demonstrates how consumers' choices can be tracked from their preferences to their contribution to aggregate demand. The third model provides a practical way of examining the effect on demand of price changes. Finally, the chapter compares the results from these simple models using heterogeneous agents with those from a 'representative agent' analysis.

Chapter 4: Social demand

Chapter 4 adds interaction between agents and dynamics. Consumers' behaviour is now not just influenced by prices and incomes but also by what others do, especially family and friends. ABM is well suited to modelling such social networks, and the first model in this chapter does this very simply using the concept of social circles. Next, we introduce threshold models and show how these can be combined with the social network model to examine possible adoption patterns of new products. The chapter then reviews the adoption of new technology by households in the United Kingdom and finally presents a case study of the adoption of fixed-line phones in the United Kingdom from 1951 to 2001.

Chapter 5: Benefits of barter

Chapter 5 demonstrates how ABM allows us to explore the dynamics of heterogeneous agents interacting by trading. Using the two-good economy much beloved of economics textbooks, agents trade by barter. We model an exchange economy broadly based on a description of trading that occurred in a prisoner-of-war camp. We start by creating a model that reproduces the Edgeworth Box to tease out the essentials of the barter process between two individuals. We explore the effectiveness of different price setting mechanisms in clearing the market and achieving Pareto optimality, starting with the theoretical Walrasian auctioneer. Then we extend this model to allow 200 agents to trade. We show that a simple stochastic peer-to-peer trading mechanism can produce a large increase in welfare, even if total utility is not maximised.

Chapter 6: The market

Chapter 6 focuses on the decisions of firms and demonstrates how ABM can easily accommodate the dynamic and interactive nature of markets. We present three models. The first is based on Cournot's classic model of duopoly and its Nash equilibrium but introduces the possibility of inaccurate information. The second model is based on small shops in the real world that do not have the benefit of the perfect foresight that is granted to firms operating under perfect competition and illustrates the dynamics of survival. The final model reflects business in the digital world, where there is no limit on capacity.

Chapter 7: Labour market

Heterogeneity and dynamics are the central themes of Chapter 7. The United Kingdom labour market is characterised by large flows and great diversity among the participants. The chapter starts with a model to generate the distribution of wages. It then adds the interaction between employers and workers as employers try to fill vacancies and workers seek jobs, touching briefly on the very skew distribution of firms by size. Finally, the various flows of workers between employers and into and out of the labour force are added to produce a simple, but interesting, model of the labour market of a small town. It also shows how micro and macro aspects can be combined in one model.

Chapter 8: International trade

Chapter 8 presents a simple model of trade between one country and the rest of the world, focusing on the determination of exchange rates. Five countries are used as examples, two with floating exchange rates and three in the Eurozone. Four scenarios are examined: inflation, depreciation, exogenous change in demand for exports and the impact of fiscal policy changes. The model focuses on dynamics. Even this simple model serves to highlight the difficulty of modelling the dynamics of international trade. It also shows clearly the constraints under which Eurozone countries operate.

Chapter 9: Banking

Chapter 9 uses a simple agent-based model to explore the basic features of fractional reserve banking and shows how the reserve and capital adequacy ratios imposed by regulators can dampen an otherwise explosive system. It illustrates how ABM can accommodate heterogeneity in that both savers and borrowers can be represented; how micro and macro aspects can be combined in one model, unlike the conventional textbook treatment of banking; and the importance of taking dynamic processes fully into account in modelling the banking system.

Chapter 10: Tragedy of the commons

Chapter 10 demonstrates how ABM can handle the interaction of agents with their environment as well as with one another by addressing the problem of the overuse of shared resources. In the 'tragedy of the commons', the pursuit of self-interest results in overuse of a common pool resource to the detriment of all. A model, inspired by English common land, is built in two stages. First, a meadow is created and its carrying capacity established. Then commoners are introduced. If there are no restrictions on the number of cows grazed on the meadow, there is overgrazing and 'the tragedy' ensues. But by following actual practice observed in England and Switzerland of setting limits on the number each commoner is allowed to graze, the model demonstrates that the tragedy can be avoided. The model can be readily adapted to accommodate other scenarios.

Chapter 11: Summary and conclusions

The final chapter summarises the models to show how ABM has addressed the weaknesses in the existing methods identified in Section 1.2 by allowing heterogeneity, facilitating dynamics and modelling interactions between people and their environments and thereby improving the link between micro- and macroeconomics. It also sets out some of the problems that need to be addressed in order for ABM's potential to make a useful contribution to economics to be fully realised.

The models

We present 19 models in Chapters 3–10, ranging from modules to be used in larger models to a real-world model. In each case, we follow Müller *et al.* (2014) who suggested 'a structured natural language description plus the provision of source code' as being 'particularly suited for academic purposes'. We describe the models in natural language in the chapters. The appendices to the chapters provide more details based on the ODD (Overview, Design concepts, and Details) protocol (Grimm *et al.*, 2010) and include pseudocode. The code itself is provided on the website http://cress.soc.surrey.ac.uk/.

References

Arthur, W.B. (1999) Complexity and the economy. *Science*, 284 pp.107–109.

Arthur, W.B. (2014) *Complexity and the Economy*. Oxford: Oxford University Press.

Axtell, R.L. (2007) What economic agents do: How cognition and interaction lead to emergence and complexity. *Review of Austrian Economics*, 20, pp.105–122.

Begg, D., Vernasca, G., Fischer, S. & Dornbusch, R. (2011) *Economics*. Tenth Edition. London: McGraw-Hill Higher Education.

Colander, D. (2006) *Post Walrasian Macroeconomics: Beyond the Dynamic Stochastic General Equilibrium Model*. Cambridge: Cambridge University Press.

CORE (2014) *The CORE project* [Online]. Available at: http://core-econ.org/ [Accessed 31 January 2015].

Economist (2010) *Agents of change: Conventional economic models failed to foresee the financial crisis. Could agent-based modelling do better?* 22nd July [Online]. Available at: http://www.economist.com/node/16636121 [Accessed 31 January 2015].

Economist (2013) *Keynes's new heirs: Britain leads a global push to rethink the way economics is taught* [Online]. Available at: http://www.economist.com/news/britain/21590555-britain-leads-global-push-rethink-way-economics-taught-keyness-new-heirs [Accessed 31 January 2015].

Epstein, J.M. (2006) *Generative Social Science*. Princeton: Princeton University Press.

Epstein, J. M. & Axtell, R. (1996) *Growing Artificial Societies. Social Science from the Bottom Up*. Cambridge, MA: The MIT Press.

Farmer, J.D. & Foley, D. (2009) The economy needs agent-based modelling. *Nature*, 460, pp.685–686.

Gilbert, N. (2007) *Agent-based Models*. London: Sage.

Gilbert, N. & Troitzsch, K. (2005) *Simulation for the Social Scientist*. Oxford: Oxford University Press.

Grimm, V., Berger, U., DeAngelis, D.L., Polhill, J.G., Giske, J., & Railsback, S.F. (2010) The ODD protocol: A review and first update. *Ecological Modelling*, 221, pp.2760–2768.

Hayek, F. (1931) *Prices and Production*. London: George Routledge & Sons Ltd.

Howitt, P. (2012) What have central bankers learned from modern macroeconomic theory? *Journal of Macroeconomics*, 34, pp.11–22.

Jevons, W.S. (1888) *The Theory of Political Economy*. Third Edition. London: Macmillan & Co. [Online]. Available at: http://www.econlib.org/library/YPDBooks/Jevons/jvnPECover.html [Accessed 31 January 2015].

Keynes, J.M. (1936/1970) *General Theory of Employment, Interest and Money*. London: Macmillan.

Kirman, A.P. (1992) Whom or what does the representative individual represent? *Journal of Economic Perspectives*, 6(2), pp.117–136.

LeBaron, B. (2006) Agent-Based Computational Finance. In Tesfatsion, L. & Judd, K.L., eds, *Handbook of Computational Economics*. Elsevier: Amsterdam, pp.1187–1233.

Leijonhufvud, A. (2006) Episodes in a Century of Macroeconomics. In Collander, D., ed, *Post Walrasian Macroeconomics*. Cambridge: Cambridge University Press, pp.27–45.

Lucas, R. (1976). Econometric Policy Evaluation: A Critique. In Brunner, K. & Meltzer, A., eds, *The Phillips Curve and Labor Markets*. Carnegie-Rochester Conference Series on Public Policy, 1. Amsterdam: North Holland, pp.19–46.

Markose, S. (2014) *Report on ESRC Conference on diversity in macroeconomics new perspectives from agent-based computational, complexity and behavioural economics:* 24–25 February 2014 [Online]. Available at: http://essex.ac.uk/economics/documents/conference-report.pdf. For papers and slides: http://www.acefinmod.com/esrc2014.html [Accessed 31 January 2015].

Marshall, A. (1920/1961) *Principles of economics*. London: Macmillan.

Morgan, M.S. (2012) *The World in the Model*. Cambridge: Cambridge University Press.

Müller, B., Balbi, S., Buchmann C.M., de Sousa, L., Dressler, G., Groeneveld, J., Klassert, C.J., Le, Q.B., Millington, J.D.A., Nolzen, H., Parker, D.C., Polhill, J.G., Schlüter, M., Schulze, J., Schwarz, N., Sun, Z.,

Taillandier, P., Weise, H. (2014) Standardised and transparent model descriptions for agent-based models: Current status and prospects. *Environmental Modelling & Software*, 55, pp.156–163.

Petty, W. (1690) *Political arithmetick*. Robert Clavel at the Peacock, and Hen, Mortlock at the Phoenix in St. Paul's Church-yard [Online]. Available at: http://socserv2.socsci.mcmaster.ca/~econ/ugcm/3ll3/petty/poliarith.html [Accessed 31 January 2015].

Ramsey, F.P. (1927) A contribution to the theory of taxation. *Economic Journal*, 37, pp.47–61.

Ramsey, F.P. (1928) A mathematical theory of saving. *Economic Journal*, 37, pp.543–559.

Royal Economic Society (2014) *New teaching for economics: The INET-CORE project* [Online]. Available at: http://www.res.org.uk/view/art3Jul14Features.html [Accessed 31 January 2015].

Samuelson, P. (1941) The stability of equilibrium: Comparative statics and dynamics. *Econometrica*, 9(2), pp.97–120.

Samuelson, P. (1948) *Economics*. New York: McGraw Hill.

Smith, A. (1776/1861) *Wealth of Nations*. Edinburgh: Adam Charles & Black.

Squazzoni, F. (2010) The impact of agent-based models in the social sciences after 15 years of incursions. *History of Economic Ideas*, xviii, pp.197–233.

Stiglitz, J.E. & Gallegati, M. (2011) Heterogeneous interacting agent models for understanding Monetary economies. *Eastern Economic Journal*, 37(1), pp.6–12.

Stockton, D. (2012) *The review of the Monetary Policy Committee's forecasting capability*. Presented to the Court of the Bank of England [Online]. Available at http://www.bankofengland.co.uk/publications/Documents/news/2012/cr3stockton.pdf [Accessed 31 January 2015].

Trichet, J-C. (2010) *Reflections on the nature of monetary policy non-standard measures and finance theory*. Speech by President of the ECB, Opening address at the ECB Central Banking Conference Frankfurt, 18 November 2010. Available at https://www.ecb.europa.eu/press/key/date/2010/html/sp101118.en.html [Accessed 24 May 2015].

Varian, H. (2010) *Intermediate Microeconomics*. Princeton: Princeton University Press.

Wickens, M. (2008) *Macroeconomic Theory: A Dynamic General Equilibrium Approach*. Princeton: Princeton University Press.

2

Starting agent-based modelling

2.1 Introduction

While it is possible just to use an agent-based model that someone else has developed, it is much better and more interesting to see what goes on 'under the hood', so that you can see and understand the program code that is making the model work. Learning how to program, as well as being a worthwhile exercise in its own right, will allow you to modify existing programs, for example, to explore the effect of different settings and different assumptions, and eventually to build your own programs. Programming used to be a matter for experts, requiring many months of study or a degree in computer science. Fortunately, advances in programming languages and interfaces have meant that programming is becoming ever more easily accessible to those without expert knowledge. In this book, we use a programming system called NetLogo (Wilensky, 1999) that was originally designed for secondary (high) school pupils and is still used, particularly in the United States, to teach science by means of simulations. The origins of NetLogo mean that a great deal of attention has been paid to making the NetLogo system easy to use and to understand. We will take advantage of that in this book, and we will also benefit from the fact that NetLogo is especially good for developing agent-based models. The authors describe it as a 'multi-agent programmable modelling environment'.

NetLogo has three parts:

- A code editor to write programs

- An interface that shows the controls to operate the program and any of a range of graphs, maps and other outputs to show what the program is doing

- A documentation editor that can be used to describe the program and what it is intended to do

Each of these is independent so, for example, you run a program that someone else has written and observe what it is doing without looking at the code. NetLogo comes with a large library of pre-built sample models taken from physics, chemistry, geography and other disciplines, as well as economics, and trying these is a good way of starting to become familiar with it.

NetLogo can be downloaded from http://ccl.northwestern.edu/netlogo/. It is open source and free and works almost identically on Windows, Mac OS and Unix systems. You might like to download it onto your computer now and follow along as you work through this chapter. There are other agent-based modelling environments (examples are Mason and RePast, both of which are open source but are based on the programming language, Java, so that using them needs some prior knowledge of that language, and AnyLogic, a commercial system), but for beginners, NetLogo is at the moment the best place to start.

This chapter explains some aspects of NetLogo, but for a fuller account, see the textbook authored by its main developer (Wilensky & Rand, 2015). Other books on agent-based modelling also include introductions, for example, Railsback and Grimm (2011) and Gilbert (2007). The NetLogo system itself includes an excellent tutorial and many code examples in its model library. There is also a NetLogo Users Group email list at https://groups.yahoo.com/neo/groups/netlogo-users/info and a StackOverflow community at http://stackoverflow.com/questions/tagged/netlogo where questions can be asked.

To illustrate how NetLogo is used, we will develop a simple model and explain the program code step by step. First, let us see the model in action (the code can be downloaded from the website: *Chapter 2*).

2.2   A simple market: the basic model

Much of this book is about modelling markets of different types. One of the simplest is a produce market, such as is often found in towns and cities selling fruits and vegetables. In this model, there are shoppers, each with a shopping list, and a number of market stalls, each selling a range of fruits and vegetables. The shoppers want to buy the items on their lists, which will differ from one shopper to the next, and may want to minimise the cost of their shopping. The stallholders sell their produce for different prices, depending on what they think the customers will pay, the prices that they paid in a wholesale market and other factors. Not all stalls sell the complete range of fruits and vegetables.

Agent-based models almost always follow a standard pattern: they are initialised with parameters that define the starting situation. Then the model is executed to simulate the passage of time. At each step, representing some short duration (e.g. a day), each agent performs some action (or does nothing), as determined by its behavioural rules. The action can include communicating with other agents, changing the environment, moving through the environment and many other things. The execution of the program continues, step by step, until either some programmed stopping condition is met or the user stops the simulation manually. While the program runs, what is happening to the agents can be measured on graphs or monitors. This will become clearer as we work through the example model.

Figure 2.1 shows the interface of the model at a point midway through the simulation. The houses represent the market stalls, and the people are the shoppers. To run the model, you first press the `setup` button at the top left, which initialises the model, and then the `go` button to run it. The top slider is used to adjust the number of shoppers before the simulation begins. The slider under it, labelled `walking speed`, adjusts the speed at which the shoppers walk from stall to stall. This slider can be adjusted while the simulation runs to make the shoppers move faster or slower. The third slider sets the number of kinds of produce that traders keep on their stall. The three sliders allow the user to adjust the parameters of the model before and during each simulation run.

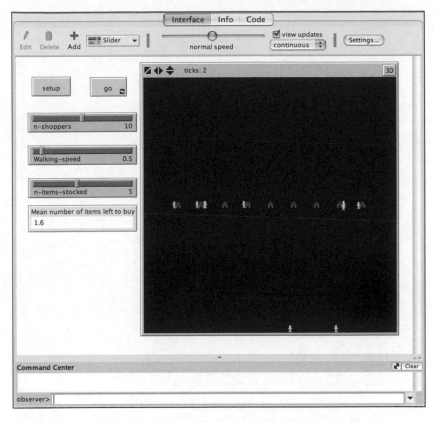

Figure 2.1   NetLogo interface window showing the market model after two ticks.

The bottom object is a monitor. It keeps a continually updated record of the average number of items on the shoppers' lists, that is, how many items have yet to be bought. Figure 2.1 shows the interface; clicking on the tab labelled 'Code' at the top takes you to the program itself (see Figure 2.2).

2.3   The basic framework

NetLogo programs have two sections: a 'setup' section which is executed once and which initialises the model to its starting state and a 'go' section which contains code that is executed again and again as the simulation runs. In addition, at the beginning, there is a header section that specifies the variables and the types of agents that will be used in the program.

The header for the example program (Box 2.1) begins by reserving two 'global' variables, fruit-and-veg and mean-items (line 1). The former will be used to hold a list of all the kinds of fruits and vegetables that any trader can offer for sale. The latter will in due course be used to hold the average number of items remaining on shoppers' shopping lists. When this variable has reached zero, everyone's shopping will have been completed. They are called global variables because they are accessible everywhere throughout the program.

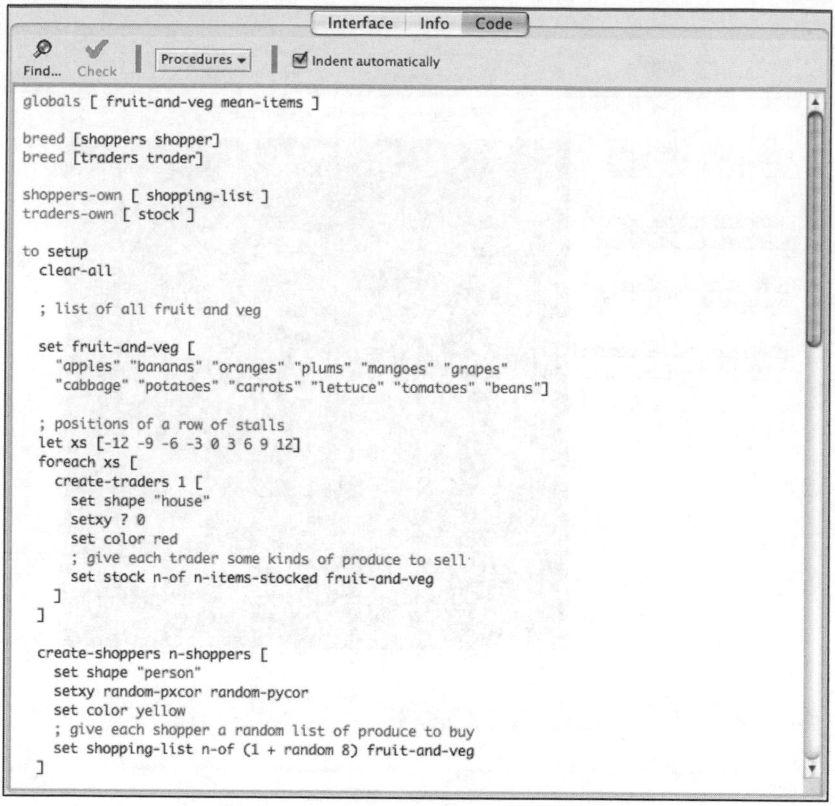

```
                    Interface │ Info │ Code
  🔍      ✔        │ Procedures ▾ │ ☑ Indent automatically
 Find...  Check

globals [ fruit-and-veg mean-items ]

breed [shoppers shopper]
breed [traders trader]

shoppers-own [ shopping-list ]
traders-own [ stock ]

to setup
  clear-all

  ; list of all fruit and veg

  set fruit-and-veg [
    "apples" "bananas" "oranges" "plums" "mangoes" "grapes"
    "cabbage" "potatoes" "carrots" "lettuce" "tomatoes" "beans"]

  ; positions of a row of stalls
  let xs [-12 -9 -6 -3 0 3 6 9 12]
  foreach xs [
    create-traders 1 [
      set shape "house"
      setxy ? 0
      set color red
      ; give each trader some kinds of produce to sell
      set stock n-of n-items-stocked fruit-and-veg
    ]
  ]

  create-shoppers n-shoppers [
    set shape "person"
    setxy random-pxcor random-pycor
    set color yellow
    ; give each shopper a random list of produce to buy
    set shopping-list n-of (1 + random 8) fruit-and-veg
  ]
```

Figure 2.2   The NetLogo code window showing the top portion of the market model code.

Box 2.1   Market simulation header section.

```
1  globals [ fruit-and-veg mean-items ]
2  breed [shoppers shopper]
3  breed [traders trader]
4  shoppers-own [ shopping-list ]
5  traders-own [ stock ]
```

Note: the line numbers have been added; they are not part of the program code.

There are two kinds of agents in the model: shoppers and market traders. NetLogo allows you to name the types of agents as breeds (by analogy to the way that breeds of dog are different types of dog). One of the points emphasised in the previous chapter is that economic models need to allow for the fact that not everyone is the same, that is, to be able to deal with heterogeneity. In this simple market model, each shopper has a different list of items to buy, and each trader has different kinds of fruits and vegetables in stock. So each shopper has its own shopping list and each trader, its own list of what it sells. Shoppers are provided with a variable, shopping-list, that will be used to store that agent's own shopping list. Similarly, each trader has a variable, stock, in which will be stored a list of items that the trader has for sale.

So far, the code has done nothing more than to define some names, of variables and agents. Next comes the setup section of code (Box 2.2), which is executed once at the beginning of the simulation, when the user presses the setup button on the interface shown in Figure 2.1. The setup section includes code that initialises the variables defined in the header section (shown in Box 2.1) and creates the agents that will populate the model.

The setup section is marked by to setup at the beginning (line 6) and end at the end (line 32). Everything in between is executed once in order from top to bottom. First (line 7), NetLogo is instructed to remove everything (including the agents) that might have been left over from a previous run. Then the fruit-and-veg variable is initialised to a list of fruits and vegetables. All the lines beginning with a semicolon are comments intended for the human reader and are ignored by NetLogo. Hence, line 8 is for our information only. The next line, line 9, does the work. The square brackets here, [and], indicate that what lies in between is a list of items. set is the command that puts a value into a variable (other programming languages often use = to mean the same). So after line 9, the value of the variable fruit-and-veg is a long list of the names of fruits and vegetables.

Now, we draw the market traders (the house shapes in Figure 2.1). First, we create another list, this time consisting of the positions of each trader on the NetLogo grid. This grid consists of

Box 2.2   Setup section.

```
 6  to setup
 7    clear-all
 8    ; list of all fruit and veg
 9    set fruit-and-veg [
10       "apples" "bananas" "oranges" "plums" "mangoes"
           "grapes"
11       "cabbage" "potatoes" "carrots" "lettuce" "tomatoes"
           "beans"]
12    ; positions of a row of stalls
13    let xs [-12 -9 -6 -3 0 3 6 9 12]
14    foreach xs [
15       create-traders 1 [
16          set shape "house"
17          setxy ? 0
18          set color red
19          ; give each trader some kinds of produce to sell
20          set stock n-of n-items-stocked fruit-and-veg
21       ]
22    ]
23    create-shoppers n-shoppers [
24       set shape "person"
25       setxy random-pxcor random-pycor
26       set color yellow
27       ; give each shopper a random list of produce to buy
28       set shopping-list n-of (1 + random 8) fruit-and-veg
29    ]
30    set mean-items mean [ length shopping-list] of shoppers
31    reset-ticks
32  end
```

squares (called `patches` by NetLogo) in a coordinate system, which in this example runs from −16 to +16 from left to right and −16 to +16 from bottom to top. Line 13 sets up the variable xs to hold the x-coordinates of each of the traders on the grid, in preparation for actually creating the trader agents. `let` is used instead of `set` because `let` does two jobs: it creates a variable and also gives the variable an initial value. `foreach` (line 14) works its way down the list of coordinates in xs and for each one executes the commands between the square brackets in lines 14 and 22. First, the leftmost trader (at x-coordinate −12) is created, then the next trader is created at −9 and so on until the last one at coordinate 12. In line 15, the command `create-traders 1` generates one new trading agent, and this agent is initialised using the commands in lines 16 to 20. The displayed shape of the agent is set to house icon (line 16), the house is positioned at the current x-coordinate (−12 on the first time through) using the placeholder ? to represent the current item in the xs list and at y coordinate 0 (i.e. on the horizontal centre line), and the colour of the house is set to red.

In line 20, the just created trader is given some stock to sell. The number of items of produce has been set as a parameter by the user by adjusting the `n-items-stocked` slider on the interface. This number is used in `n-of`, which selects a random selection of that number of items from the `fruit-and-veg` list. That concludes the first time through the loop that started at line 14. Each further pass through lines 14 to 22 creates another agent, located at successive x-coordinates taken from the list of xs.

This part of the code has demonstrated some basic building blocks of NetLogo programming:

- A variable can be given a value using the set command.

- A list can be laid out between square brackets; the list can contain anything, for example, numbers or symbols such as 'apple'.

- Agents are generated using the `create-`*breed* command. As part of the agent creation process, commands enclosed in square brackets following the `create-`*breed* command are executed to initialise the agent (e.g. to set its shape, position and colour).

- You can iterate down a list, one item at a time, with the `foreach` command.

These building blocks are used in many of the programs later in the book.

The next part of the setup code (lines 23 to 29) is concerned with creating the shopper agents. This follows the pattern for creating the traders. The number of shoppers is set by the slider called `n-shoppers` (see Figure 2.1). Once created, each agent is set to a 'person' shape and located at a random location on the grid (line 31). `random-pxcor` chooses a random x-coordinate somewhere on the grid, and `random-pycor` does the same in the y direction. The colour of the agent is set to yellow, and finally, the shopper is given a shopping list selecting items from the `fruit-and-veg`. The number of items on the shopping list is calculated as a random number. This is done by using a NetLogo reporter, which is code that returns some value. The reporter `random` returns a random integer between zero and the number given: in this case up to but not including eight. Adding one ensures that there is at least one item on every shopper's list.

All the agents, both traders and shoppers, have now been created and placed on the grid. As a final step, the mean number of items on the shopping lists is calculated in line 30. Line 30 introduces further NetLogo constructs. Recall that each shopper has its own shopping list. The length of the shopping list is obtained using the reporter `length` that provides the number of items in a list.

`shoppers` refers to what NetLogo calls an `agentset`. An agentset is, unsurprisingly, a set of agents, in this case the set of all the shoppers that were created earlier. Agentsets are very useful in NetLogo, as they are an easy way to refer to groups of agents. `of` works with agentsets and returns a list composed of what is returned by the preceding reporter (i.e. `[length shopping-list]`).

So, the construct [length shopping-list] of shoppers produces a list of the lengths of the shopping lists of all the shoppers. This is fed to the mean reporter, which finds the average of a list of numbers. Thus, taking the command as a whole, mean-items is set to the value of the mean length of the shoppers' shopping lists.

Lastly, in line 31, the NetLogo clock, which counts steps or ticks, is reset to zero, and the setup is complete. (Using the NetLogo's tick command is the simplest approach, but you can easily devise your own time counter, which is more flexible.)

The final section of the program is the part that gets executed repeatedly, once for every time step (Box 2.3). It is bounded by to go (line 33) and end (line 59). It is an example of a procedure; the setup section also consisted of a procedure. Procedures start with to and the name of the procedure and end with end. Procedures can have any name you wish, but by convention, the initialisation is carried out by a setup procedure, and the main part of the simulation is called the go procedure. Execution of the go procedure starts when the user presses the go button on the user interface (Figure 2.1).

Most of the go procedure consists of an ask command: each of the shoppers that still have some items to buy is asked to carry out some commands. When ask is executed, each of the

Box 2.3 The go section.

```
33  to go
34     ; for each  shopper in turn that still has something to
          buy
35     ask shoppers with [not empty? shopping-list] [
36        ; choose a stall
37        let stall one-of traders
38        ; go to that stall
39        face stall
40        while [ patch-here != [patch-here] of stall ]
41           [ forward 0.005 * walking-speed ]
42        ; buy everything on my shopping-list that is for sale
43        ; at this stall
44        let purchases filter [ member? ? [stock] of stall]
             shopping-list
45        foreach purchases [
46           ; delete the items bought from the shopping list
47           set shopping-list remove ? shopping-list
48        ]
49        ; when shopping is done, go home
50        ; (move to the edge of the grid)
51        if empty? shopping-list [ set ycor -16 ]
52     ]
53     ; calculate the average number of items on the shopping
          lists
54     set mean-items mean [ length shopping-list] of shoppers
55     ; if no one has anything left to buy, stop
56     if mean-items = 0  [ stop ]
57     ; count the iterations
58     tick
59  end
```

agents mentioned immediately after the command, in this case all the shoppers that have items still to buy on their shopping list, are given the set of commands that follow the square brackets (lines 36 to 51). ask is equivalent to writing out some instructions on a sheet of paper, copying the instructions as many times as there are agents and then asking each agent to carry out those instructions independently. In principle, the agents carry out the instructions simultaneously, but since this is difficult to implement on a single computer, they act one after another but with the order of agents assigned randomly (and in a different order with every ask).

First, each shopper chooses a trader to buy from using one-of, which selects one agent (a trader) from an agentset (all the traders). Then the shopper changes the direction in which it is pointing on the grid until it is facing the selected trader's stall and moves in that direction. The forward command (line 41) moves the agent in the direction it is facing. The movement continues while the patch on which the shopper is walking remains different from the patch on which the trader's stall is located. The speed of movement is controlled by the walking-speed slider on the user interface: higher values of walking speed mean that the agent moves further each time around the while loop. (The constant 0.005 is there to make the agents walk sufficiently slowly that their movement is visible. It may need adjustment to suit the speed of your computer.)

Eventually, the shopper arrives at the stall and can buy anything on its shopping list that the stall sells. (Recall that a stall doesn't necessarily stock everything that might be on the agent's shopping list). The agent is assumed to buy everything it wants that is available from the trader. This is the purpose of line 45. filter works along a list, item by item, and makes a new list, purchases, of those items in the shopping list for which a reporter (in this case [member? ? [stock] of stall]) is true. The item being considered is represented by the placeholder ?. So, the reporter asks whether the item (?) is a member of the stall's stock list and reports true if it is, which is just what we want to happen. Traders can always meet shoppers' demand and do not run out of stock.

This may leave some items not available on this stall and therefore yet to be bought. To find which items were not bought, because they were not in the stall's stock, we take the list of purchases, work through it item by item and remove from the shopping list those items that have been bought (lines 45 to 48). Now that the shopper has bought everything it wants that is available from this trader, it is time to check whether there is more shopping to do. If the shopping list is now empty, the shopper is moved to the edge of the grid to be out of the way.

That is the process for one agent. The ask command gets all the agents to go through this process once. Then the mean number of items left on the shoppers' lists is calculated. If everyone has done all their shopping (the mean number of items on the lists is zero), the simulation stops. If not, the simulation clock is incremented by one. That completes one step of the simulation, and the loop is repeated. On the second time around, those agents with more shopping to do will again choose a trader's stall and buy items that the trader has in stock. Eventually, all the shopping will have been completed, all the shoppers will have gone home, and the simulation stops.

The go procedure demonstrates some common features of NetLogo programs. Most of the procedure consists of an ask command and inside this command is a list of the behaviour rules that the agents carry out. The actions can include movements around the environment, represented by the grid, manipulation of the agents' state (here, a shopping list) and the calculation of variables such as mean-items.

2.4   Enhancing the basic model: adding prices

The model described so far is intentionally rather simple to make it easier to explain the general structure of agent-based models. As you may have noticed, it does not include any economic variables as yet. But once a basic model is working, it can be modified and enhanced with further details, and often, this is the best way to develop models: one stage at a time. Indeed, it is very important to check that a model is doing what you intended as you develop it. If this process, called verification, is left until the model is large and complicated, it may well be almost impossible to do. NetLogo makes this approach to development easy because it is simple to edit a program and see the effect of changes.

For our first enhancement, we shall add prices to the model. Each kind of fruit and vegetables will have a price set by the market trader.

The following changes and additions are needed:

```
1  globals [ fruit-and-veg fruit-and-veg-prices mean-items ]
...
4  shoppers-own [ shopping-list spent]
5  traders-own [ stock prices ]
```

As well as having a global variable to hold the full range of fruits and vegetables, there is a variable that stores a list of the prices of each of these (e.g. the wholesale price). These prices are arranged in the same order as the produce in fruit-and-veg, so, for example, if oranges is the third item in fruit-and-veg, the price of oranges will be the third item in fruit-and-veg-prices. Both shoppers and traders need additions to their own variables: shoppers record the money that they spend for their fruit and vegetables in the variable spent, and traders have a price list containing the prices of each of the kinds of produce they have in stock.

Traders add a markup to the wholesale prices. The mark varies between traders and is a random percentage between 1 and 30%. The following lines calculate the markup and generate a list of the prices, including the markup, arranged in the same order as the traders' list of produce in stock:

```
let mark-up (1 + random 30) / 100
foreach stock [
    set prices lput ((1 + mark-up) *
            (item (position ? fruit-and-veg) fruit-and-veg-prices))
            prices
    ]
```

The foreach works down the list of stock items. For each one, it puts the price of the item on the end of a list of prices using lput. The price of the item is determined by finding the position of the item in the list of fruits and vegetables (position ? fruit-and-veg), then extracting the price found at that position in the list of wholesale prices and adding the markup:

```
45  foreach purchases [
            set spent spent +
                    item (position ? [stock] of stall) [ prices ]
                    of stall
46      ; delete the items that have been bought from the shopping
            list
47      set shopping-list remove ? shopping-list
48  ]
```

This block of code is inserted after line 45 in the go procedure. For each purchase ('oranges', 'bananas' or whatever), the price of that purchase is looked up in the trader's price list and added to the sum spent by the shopper. It is assumed that the shopper buys only one unit of each item. The lookup is done in two parts: first the position of the item in the trader's stock list is found. For example, if the stock list is ["apples" "bananas" "oranges" "plums" "car-rots" "lettuce" "tomatoes"] and the shopper has bought carrots, (position ? [stock] of stall) will yield four (the first position in a list is position 0). Then the item reporter returns the price at the corresponding position in the trader's price list (e.g. the price at position 4).

Finally, it would be helpful to be able to observe the amounts being spent by the shoppers as they go about their shopping. This can be done by drawing a plot of the average amount spent against time, measured in ticks. The result is shown in Figure 2.3.

This first enhancement shows how to augment a model by adding just a few lines of code, in this case to calculate the amount the shopper is spending, and how you can instrument a model by adding a plot showing how the agents' behaviour changes over time. We have also seen other list processing commands to filter lists and remove items. There are many more such commands available in NetLogo, all of which are described in the NetLogo dictionary.

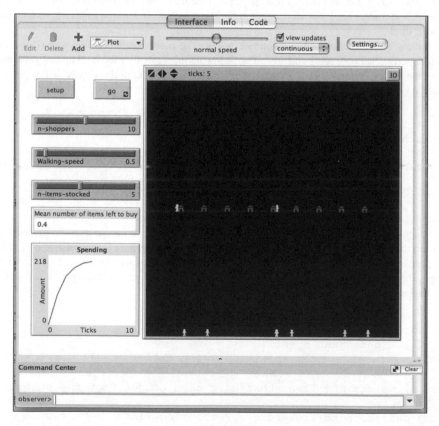

Figure 2.3   The interface of the model enhanced with a plot of the average amount spent.

2.5   Enhancing the model: selecting traders

In this and the basic version of the model, the shoppers choose the stall they go to at random, and then if their shopping is not yet done, they choose another stall at random. The problem with this is that it is possible for the shopper to choose the same stall twice, which seems somewhat stupid. This can be avoided if the shoppers are given some memory to record where they have been so that they can then choose their next stall from those they have not yet visited.

The third version of the model does this. A new variable for each agent to store those stalls it has not yet visited is added to the setup procedure for the agentset of all the shoppers:

```
4   shoppers-own [ shopping-list not-yet-visited spent ]
...
23  create-shoppers n-shoppers [
24      set shape "person"
25      setxy random-pxcor random-pycor
26      set color yellow
        set not-yet-visited traders
27      ; give each shopper a random list of produce to buy
28      set shopping-list n-of (1 + random 8) fruit-and-veg
29  ]
```

In the go procedure, the agent selects a stall to visit, not from every stall as before, but from the agentset of those not yet visited (line 37):

```
36  ; choose a stall
37  let stall one-of not-yet-visited
38  ; go to that stall
39  face stall
40  while [ patch-here != [patch-here] of stall ]
41      [ forward 0.005 * walking-speed ]
    ; remember that I have been to this stall, so I don't come
      again
    set not-yet-visited not-yet-visited with [ self != stall ]
```

The agent needs to remember where it has been, so there is an additional line after line 41. This line needs some explanation. We want to remove the trader whose stall the agent has visited from the not-yet-visited agentset. This can be done with the NetLogo primitive, with, which was used before to select shoppers with non-empty shopping lists (line 35). with is followed by a condition (here, [self != stall]): an agentset is created containing a copy of the original but including only those agents for which the condition is true. In this case, the condition uses the special name, self, which refers to the agent for which the condition is being tested. So the condition in square brackets can be translated as meaning 'select only those stalls from the not-yet-visited agentset that are not equal to the current market stall'. While this may be difficult to follow at first, filtering agentsets in this way can be very powerful and concise.

That is all that seems to be needed to allow agents to remember where they have been and to avoid returning to the same stall again. However, under certain circumstances, the code produces an error (see Figure 2.4).

Getting errors such as this one is an almost inevitable part of programming. To find the source of the problem requires working through the program, command by command. It is part of the all-important process of verification, mentioned previously. It is often useful to add commands to

Figure 2.4   A NetLogo runtime error.

display intermediate values, such as the `show` command (which prints values in the command centre that is visible at the bottom of the interface; Figure 2.1).

In this case, the error arose because the agent had already visited all the stalls in the market but still had items on its shopping list. For such an agent, the `not-yet-visited` agentset is empty – in NetLogo parlance, it contains `nobody`. This must be because the items the agent has not yet managed to buy are in fact not sold by any trader (remember that each trader sells a random selection of items, and sometimes no trader selects one of the fruits or vegetables in the `fruit-and-veg` list). So the variable `stall` has the value `nobody`, the agent tries to face in the direction of `nobody`, and NetLogo complains and halts the program.

What can we do? One possibility is to arrange matters so that all the kinds of produce are sold by at least one trader. Another is to allow the shopper to give up if it cannot find a trader to sell it the remaining items on its list. The latter seems more useful, so the following code is added after line 43:

```
42  ; choose a stall
43  let stall one-of not-yet-visited
    if stall = nobody [
      show (word "No one sells " shopping-list)
      set shopping-list []
      stop
    ]
```

Notice here the use of the show command, and the reporter word, which joins two or more things together to form one string of characters. This might print something like (shopper 12): "No one sells [lettuce]" in the 'command centre'.

In this third version, we have shown how to use the with keyword to create tailored sets of agents and how to deal with runtime errors. In the final enhancement, we shall explain more about procedures in NetLogo.

2.6   Final enhancement: more economically rational agents

While the agents now do not keep going back to the same trader, they still behave in a rather implausible way, choosing stalls randomly. It would be more interesting if they were able to plan ahead and buy from the stalls that would give them the best price. (Recall that each trader offers its stock at its own price; there is no uniform market price in this model). The agents should view the price lists of the traders, calculate what their shopping lists would cost if they bought from those traders and then go for the cheapest. In principle, it would be possible for agents to do this exhaustively, checking every price list, but we will also assume that the shoppers have limited time and energy and so will only check a few traders.

In this version of the model, before an agent buys anything, it tries out one or more potential purchases from traders. For example, it sees what would be the cost of buying its shopping list from trader 1, trader 10 and trader 5 and compares that with the cost of buying the same shopping list from, for instance, trader 3, trader 2 and trader 7. It does this for n-scans different sets of traders, selecting the set that gives the cheapest outcome. Then it actually buys what is on its shopping list from that cheapest set.

We can think of this as giving the agent some additional 'intelligence' so that it can plan ahead. Clearly, to minimise the cost of the purchases, the agent could find the prices at every stall and engage in some calculation to minimise its outgoings (although this might be quite complicated and time consuming, since not all traders sell all the kinds of produce, so the shopper would have to find the trader with the minimum price for each item on the shopping list and go to that trader's stall). We shall assume that such an optimising strategy, which requires knowledge of every trader's prices for every kind of produce (i.e. perfect information) and potentially visiting as many traders as there are items on the shopping list (i.e. unbounded time and energy), is not possible for these agents. Instead, we make them boundedly rational: able to visit only a few stalls and to compute only a few possible permutations of where to buy what.

To implement this, we write an additional procedure. This procedure, called search-before-buying, will be similar to the code used before, except that the agent will just note the potential cost of its purchases, rather than actually buying. It does this a number of times (as set by a slider on the interface called n-scans) and returns to the main section of code a list of the stalls that yields the lowest total price of all that it has tried. The go procedure has then just to visit those stalls in order.

Procedures are of two kinds: those, such as the go procedure we have seen already, which carry out a set of commands, and those, called reporters, that compute and return a value. search-before-buying is of the second kind, because it returns a list of the best stalls to buy from. A reporter must start with the keyword to-report and must have within it the command report followed by some value, which it returns to the calling procedure. For example, we could write let route search-before-buying, and the variable route would then be set to the best list of stalls as calculated by search-before-buying.

It is often more convenient and clearer to extract distinct parts of a program and put them into a procedure. Another example is the code to look up the price of product from a stall. In the

Box 2.4   Additional procedures to implement finding the cheapest stalls, under bounded rationality.

```
36  to-report search-before-buying
37    ; see how much it would cost to purchase using n-scans
        sequences
38    ; of traders' stalls and report the cheapest
39    ; initialise cheapest with a very large number
40    ; so every purchase will be cheaper
41    let cheapest-price 100000
42    let cheapest-route []
43    repeat n-scans [
44      let this-route []
45      let cost 0
46      let to-buy shopping-list
47      let visited []
48      while [ not empty? to-buy] [
49        let stall one-of traders with [ not member? self
            visited ]
50        if stall = nobody [
51        show (word "Trying to buy " to-buy ", but no trader
            sells it.")
52        set shopping-list []
53        report []
54        ]
55      set visited lput stall visited
56      let purchases buy-from-stall to-buy stall
57      if not empty? purchases [
58        set this-route lput stall this-route
59        foreach purchases [
60          set cost cost + produce-price ? stall
61          ; delete the items that have been bought
62          set to-buy remove ? to-buy
63          ]
64        ]
65      ]
66      if cost < cheapest-price [
67        set cheapest-price cost
68        set cheapest-route this-route
69      ]
70    ]
71    report cheapest-route
72  end
73  to-report produce-price [ produce stall ]
74    report item (position produce [stock] of stall)
      [ prices ] of stall
75  end
76  to-report buy-from-stall [ what-to-buy stall ]
77    report filter [ member? ? [stock] of stall] what-to-buy
78  end
```

previous version of the program, this was written as item (position ? [stock] of stall) [prices] of stall. It takes a little thought to work out what that code does. It is clearer if you create a new reporter with a helpful name:

```
to-report produce-price [ produce stall ]
  report item (position produce [stock] of stall) [ prices ] of
    stall
end
```

The items after the procedure name in square brackets ([produce stall]) are the procedure's arguments. When the procedure is called, the appropriate values are passed to the procedure. For example, we could execute produce-price "oranges" trader 1, and the procedure would report the price of oranges at trader 1's stall.

These two procedures are shown in Box 2.4, as well as one that reports what from a shopping list can be bought from a particular stall.

The go procedure has to be amended to get the best route through the market stalls and to follow that route:

```
35  ask shoppers [
36    let route search-before-buying
37    foreach route [
38      let stall ?
39      ; go to that stall
40      face stall
```

The rest of the code is the same as before (although we can if we wish use the produce-price and buy-from-stall reporters to make the code more readable).

2.7 Running experiments

The amount of scanning that agents do to find the cheapest stalls should be correlated with a reduction in the average price that they pay: the more they search, the more likely that they will find the optimum set of prices. However, it is not easy to see this by running the model once for each of several values of the n-scans slider. This is because the prices of the fruits and vegetables, the markups that the traders apply, the range of stock that each stall has, the shoppers' lists of what to buy and the choices of stalls to visit all vary randomly from run to run, and all affect the average price paid. This is typical of many agent-based models. They are stochastic, with behaviour that varies randomly. The usual method of assessing such models is to run them many times and take the average of the outcomes. (How many is enough runs to yield a reliable average can be complicated to work out, but as a guide, it is useful to calculate the standard deviation of the mean and continue the runs until this is no longer reducing).

Let us assume that 100 runs is enough. We should run the model 100 times with the agents each scanning one route, find the average price of the agents' shopping lists, then repeat for another 100 times with the agents scanning for the best of two routes and so on. This will clearly require running the model several hundred times, and it would be impracticable to do this manually, pressing the setup and go buttons and calculating the average of the runs hundreds of times. Fortunately, NetLogo can do the work for us. Since both setup and go are procedures, we can write some additional code that calls these procedures and calculates the desired mean of the average cost of the shopping baskets (see Box 2.5).

Box 2.5   Code to run an experiment to test the effect of varying the number of times agents scan for the cheapest combination of stalls to purchase from.

```
to run-experiment
 set n-scans 1
 let runs-per-trial 100
 while [ n-scans <= 10 ] [
  let total-of-averages 0
  repeat runs-per-trial [
   setup
   go
   set total-of-averages total-of-averages + mean [ spent ]
   of shoppers
  ]
  show (word "Mean of average of cost of shopping lists over "
runs-per-trial " runs for " n-scans " scans = " (total-of-
averages /runs-per-trial))
  set n-scans n-scans + 1
 ]
 show "Finished."
```

The run-experiment procedure can either be executed by typing run-experiment into the command centre and pressing the return key or a button can be added to the interface with run-experiment as the command to run when the button is pressed (this is similar to the way that the setup and go procedures are run when their buttons are pressed). Code like run-experiment can also save the results to a file for later analysis using a statistical program, and this is the approach used in many of the examples in this book.

An alternative to use when many runs are needed is to restructure the program so that all the initialisation is done from the go command. NetLogo also provides a tool called BehaviorSpace that can run such experiments without writing code, and often, this is easier to use than code such as in Box 2.5, but it is less flexible and has not been used for this book.

2.8   Discussion

This chapter has aimed to provide an idea of what the internals of an agent-based model looks like, as well as providing an introduction to some of the most common constructs and commands in NetLogo. Although the example we have dissected is rather simple (as it had to be in order that it could be explained within the confines of one chapter), it does illustrate the characteristics of agent-based models that were mentioned in Chapter 1. The agents were heterogeneous: the range of fruits and vegetables stocked differed between market traders, and every shopper had a different shopping list. Consequently, the behaviour of each agent differed. The dynamics of the system were important: there is no notion of equilibrium in the model, but we can observe agents proceeding through time to purchase their shopping. Thirdly, the agents interacted: shoppers bought from traders. Furthermore, agents were endowed with some rationality that allowed them to attempt to optimise but within constraints imposed by limited information and limited resources of time and effort.

At the end of each of the following chapters, there are appendices that summarise the models introduced in the chapter using a standard structure and a listing in 'pseudocode', a version of the program code that is closer to natural language. This chapter does the same to show for the example that we have described in detail what the pseudocode version looks like.

Appendix 2.A   The example model: full version

Purpose: The aim of the model is to illustrate some of the basic features of NetLogo using a simple model of a fruit and vegetable market as an example.

Entities: There are two types of agents: shoppers and traders.

Stochastic processes: The items in the shoppers' lists, the items stocked by traders and prices charged by traders are selected randomly (within set limits).

Initialisation: For shoppers, select the number of shoppers, the speed at which they walk and the number of alternative buying options they are willing to consider. For traders, select the number of items stocked.

Output: A graph showing the amount spent over time and two reporters: the mean number of items left to buy and the average spend.

A screenshot is shown in Figure 2.A.1. The pseudocode is in Box 2.A.1.

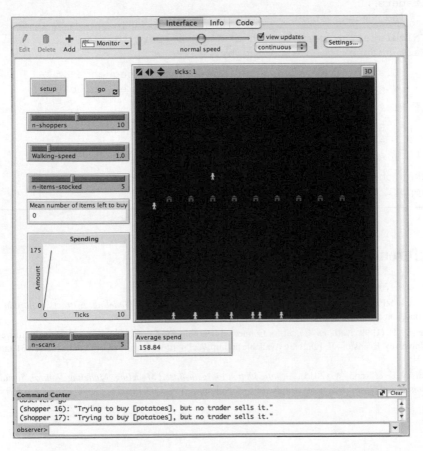

Figure 2.A.1   Screenshot of the interface of the final version of the model.

Box 2.A.1   Pseudocode for the final version of the model.

```
Set the list of 12 fruit and vegetables the traders are to sell.
Set the (wholesale) prices of the items randomly between 1
and 100.
Generate nine agents to represent traders with the shape
'house', coloured red and placed in a line across the middle.
Allocate randomly to each trader:

    Stock: which of the 12 possible items are stocked, given
    that the number of items to be stocked is set by the slider.
    Prices: based on wholesale prices plus a random mark-up
    of between 1 and 30%.

Generate the number of agents selected with the slider to
represent shoppers with the shape 'person', coloured yellow,
and distributed randomly.
Allocate three attributes to each shopper:

    A shopping list of between 1 and 8 items, selected randomly.
    A list of traders not yet visited: initially this is all
traders
    The amount spent: initially this is nil.

Calculate the mean length of the shoppers' lists.
Each shopper goes shopping by:

    Scanning the stalls for the cheapest sequence of
    stalls. It does this the number of times selected.

    Visiting the selected stalls:

        Ensuring that no stall is visited twice
        Recording what is bought
        Adding up how much is spent.

When the shopping list is empty, the shopper goes home.
Report the results and plot the graph.
```

References

Gilbert, N. (2007) *Agent-Based Models*. London: Sage.

Railsback, S.F. & Grimm, V. (2011) *Agent-Based and Individual-Based Modeling: A Practical Introduction*. Princeton: Princeton University Press.

Wilensky, U. (1999) *NetLogo*. Center for Connected Learning and Computer-Based Modeling, Northwestern University, Evanston, IL [Online]. Available at: http://ccl.northwestern.edu/netlogo/ [Accessed 31 January 2015].

Wilensky, U. & Rand, W. (2015). *An Introduction to Agent-Based Modeling: Modeling Natural, Social and Engineered Complex Systems with NetLogo*. Cambridge, MA: MIT Press.

3

Heterogeneous demand

3.1 Introduction

Economics is about the allocation of scarce resources. In other words, it is about making choices. Like most introductory economics textbooks, this book starts with the choices faced by consumers and the determinants of consumer demand.

Consumers spend money on many different things. And different households will have very different spending patterns: a pensioner living alone will not buy the same things as student living alone nor as a family with children. In the United Kingdom, the Office for National Statistics (ONS) undertakes an annual survey of households' spending (ONS, 2011). The information collected is very detailed as it is used to set the appropriate weights for the retail and consumer price indices. In the United States, the Bureau of Labor Statistics conducts the similar *Consumer Expenditure Survey*.

Figure 3.1 shows what the UK 2010 *Family Spending* survey found in broad terms: housing, food and fuel accounted for 40% of the average household's budget. It also shows the spending pattern for the poorest, defined as those in the bottom 10% of the distribution of gross household income, and for the richest, in the top 10%. For some expenditure categories, such as housing, the budget share varied little from the richest to the poorest households. However, the poorest households spent much higher proportions of their budgets on food, fuel and power than the richest, while the opposite was the case for transport.

Looking at expenditure patterns in more detail, consumption is even more varied. For example:

- While 99% of households reported spending on food during the survey period, and four out of five reported buying fresh fruit, only 45% reported buying apples.

- While 99% of households reported spending on recreation and leisure during the survey period, only about a third reported buying pet food and only a fifth, books.

Agent-Based Modelling in Economics, First Edition. Lynne Hamill and Nigel Gilbert.
© 2016 John Wiley & Sons, Ltd. Published 2016 by John Wiley & Sons, Ltd.

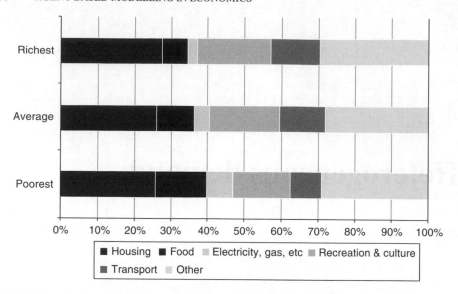

Figure 3.1   Budget shares by household income: United Kingdom, 2010. Source: ONS (2011).

Thus, households have different incomes, different tastes and different spending patterns. While the spending pattern of the average household may be useful for certain purposes, such as constructing a consumer price index, it is very likely that no household actually spent their budget in that way. Consumers are heterogeneous.

One of the key benefits of agent-based modelling is its ability to deal with heterogeneity, and this chapter demonstrates how this can be done. In Section 3.2 an agent-based model for basic textbook consumer demand theory is developed. Then practical models to examine the impact of price changes in the real world are presented. The chapter ends with a summary and an assessment of models based on heterogeneous agents with those that use representative agents. The Appendix to the chapter describes the models in detail and suggests ways of using them.

3.2   Modelling basic consumer demand theory

A household's demand for a good depends on its tastes, its budget, the price of the good in question and the prices of other goods. Tastes, or more formally preferences, can be modelled by a utility function, from which indifference curves are generated, showing which combinations of goods generate the same level of utility. The slope of an indifference curve therefore shows how much of one good the household is willing to give up for more of the other or, put formally, the marginal rate of substitution (MRS).

To maximise utility subject to a budget constraint, the slope of the indifference curve, which, as just explained, is the MRS, must equal the slope of the budget constraint. The slope of the budget constraint is determined by relative prices. If prices change, the slope of the budget constraint changes and so does the utility-maximising choice. Tracking these choices as prices are changed traces a demand curve.

An example shows how this works. There are two goods, *A* and *B*. Good *B* is defined as a 'composite commodity' that comprises all the things that are bought except good *A*. Furthermore, the units of this composite commodity are defined as all that can be purchased for one unit of currency (be it £1, $1 or €1). In other words, the price of *B* is always 1. (In some texts, this composite commodity is described as a numeraire.) In this way, a two-good analysis can be applied to many choices.

Specifically, consider a household with a budget of £100, the price of *A* and the price of *B* are both £1, and this particular household's utility is maximised when it buys 50 of *A* and 50 of *B*. However, if the price of *A* in terms of *B* doubles (from 1 to 2), then to continue to maximise its utility, given the assumed utility function, the household's demand for *A* falls from 50 to 25. Because it can now afford less *A*, the household has moved to a lower indifference curve. This is shown in the top of Figure 3.2. This analysis generates two points on the demand curve: when the price of *A* is 1, demand is 50 and when price is 2, demand is 25. Repeating this analysis gives more points to plot the demand curve shown at the bottom of Figure 3.2. (Note that because of the form

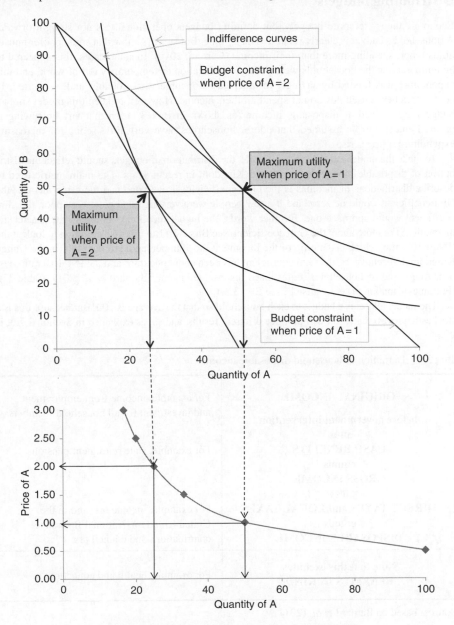

Figure 3.2   Effect of a change in price on demand.

of the utility function assumed, the demand for B is not affected by price changes in this example because total expenditure on A does not change, remaining at £50. This is discussed further later.)

To create an agent-based model using this theory, agents representing households are each allocated a budget and a utility function. To draw demand curves, each household is asked how much of the good in question it would buy at that price. First, we show how to model budgets, and then we add a utility function and generate demand curves.

Distributing budgets

Economic theory refers to budgets, but defining budgets operationally is not straightforward. A household's budget is clearly related to its income. But surveys show that some poorer households report spending more than their income (Carrera, 2010). In some cases, this appeared to be temporary as the households were young, in education or temporarily out of work, and this expenditure was funded by savings. In other cases, income was probably under-reported. In contrast, richer households do not spend all their income. However, to keep this model simple, budgets are defined as disposable income (as shown in Box 3.1), so that any borrowing is ignored and it will be assumed that poorer households have very little scope for increasing expenditure if prices rise.

To make the model as realistic as possible, the distribution of budgets should reflect the distribution of disposable income in the United Kingdom in recent years. The main metric used to describe distributions of incomes is the Gini coefficient: if everyone had the same income, the Gini coefficient would be zero, and if a few people were very rich and most very poor, the Gini coefficient would approach one. In other words, the higher the Gini coefficient, the greater the inequality. (For more about the Gini coefficient, see Box 3.2.) But it is also common to look at the 'P90/P10' ratio, which is the ratio of the income at the 90th percentile to the 10th. In the United Kingdom in recent years, the Gini coefficient has been about one third and the P90/P10 ratio, just over four based on households' equivalised disposable income (Barnard et al., 2011: Table 27). (For an explanation of 'equivalised', see Box 3.3.)

The model allocates a budget to each household so that the average is 100. But because this is a stochastic process, each run will produce different results, and so, as explained in Section 2.7, it is

Box 3.1   Definition of household disposable income.

ORIGINAL INCOME **before government intervention** plus **CASH BENEFITS** equals **GROSS INCOME** less **DIRECT TAXES and LOCAL TAXES** equals **DISPOSABLE INCOME**	For example, income from employment and investment for all household members For example, state retirement pensions For example, income tax, and in the United Kingdom, National Insurance contributions and council tax
Note that this excludes **BENEFITS IN KIND**	For example, health and education

Source: based on Barnard et al. (2011).

Box 3.2 The Gini coefficient.

If income were distributed evenly, then, for example, 50% of households would have 50% of the total income. In practice, the distribution is skewed and the poorest half receives much less than half the total income. Graphically, the income distribution can be represented by the Lorenz curve.

The Gini coefficient is the ratio of the area between the Lorenz curve and the straight line that represents an equal distribution (indicated by the darker shaded area A) and the total area below the straight line (area A + area B).

In other words, the Gini coefficient measures the extent to which the actual distribution of income deviates from complete income equality: the lower the coefficient, the more even the distribution.

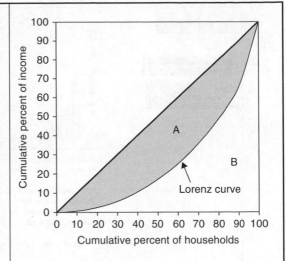

Box 3.3 Equivalised disposable income.

Equivalisation is a process of adjusting incomes to reflect the common sense view that, in order to enjoy a comparable standard of living, a household of, for example, two adults will need a higher level of income than a household of one person.

The data presented here is based on the modified OECD scale using the following weights:
First adult: 0.67
Second and subsequent adults: 0.33 (per adult)
Child aged 13 and under: 0.20
Child aged 14 and over: 0.33
The values for each household member are added together to give the total equivalence number for that household. Disposable income is then divided by this number to give equivalised disposable income for the household.

For example, take a household comprising a married couple with two children under 14. The household's equivalence number is

$$0.67 + 0.33 + 0.20 + 0.20 = 1.40$$

If the household's disposable income is £20 000, its equivalised disposable income

$$= £20\,000 / 1.40 = £14\,286$$

Source: Barnard *et al.* (2011).

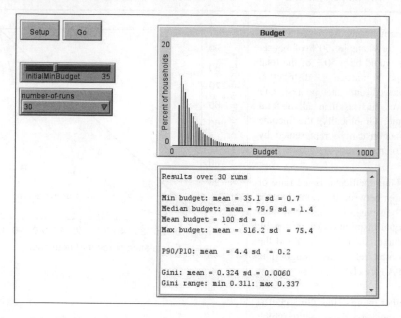

Figure 3.3   The budget distribution model (based on 30 runs, each with 1000 agents).

necessary to take averages over several runs. Figure 3.3 shows an example of the output based on 1 000 agents over 30 runs: the distribution is based on all 30 000 agents, while metrics – the minimum, median, mean and maximum – are the means of these metrics taken from each run. This shows that while there is little variation in the minimum budgets between runs, the maximum varies a great deal. Because the distribution is normalised, the mean budget is the same in all runs (100), so the standard deviation of the mean is zero. The Gini coefficient is simply the average over 30 runs. Overall, the model broadly replicates the distribution of household equivalised disposable income in the United Kingdom in recent years: the median budget is below the mean budget, the Gini coefficient is around third and the P90/10 ratio just over 4. The model is described in Appendix 3.A.

Giving preferences to households

In economic theory, preferences are modelled by utility functions. A Cobb–Douglas utility function has been chosen because it offers a very simple analysis that may already be familiar. The Cobb–Douglas utility function for two goods is

$$U = A^\alpha B^{1-\alpha}$$

where U is utility, A and B are the quantities of goods A and B, respectively, and alpha (α) must lie between zero and one. Each agent's tastes are controlled by alpha: the higher alpha, the stronger the preference for good A. When utility is maximised subject to the budget constraint, the demand for A, A^* is given by alpha (α) multiplied by the agent's budget (m) and divided by the price of A (P_A):

$$A^* = \frac{\alpha m}{P_A}$$

Further, this means that when utility is maximised, the share of the agent's budget spent on good A is alpha. See Box 3.4 for details.

Box 3.4   Mathematics of the Cobb–Douglas utility function.

The Cobb–Douglas utility function for two goods is

$$U = A^{\alpha} B^{(1-\alpha)} \tag{3.1}$$

where U=utility, A and B are the quantities of goods A and B and $0<\alpha<1$. (The higher α, the stronger the preference for good A.)

$$\text{The marginal rate of substitution}\,(\text{MRS}) = \frac{\partial U / \partial A}{\partial U / \partial B} \tag{3.2}$$

where the deltas (∂) represent partial derivatives to measure what happens when one variable changes and the others remain the same. (For an explanation of partial derivatives, see, e.g. Bradley and Patton, 2002, pp.336–340.) Differentiating gives

$$\text{MRS} = \frac{\alpha A^{(\alpha-1)} B^{(1-\alpha)}}{(1-\alpha)A^{\alpha} B^{(1-\alpha-1)}} = \frac{\alpha B}{(1-\alpha)A} \tag{3.3}$$

Note that if α were to equal 1, the denominator of the MRS would be 0, and so α is always less than 1.

The budget constraint can be written as

$$m = P_A A + P_B B \tag{3.4}$$

where m is the budget, P_A is the price of A and P_B is the price of B and P_A and P_B are independent.

Rearranging (3.4) gives

$$B = \frac{m - P_A A}{P_B} \tag{3.5}$$

So the slope of the budget line is the price of A divided by the price of B. Utility will be maximised when this equals the MRS. So from (3.3):

$$\frac{\alpha B}{(1-\alpha)A} = \frac{P_A}{P_B} \tag{3.6}$$

Substituting (3.5) in (3.6) gives

$$\frac{\alpha \dfrac{m - P_A}{P_B}}{(1-\alpha)A} = \frac{P_A}{P_B} \tag{3.7}$$

Rearranging (3.7), the P_B s cancel out and so utility is maximised when

$$A = \frac{\alpha m}{P_A} \tag{3.8}$$

Rearranging (3.8) gives

$$\alpha = \frac{P_A A}{m} \tag{3.9}$$

In other words α equals the budget share of A when utility is maximised subject to the budget constraint.

At this point, the model is populated by 1000 household agents having budgets distributed in roughly the same way as the UK population. Taking food as an example, the next step is to find out what proportion of their budgets each allocates to the purchase of food; in other words, the households' budget share for food. The average budget share for food was about 10% in the United Kingdom in 2010 although the shares varied from nearly 15% in the bottom quintile of households – the poorest 20% – to 8% in the top quintile – the richest 20% (ONS, 2011). But these are only averages, and within each quintile, there will have been variation too: so some of the poorest may spend more than 15% and some of the richest, less than 8%. To model these variations, a mean budget share (or alpha) is allocated to each budget quintile group together with the same standard deviation for all groups; and for each group, budget shares are distributed normally using those two parameters. For example, for the bottom quintile, the budget share is allocated randomly using a normal distribution with a mean of 15% (or 0.15) and a standard deviation of 2% (or 0.02). This means that two thirds of the households in the bottom quintile will have budget shares of between 13% (or 0.13) and 17% (or 0.17) and almost all will have budget shares between 9% (0.09) and 21% (0.21). This is illustrated in Figure 3.4.

Figure 3.5 shows an example (based on a single run) of the distribution of budget shares generated by the model using 1000 agents: the shares range from 2.6% (0.026) to 20.1% (0.201), with a median of 11.6% (0.116) and an average of 10.2% (0.102).

Each household is then asked how much it would buy at a given price, following through the process illustrated in Figure 3.2. This means that for every price, a set of demands are generated, as shown in the example in the left panel of Figure 3.6. Repeating this process for different prices and adding together the demand from each household produces an aggregate demand curve as shown in the right panel of Figure 3.6. Each point of the demand curve on the right was found by summing the demands of households, as shown on the left of Figure 3.6, and plotting the total against the price to generate that total. In other words, the macro aggregate demand curve has been created from micro assumptions about households' budgets and utility functions.

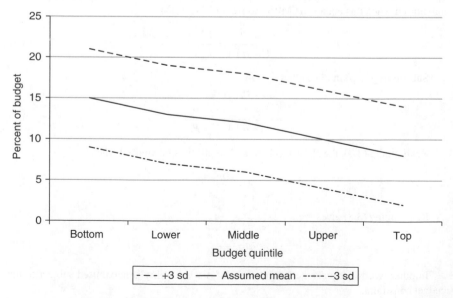

Figure 3.4   Assumed budget shares (alphas) for food.

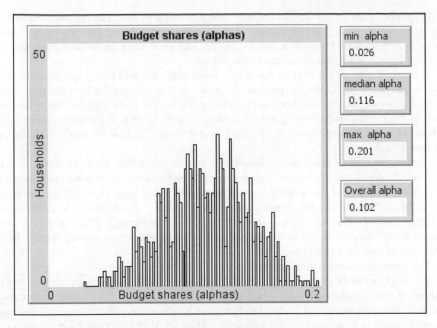

Figure 3.5   Results: distribution of budget shares generated by model (based on a single run using 1000 agents). (A single run is used as this model serves only to illustrate the methodology and has no practical value.)

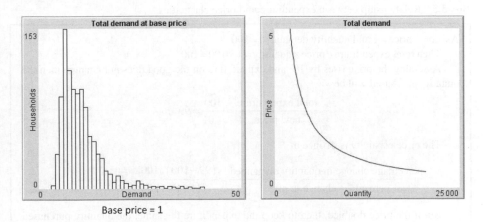

Figure 3.6   Results: demand for food based on a Cobb–Douglas utility function (based on a single run of 1000 agents).

The impact of price changes on demand is measured by the own-price elasticity (called 'own-price' to distinguish it from cross-price elasticities, which measure the effect of a change in the price of one good on the demand for another and which are not used here). The own-price elasticity is given by

$$\frac{\text{percentage change in quantity demanded}}{\text{percentage change in price}}$$

If the price rises by 1% and the quantity demanded falls by 1%, then the price elasticity is said to be one or, strictly, −1. In this case, the expenditure on the good does not change. But if the own-price elasticity is less than one, total expenditure will rise if the price is increased; and if the elasticity is more than one, expenditure will fall.

Given the Cobb–Douglas utility function, a household's demand for a good depends on the good's price, the household's budget, and the good's budget share in that household (as previously discussed). Because neither the budget nor the budget share changes when the price changes, the amount spent on the good in question does not change, so the own-price elasticity is always (−) one for small changes. (To see why this is only the case for small price changes, see Box 3.5.)

Because the Cobb–Douglas utility function is used in this model, the price elasticity is the same for all agents, the percentage change in demand is the same for all households, and total expenditure on the good whose price has increased does not change. However, the percentage change in utility will differ between households. The model plots the change in utility against budget for each of 1000 households as shown in the example in Figure 3.7. The figure also shows that the poorest households suffer the greatest reductions in utility because they spend a higher proportion of their income on food.

This model is described in Appendix 3.A.

The simplicity of the Cobb–Douglas utility function has a basic disadvantage, namely, that the share of an agent's budget that is spent on a particular class of goods is fixed whatever happens to prices. If price changes are small, a fixed budget share may be a reasonable assumption, and much economic analysis is based on marginal decisions. However, if, for example, food becomes very expensive, people will buy cheaper or less food, but they are also likely to cut down on non-food

---

Box 3.5   Relationship between expenditure and price elasticities.

Assumed price = 1 and quantity demanded = 100

Then total expenditure = price × quantity = 1 × 100 = 100

Assuming the price rises by 1% and expenditure on the good does not change, then the quantity purchased will be

$$\frac{\text{total expenditure}}{\text{new price}} = \frac{100}{1.01} = 99$$

The price elasticity is defined as

$$\frac{\text{percentage change in quantity demanded}}{\text{percentage change in price}} = \frac{(99 - 100)/100}{(1.01 - 1)} = \frac{-0.01}{0.01} = -1$$

But if the price doubled, then to keep the expenditure the same, the quantity purchased would have to halve:

$$\frac{\text{total expenditure}}{\text{new price}} = \frac{100}{2} = 50$$

Thus, the own-price elasticity =

$$\frac{(50 - 100)/100}{(2 - 1)} = \frac{-0.5}{1} = -0.5$$

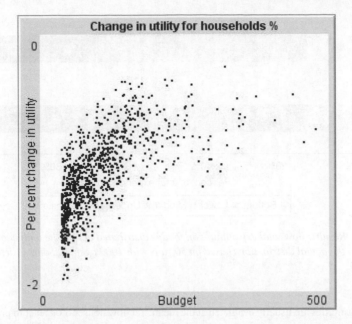

Figure 3.7   Results: change in utility by budget following a 10% increase in the price of food (based on a single run with 1000 agents).

expenditure so as to be able to spend more on food. In other words, alpha should vary with the price of the good in question. More complicated utility functions, such as the constant elasticity of substitution, have been developed to overcome these problems. But in the real world, households do not have observable utility functions. Indeed, it is arguable whether households even have utility functions of the kind envisaged by economic theory, based on rational or consistent choices (see, e.g. Kahneman, 2011) let alone the continuously differentiable utility function described in textbooks. For these reasons, we shall leave the Cobb–Douglas utility for now, though we shall be returning to it in Chapter 5. The next section presents more pragmatic models to use to examine the effect of price changes in the real world.

3.3   Practical demand modelling

It is possible to model the effect of changes in prices without making any assumptions about an underlying utility function by using just budget shares and price elasticities. As in the previous model, agents represent households and budgets are distributed to generate a Gini coefficient of about a third and a P90/P10 ratio of about 4. But instead of relying on a utility function to generate price elasticities, these are selected by the modeller.

Again, food is taken as the example, and budget shares are allocated in the same way. As realism is now important, to check that the chosen parameter values 'add up' to what is observed in the real world, the overall distribution of total expenditure on food between quintiles generated by the model is compared to that shown in the ONS survey in Figure 3.8. The model does yield a pattern of overall budget shares for each quintile that is similar to the observed pattern: for example, in 2010, the top quintile – the darkest section of each bar – accounted for 30% of the total expenditure on food, while in the model, the top quintile accounts for 32%.

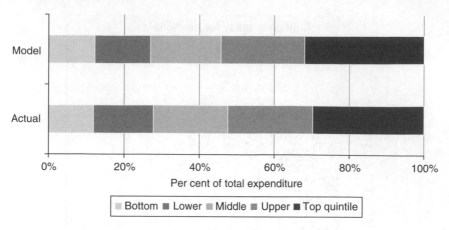

Figure 3.8   Results: how total expenditure on food is distributed across the budget quintiles compared to the actual distribution (based on 30 runs with 1000 agents). Source (actual): ONS (2011).

Price elasticities are usually evaluated at the mean. Yet how households react to price changes will depend on their income. For a basic good, such as food, richer households may not react at all to an increase in prices, funding the additional expenditure by saving less, while poorer households may have to cut consumption because they cannot afford to spend more. Put formally, price elasticities (for small price changes) could vary between 0 for the richest households, who consume as they did before the price rise, and (–) 1 for the poorest, whose total expenditure on food does not change but who have to consume less. Although this is rather obvious, surprisingly, estimates of price elasticities for different income groups are rare. One of these rare examples is Blundell *et al.* (1993). They estimated that the own-price elasticity for food varied from an average of about (–) 0.6 for those in the bottom quartile of the expenditure distribution to an average of (–) 0.3 for those in the top decile, while the overall elasticity was (–) 0.5. (These are averages and within each expenditure group, the elasticity will vary between households.)

Based on Blundell *et al.*'s (1993) estimates, we have assumed the elasticities shown in the top panel of Box 3.6. Again, the model allows for variation both between quintile groups and within quintile groups. The same method is used to allocate elasticities as for allocating budget shares. For each quintile group, a mean is set and the elasticities are allocated normally using these means and an overall standard deviation. So, for instance, if the mean own-price elasticity of the upper quintile is set at (–) 0.4, with a standard deviation of 0.1, then two thirds of the upper quintile households will have elasticities lying between (–) 0.3 and (–) 0.5, while almost all will have elasticities between (–) 0.1 and (–) 0.7. On the basis of all these assumptions, the model produces an overall elasticity of (–) 0.5, but ranging from 0 to (–) 0.9. The resulting distribution of elasticities is shown in the top panel of Box 3.6.

On this basis, a price rise of 10% will reduce demand by 4.4%, and total expenditure will rise by 5.1%. However, this increase in expenditure will vary from 3.4% among the poorest to 6.7% among the richest households. Overall, the budget share rises from 10.3 to 10.8%. The details are shown in the lower panel of Box 3.6.

This model is adequate for examining the consumption of things that are consumed by everyone, such as food in general. But the more narrowly consumption is defined, the less likely

Box 3.6 Practical demand model: food (based on 30 runs with 1000 agents).

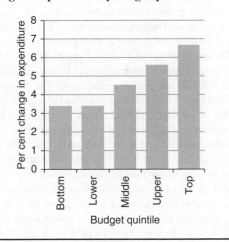

Own-price elasticities	
Assumed mean price elasticities	**Distribution of elasticities**
Bottom quintile −0.6 Lower quintile −0.6 Middle quintile −0.5 Upper quintile −0.4 Top quintile −0.3 (All with sd of 0.1)	Mean −0.48 (sd 0.05) ($N = 30\,000$, i.e. 1000 agents over 30 runs)
Effect of 10% price rise	
Average per cent change in: • Demand: mean −4.41 (sd 0.04) • Expenditure: mean +5.15 (sd 0.05) Budget share (per cent): • Before: mean 10.29 (sd 0.08) • After: mean 10.82 (sd 0.09) *Note: $N = 30$ i.e. on each run, we took the average and here we report the average of those 30 averages.*	**Change in expenditure by budget quintile**

it is that all households consume the item in question. To contrast with the example of food, the next example is a luxury good mostly consumed by better-off households, which has an own-price elasticity of more than (−) 1. The example taken is expenditure on 'cinema, theatre, museums, etc.'. In the United Kingdom in 2010, the average budget share of this category was ½%, rising from ¼% for the poorest income decile to ¾% for the richest (ONS, 2011). This pattern means that the expenditure is concentrated in the two top quintiles: indeed, 40% of households account for nearly three quarters of the total expenditure. However, only 16% of households reported any expenditure on these outings during in the survey period.

Because not everyone consumes these entertainment services, a two-stage model is required. The first stage determines who consumes, while the second stage determines how much those households that consume do consume. Ideally, we would determine which households consume by taking into account income and other characteristics such as age, education or class. We shall do this in Chapter 4, but here, for simplicity, the first stage is simplified by setting the initial proportions of each budget quintile group that consumes, together with a minimum consumption level below which consumption is rounded down to zero. This minimum is required so that when prices rise, some households will actually stop consuming.

The method is the same as used for allocating budget shares and own-price elasticities: for each budget quintile group, a mean is set and allocations are made randomly within a normal distribution with an overall standard deviation for all quintiles. There are therefore three sets of parameters for which the mean for each budget quintile and a common standard deviation for all must be set:

• For the budget shares

• For the initial percentage consuming

• For the price elasticities

The levels are chosen to reflect the overall distribution of the expenditure between quintiles and produce the overall budget shares noted in the Introduction to this chapter. The details are shown in Box 3.7.

On this basis, the model showed 16.7% of households consumed, which is in line with the 16% observed; and the overall budget share, including non-consumers, was 0.47%, again in line with the observed budget share of 0.5%. The bottom panel of Box 3.7 shows how the model replicated the observed pattern of total expenditure across the quintiles.

Turning now to the impact of price changes, Macmillan and Smith (2001) found 'a strong inverse relationship between cinema admissions and price' in the United Kingdom, but did not offer a figure for the price elasticity. The nearest figure we have found is Dewenter and Westermann's (2005) estimate that the price elasticity of cinema visits in Germany was over (−) 2. This means that if the price rises by 10%, the demand will fall by more than 20% and total expenditure will fall by more than 12% ($1.10 \times (1 - 0.2)$). But each household will have a different elasticity depending on its income and its priorities. For a luxury such as these outings, the poorer households will probably reduce their expenditure by more. However, we do not have any estimates of price elasticities by income group and so have assumed somewhat arbitrarily that the price elasticities vary from (−) 2.5 for the poorest to (−) 1.5 for the richest with a standard deviation for all groups of 0.5 (as shown in the left top panel of Box 3.8). On this basis, the average elasticity is (−) 2 varying from (−) 4.4 to 0 (as shown in the right top panel of Box 3.8).

If the price rises by 10%, the model suggests that demand will fall by 17% and total expenditure by 8%. A few (0.1%) households will stop consuming altogether, all of these being in the bottom two quintiles. As a result, according to the model, the fall in expenditure will vary from a reduction in expenditure of 20% among the poorest to only 6% among the richest households. Overall, the budget share falls from 0.47 to 0.43%. The full results are shown in the lower panel of Box 3.8. In effect, the increase in price concentrates expenditure even more in the higher income groups.

Box 3.7   Results: Expenditure on cinema and theatre visits (based on 30 runs with 1000 agents).

Assumptions		
	Initial per cent consuming[a]	Mean budget share of consumers (per cent)[b]
Bottom quintile	15	1.0
Lower quintile	10	1.0
Middle quintile	15	2.0
Upper quintile	25	2.0
Top quintile	25	3.0

[a] Minimum consumption level (below which consumption is rounded down to zero) = 0.1.
[b] sd for all quintiles = 0.5%.

How total expenditure on cinema and theatre visits is distributed across the income/ budget quintiles compared to the actual observed distribution.

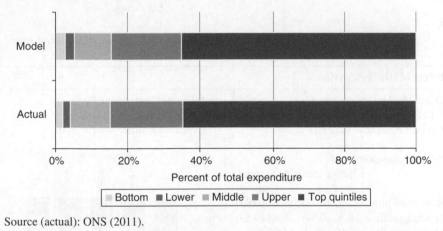

Source (actual): ONS (2011).

3.4   Discussion

Economic theory postulates that households' demand depends on their budgets and their preferences. An agent-based model using this theory was created, with agents representing households. It was done in two stages. In the first stage, a model was built to generate a budget distribution to reproduce the income distribution observed in the United Kingdom, with a Gini coefficient of about a third and a P90/P10 ratio of about four. The second stage was to add a Cobb–Douglas utility function to generate preferences. Each household was then asked how much it would consume at different prices, and these were summed to produce an aggregate demand curve. This process established a traceable path from households' utility functions and budgets to aggregate demand. But while utility functions provide a nice logical framework, they are not observable in practice. So the next model made no assumptions about underlying utility but used just budgets

Box 3.8   Effect of a price rise on demand for cinema and theatre visits.

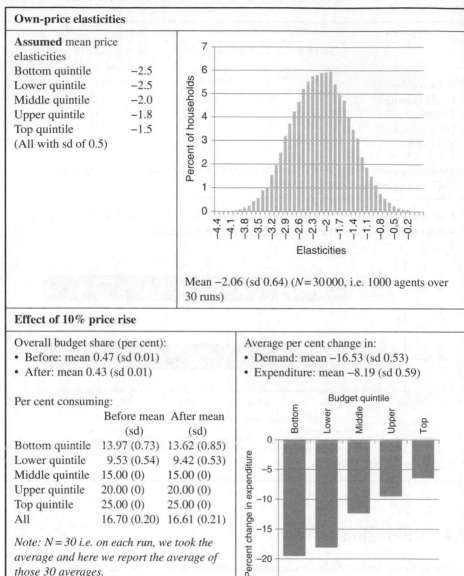

Own-price elasticities	
Assumed mean price elasticities	

Bottom quintile   −2.5
Lower quintile   −2.5
Middle quintile   −2.0
Upper quintile   −1.8
Top quintile   −1.5
(All with sd of 0.5)

Mean −2.06 (sd 0.64) (N = 30000, i.e. 1000 agents over 30 runs)

Effect of 10% price rise

Overall budget share (per cent):
- Before: mean 0.47 (sd 0.01)
- After: mean 0.43 (sd 0.01)

Average per cent change in:
- Demand: mean −16.53 (sd 0.53)
- Expenditure: mean −8.19 (sd 0.59)

Per cent consuming:

	Before mean (sd)	After mean (sd)
Bottom quintile	13.97 (0.73)	13.62 (0.85)
Lower quintile	9.53 (0.54)	9.42 (0.53)
Middle quintile	15.00 (0)	15.00 (0)
Upper quintile	20.00 (0)	20.00 (0)
Top quintile	25.00 (0)	25.00 (0)
All	16.70 (0.20)	16.61 (0.21)

Note: N = 30 i.e. on each run, we took the average and here we report the average of those 30 averages.

and price elasticities to estimate the effect of price changes. To sum up, this chapter has presented three models:

- To generate an budget distribution
- To model demand using a Cobb–Douglas utility function
- To model the impact of price changes without using a utility function

How do these models compare with models based on averages, such as the 'representative agent' discussed in Chapter 1? For example, if we take an average household and the average price elasticity for food of (−) 0.5, a price rise of 10% will result in an increase in total expenditure of 4.5% $(1.1 \times (1 - 0.05) = 1.045)$. The model using heterogeneous agents suggested expenditure will rise by 5.1%, more than the representative agent method suggests. This may seem surprising. It arises because of the skewness of the budget distribution. Even though most households have a below average budget – the median is less than the mean – and despite the fact that richer households spend a lower proportion of their budgets on food, the households in the top 20% of the budget distribution account for 30% of the expenditure (as shown in Figure 3.8). As richer households have lower price elasticities, their expenditure will rise by more: according to the model, the rise in expenditure varies from 3% in the poorest quintile to 7% in the richest. In both cases, expenditure rises less than the price has risen, which means that demand has fallen, by 6% in the poorest households but only 3% among the richest. This depth of understanding is just not available from a method relying on averages.

To show how this depth might be useful, imagine that the 10% increase in the price of food was the result of the imposition of value-added tax. (In the United Kingdom, most food is not taxed.) Not surprisingly, the practical demand model shows that the tax is regressive. The tax paid amounts to an average of 1.4% of the budget of the poorest quintile and 0.8% of the richest (because the poor spend a higher proportion of their budget on food than do the rich). Nevertheless, the richest quintile actually pay 32% of the total tax revenue compared to only 12% paid by the poorest because the rich spend more on food. See details in Table 3.1.

Furthermore, the representative agent approach is especially weak in the case of the luxury good which the average household does not consume at all. If the average price elasticity of (−) 2 were applied, demand would fall by 20% and expenditure by 12%. The model using heterogeneous agents suggested a few households would actually stop consuming altogether and total expenditure would fall by 8%, less than the 12% suggested by the representative agent model. However, these figures were derived using price elasticities that were assumed because no estimates are available. If we are to move away from using representative agents, we need estimates of price elasticities for different income groups and not just at the mean.

It would be surprising if both methods produced the same results because for that to be the case, the Engel curves (i.e. the relationship between income and consumption) must be linear. Clearly, this is rarely so. The heterogeneous agent model provides more detailed results and can throw light on possible distribution effects. For further discussion, see Blundell et al. (1993).

We noted at the beginning of this chapter that households have different budgets and different preferences and different consumption patterns and that the average household in this sense does not exist. Why, then, should analysis be based on averages? We noted in Chapter 1 that Hayek (1931,

Table 3.1   Results: estimated effect of the imposition of a 10% ad valorem tax on food.

	Effective tax rate (%) Mean (sd)	Share of revenue (%) Mean (sd)
Bottom quintile	1.4 (0.016)	12.0 (0.2)
Lower quintile	1.2 (0.013)	14.4 (0.3)
Middle quintile	1.1 (0.022)	18.7 (0.4)
Upper quintile	1.0 (0.015)	22.5 (0.4)
Top quintile	0.8 (0.013)	32.3 (0.7)
Overall/total	1.0 (0.010)	100

Based on 30 runs with 1000 agents.

p.5) argued averages were of no value. Yet 80 years later, when ONS tried to use its data to assess the impact of the post-2008 recession on expenditure, it seemed rather surprised to find that analysis based on an average household does not work: 'It appears that it is difficult to define the impact of the recession on the typical household, with the effect depending greatly on household circumstances and preferences' (ONS, 2011, p.86). With twenty-first century computing power, there is no longer any need to rely on averages. The simple models presented in this chapter show how a few micro assumptions can be used to reproduce macro patterns observed in the real world, taking heterogeneity into account.

To sum up, in this chapter, we have shown how agent-based models can produce heterogeneity. There are some situations for which the representative agent may be sufficient, but for others, such as when goods are not widely consumed or there is interest in the distributive impact of the price (or tax) change, the representative agent approach is inadequate. But what we have done here could have been achieved using microsimulation. We have not utilised the unique characteristic of agent-based modelling, namely, the ability of agents to interact with one another. In the next chapter, we will start to see what happens when agents do influence each other's behaviour.

Appendix 3.A   How to do it

Budget distribution

Purpose: The aim of the model is to generate a set of agents to represent households and to allocate to each household a budget to meet certain macro distribution metrics, normalised so that the average budget equals 100.

Entities: Agents are created to represent households, and each household is given just one characteristic: its budget.

Stochastic processes: The model distributes budgets randomly using an exponential function, shifted 'right' to avoid very low budgets. The exponential is used because the median is below the mean and it generates some high values in the tail. It also has the advantage that there is a ready-made function in NetLogo to create an exponential random distribution and that only one parameter is required, the mean. However, as the budgets are normalised to 100, this is preset.

Initialisation: Only one value has to be entered: a minimum budget level, to determine how far to the right the distribution is shifted.

Output: The model calculates the Gini coefficient and the P90/P10 ratio.

A screenshot is shown in Box 3.3. The pseudocode is in Box 3.A.1. For the full code, see the website: *Chapter 3 – Budget distribution*.

Things to try using the budget distribution model

- You have been asked to assess the impact of a sales tax change in the United States where the Gini coefficient is about to 0.45. To do this, you need to generate a set of households with a suitable distribution of income. How would you do that using this model?

- In Sweden, the Gini coefficient (based on equivalised disposable income) is 0.25. How would you create that distribution using this model?

- The model uses an exponential distribution. NetLogo provides other types of distributions. What is the effect of using other NetLogo distributions such as the Poisson distribution? Try creating other distributions, such as log-normal. How would you determine which distribution is the closest to the actual distribution?

Box 3.A.1   Pseudocode for the budget distribution model.

Generate 1000 agents called households and give each one attribute: budget.
Distribute a budget to each agent using a random-exponential function and the two parameters: a minimum and mean.
Normalise the budgets so that the mean is always 100.
Ensure no household has a budget of zero.
Calculate the Gini coefficient (based on Wilensky, 1998):

Sort the households by income.
Accumulate for each household in turn from the poorest to the richest:
(The rank of the household minus the proportion of the sum of the incomes of all households
up to and including this household) as a proportion of (the total income of all households).
Calculate the Gini coefficient.

Calculate the P90/P10 ratio:

Using the sorting measures generated in the calculation of the Gini coefficient, identify the
bottom and top decile boundaries and take the ratio.

Report the metrics and plot the budget distribution, sending output to the interface and to a csv file.

Utility function-based demand model

Purpose: The aim of the model is to use a Cobb–Douglas utility function together with the budget
distribution model described earlier to produce demand curves.

Entities: Agents are created to represent households, and each household is given a set of characteristics: its budget and the value of alpha to reflect its preferences. From these, additional
attributes are calculated: demand, expenditure and utility.

Stochastic processes: There are just two processes:

- The model distributes budgets randomly using an exponential function (as described previously) using preset parameters to generate a distribution with a Gini coefficient of about
  a third and a P90/P10 ratio of about 4.

- The model allocates alphas according to households' budgets. A mean alpha is allocated to
  each quintile group together with a standard deviation that applies to all quintiles. Within
  each quintile group, alpha is distributed and allocated randomly using a normal distribution
  using these parameters.

Initialisation: Two groups of parameters to be set:

- Mean budget shares (alphas) for each quintile plus a standard deviation to apply to all.
  For food, the values used (in Figure 3.4) were:

Bottom quintile	0.15
Lower quintile	0.13
Middle quintile	0.12
Upper quintile	0.10
Top quintile	0.08
Standard deviation	0.02

- Prices: the initial price and the percentage change price.

Box 3.A.2   Pseudocode for the utility function-based demand model.

Generate 1000 agents to represent households with these attributes:

The budget and which quintile it lies in
The parameter of the Cobb–Douglas function, alpha
The demand for good *A* at the initial price and new price and the difference between the two
The initial and new expenditure on good *A*
The initial and new utility levels and the percentage change

Allocate budgets to households (as in previous model) and define quintiles.
Calculate the Gini coefficient (as in Box 3.A.1).
Allocate an alpha to each household.
Ask each household how much of good *A* it would demand at each price, total and draw the
demand curve.
Calculate the change in demand from a given price and the effect on expenditure (even
though total expenditure will not change as the own-price elasticity is one).
Calculate the utility at the initial price and the new price and the percentage change for each
household.
Report the metrics and plot the graphs.

Output: Four graphs are plotted: the distribution of alphas, an aggregate demand curve, the distribution of demand at a given price and a scatter diagram plotting the change in utility against budget (see Figures 3.5, 3.6 and 3.7).

The pseudocode is in Box 3.A.2. For the full code, see the website: *Chapter 3 – Utility function-based demand.*

Things to try using the utility function-based demand model

- What happens when all agents have the same budget share or alpha? (Set all the means to the required alpha and the standard deviation to zero.) Note that this is not the same as using a representative agent as each household has a different budget.

- What happens when alpha rises with income? Take, for example, transport where the budget shares in the United Kingdom in 2010 give the following alphas:

Bottom quintile	0.09
Lower quintile	0.11
Middle quintile	0.12
Upper quintile	0.14
Top quintile	0.14
Overall	0.13

Source: ONS (2011).

Practical demand model

Purpose: The aim of the model is to use the budget distribution model described previously with assumptions about the proportion of households consuming and about own-price elasticities to estimate the impact of changes in price.

Entities: Agents are created to represent households, and each household is given a set of characteristics: its budget, its budget share (which may be zero) and its own-price elasticity. From these, additional attributes are calculated: demand and expenditure.

Stochastic processes: There are four stochastic processes:

- The model distributes budgets randomly using an exponential function (as previously described) using preset parameters to generate a distribution with a Gini coefficient of about a third.

- Initial mean percentages consuming are allocated according to households' budgets randomly using a normal distribution.

- The model allocates budget shares according to households' budgets randomly using a normal distribution.

- The model allocates own-price elasticities randomly using a normal distribution.

Initialisation:

- For budget shares: mean budget shares for each quintile plus a standard deviation to apply to all.

- For initial mean percentages consuming for each quintile group, a mean is set, and an overall standard deviation:

    ○ If all households do consume, these means should be set to 100%, and the standard deviation set to zero, and the minimum consumption set to zero.

    ○ If the model is to allow some households not to consume, the minimum consumption level has to be set so that for households estimated to consume below this level, consumption is rounded down to zero.

- For the own-price elasticities: mean own-price elasticities for each budget quintile plus a standard deviation to apply to all.

- Prices: the initial price and the percentage change price.

These are shown in Figure 3.A.1.

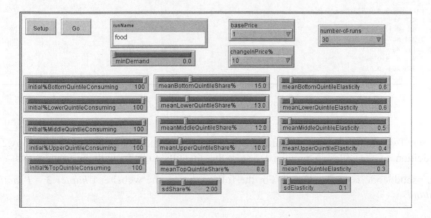

Figure 3.A.1   Screenshot of inputs for the practical demand model: food.

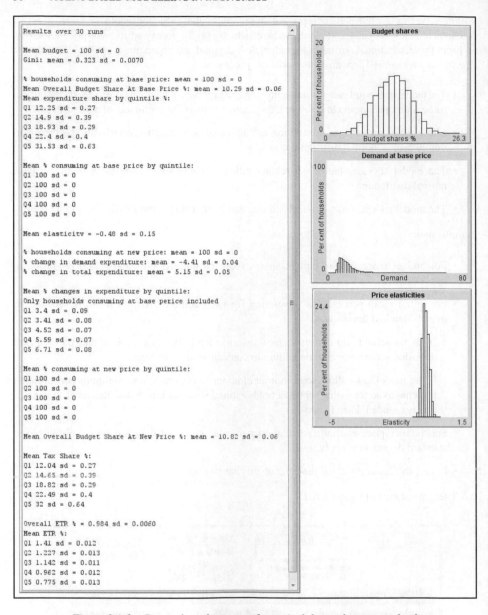

Figure 3.A.2   Screenshot of outputs of practical demand program: food.

Output: Two graphs and a large number of results are produced, as shown in Figure 3.A.2. In addition, two csv files are produced to store these results, together with the assumptions.

The pseudocode is in Box 3.A.3. For the full code, see the website: *Chapter 3 – Practical demand*.

Box 3.A.3   Pseudocode for the practical demand model.

Generate 1000 agents to represent households with these attributes:

Budget and which quintile it lies in
Initial budget share and new budget share
Price elasticity
The demand for good at the initial price and new price and the difference between the two
The initial and new expenditure on good and the difference between the two
Tax paid and effective tax rate

Allocate budgets to households and groups by quintiles.
Calculate the Gini coefficient (as in Box 3.A.1).
Allocate budget share to each household (as for alphas in Cobb–Douglas model).
Allocate elasticity to each household.
Calculate the change in demand from a given price and the effect on expenditure.
Calculate the tax paid and the effective tax rate (as if the price rise were a tax).
Report the results and plot the graphs, sending output to the interface and to two csv files.

Things to try with the practical demand model

- Use the budget data for food (given in the previous section) and try changing the price elasticities.

   For example, what happens when all agents have the same budget shares and elasticities? (Set all the means the same and the standard deviation to zero.)

- What happens with clothing and footwear, given the data below?

	Budget share (per cent)	Per cent of total expenditure on clothes and footwear	Own-price elasticity
Bottom quintile	4	6	−0.5
Lower quintile	4	11	−0.6
Middle quintile	5	17	−0.6
Upper quintile	5	25	−0.6
Top quintile	5	41	−0.6
Overall	5	100	−0.6

Sources: expenditure data: ONS (2011), elasticities based on Blundell *et al.* (1993).

- What happens when different elasticities are used for the cinema example?

- Imagine that you are looking at the consumption of a good which is considered to be 'bad' like tobacco. What could you do to reduce consumption and what would be the effects of different groups? Here is some data for tobacco consumption:

	Mean own-price elasticity = -0.9 to -1 Per cent consuming = 24	
	Budget share (%)	Per cent of total expenditure
Bottom quintile	2	19
Lower quintile	2	20
Middle quintile	1	26
Upper quintile	1	20
Top quintile	0.5	15
Overall	1	100

Sources: elasticity data: Czubek and Johal (2010); expenditure data: ONS (2011).

References

Barnard, A., Howell, S. & Smith, R. (2011) *The effect of taxes and benefits on household income, 2009/10*. Office for National Statistics [Online]. Available at: http://www.ons.gov.uk [Accessed 2 January 2015].

Blundell, R., Pashardes, P. & Weber, G. (1993) What do we learn about consumer demand patterns from micro data? *The American Economic Review*, 83(3) pp.570–597.

Bradley, T. & Patton, P. (2002) *Essential Mathematics for Economics and Business*, Chichester: John Wiley & Sons, Ltd.

Carrera, S. (2010) An expenditure-based analysis of the redistribution of household income. *Economic & Labour Market Review*, 4(3) pp.18–27. [Online]. Available at: http://www.ons.gov.uk [Accessed 2 January 2015].

Czubek, M. & Johal, S. (2010) *Econometric analysis of cigarette consumption in the UK*. HMRC Working Paper Number 9 [Online]. Available at: http://www.esrc.ac.uk/_images/Day2-Session6-Czubek-Johal-Econometric-Analysis-paper_tcm8-33130.pdf [Accessed 2 January 2015].

Dewenter, R. & Westermann, M. (2005) Cinema demand in Germany. *Journal of Cultural Economics*, 29, pp.213–231.

Hayek, F. (1931) *Prices and Production*. London: George Routledge & Sons Ltd.

Kahneman, D. (2011) *Thinking, Fast and Slow*. London: Allen Lane.

Macmillan, P. & Smith, I. (2001) Explaining post-war cinema attendance in Great Britain. *Journal of Cultural Economics*, 25, pp.91–108.

Office for National Statistics (ONS) (2011) *Family spending: A report on the 2010 living costs and food survey* [Online]. Available at: http://www.ons.gov.uk [Accessed 2 January 2015].

US Bureau of Labor Statistics consumer expenditure survey [Online]. Available at http://www.bls.gov/cex/ [Accessed 2 January 2015].

Wilensky, U. (1998) *NetLogo Wealth Distribution model*. Center for Connected Learning and Computer-Based Modeling, Northwestern University, Evanston, IL [Online]. Available at: http://ccl.northwestern.edu/netlogo/models/WealthDistribution [Accessed 2 January 2015].

4

Social demand

4.1 Introduction

The previous chapter looked at the conventional modelling of consumer demand where purchases depend on incomes, prices and preferences. Conventional economics 'assumes, either implicitly or explicitly, that agents interact only indirectly, through economic variables like prices and interest rates, instead of directly with one another through social networks' (Axtell, 2006, p.209). While conventional economics can be used to assess the short-term impact of changes in prices and incomes, it cannot be used to address the longer-term question of why some goods come to be adopted by the majority of the population while others do not (Douglas & Isherwood, 1979, p.99). Deaton and Muellbauer (1985, pp.71–72) noted that 'the most important and obvious shifts in the pattern of demand in Britain in this [twentieth] century…cannot apparently be explained in terms of changes in real income or price structure'. This chapter shows how agent-based modelling can be used to explore what might happen to consumption when consumers influence each other so that what they buy depends on what others buy.

4.2 Social networks

Relationships between people can be aggregated into social networks. There are many different types of relationships between people such as kinship and affection and business and political relationships, and so there can be many different types of social networks. There is a very large literature on social networks (see, e.g. Bruggeman (2008) for an accessible introduction and Jackson (2010) for a mathematical approach). In this section, we present the basics that are needed to model how consumers might influence one another in their consumption choices. We start with some definitions.

Agent-Based Modelling in Economics, First Edition. Lynne Hamill and Nigel Gilbert.
© 2016 John Wiley & Sons, Ltd. Published 2016 by John Wiley & Sons, Ltd.

Personal networks consist of the relationships of one person. A model of personal networks should reproduce certain characteristics:

- Personal networks are of limited size, the limit depending on the type of relationships being studied; for example, for close friends, the size will be small, and for acquaintances, large.

- Personal networks vary in size between individuals, with the possibility of some individuals having much larger personal networks than average (except for very close relationships, where it is not possible for a large number to be sustained).

- Members of an individual's personal network tend to know each other: in network jargon, this is called 'high clustering'.

- Personal networks change over time, as relationships change: people leave and new people join.

Social networks are the aggregation of personal networks. A social network model should reproduce certain characteristics of social networks too:

- Only a very few of the potential links in a social network actually exist; that is, it is far from the case that everyone has a relationship with everyone else. Technically, there is a low 'whole network density'.

- Those with large personal networks tend to know others with large personal networks – a feature known as 'positive assortativity'.

Box 4.1   Mathematics of social circles.

Area of a circle = πr^2, where r is the radius or social reach.

The number of agents in the circle will depend on the population density. For example, if the density is approximately 1% and the social reach is 10, then the average number in the circle will be $\pi \times 10^2 \times 0.01 = 3.14$.

Trebling the social reach to 30 will give an area of $900\,\pi$, which, with the population density of about 1%, will give an average number in the circle of 9π or 28.

$$\text{Average number in the social circle} = \text{density} \times \text{area} = \frac{\text{no. of agents}}{\text{area of world}} \times \pi \times r^2$$

A density of about 1% is achieved by spreading 1000 agents over an area of 315 by 315 (or 99 225 patches). Reducing the number of agents in the world or increasing the size of the world will reduce the population density and reduce the average number in a circle of given reach accordingly.

For example, to work out how to attain the same average circle size with only 500 agents – to make the program run faster, for instance – would mean rearranging the equation to calculate the area of the world:

$$\text{Area of the world} = \frac{\text{no. of agents}}{\text{average circle size}} \times \pi \times r^2 = \frac{500}{3.14} \times \pi \times 10^2 = 500 \times 100 = 50\,000$$

Taking the square root of the area to find the dimensions of a square world gives 223 (instead of 315 as used for 1000 agents).

- Social networks include communities, sometimes known as 'cliques', that is, groups of people who have many connections within the group but few connections outside it.

- Social networks are structured so that any other person can be reached by following a small number of links, that is, have short 'path lengths'.

To reproduce these characteristics in agent-based models, we have developed a simple approach based on the idea of social circles. Agents are distributed across social space, and each agent has its personal network defined by a circle drawn round it. The circumference of the circle contains all those points within a distance set by the radius – which we call the 'social reach' – and creates a cut-off, limiting the size of personal networks. This approach enables us to rely on the mathematics of the circle, as shown in Box 4.1. If the social reach is small, it replicates a network of close family and friends: if bigger, it becomes a model for larger personal networks including acquaintances. Because agents are distributed unevenly across the social space, they will automatically have personal networks of different sizes. Examples are shown in Box 4.2. This simple model of social networks also displays the other characteristics of static personal and social networks. (For more on this model, see Hamill and Gilbert (2009 & 2010) and Hamill (2010).) In the rest of this chapter, we use the terms 'personal network' and 'social circle' interchangeably.

However, except for short time periods, social circles change: people drift apart, either by physically moving away or by changing behaviour, or they die and are replaced by a new generation. Unfortunately, although not surprisingly given the obvious difficulties, longitudinal studies of social networks are rare. However, two studies (Suitor & Keeton, 1997; Wellman *et al.*, 1997) found that over a period of 10 years, around three quarters of close ties disappear and that non-kin are more likely to change than kin.

In the social circles model, a simple way to allow for change is to ask a proportion of agents to move one unit (patch) each time step: we call this 'social shifting'. If this change is random, the size and composition of individual agents' networks will change, but the overall structure of the 'society' will not. When an agent moves, its personal network may change in size, composition or both. Furthermore, moves may affect others who do not themselves move. Indeed, the larger the social reach, the more agents will potentially be affected by another agent's move. In this model, agents do not die. This simplification is not uncommon in economic models; for example, see Wickens (2008, Chapter 4, especially p.71).

Figure 4.1 shows the proportion of agents whose personal networks change in size, composition or both when social shifting is set at 5%, that is, one in 20 agents move one unit at every step:

- If the social reach is set at 10, giving an average personal network size of about 3, then after 10 time steps, the personal networks of 28% of agents are changed; after 50 steps, 75% of networks are changed.

- If the social reach is set at 15, giving an average personal network size of about 7, then after 10 time steps, the personal networks of 39% of agents are changed; after 50 steps, 88%.

- If the social reach is set at 30, giving an average personal network size of about 28, then after 10 time steps, the personal networks of 60% of agents are changed; after 50 steps, 98%.

Of course, if a lower rate of social shifting is assumed, then the proportion of agents affected is less; if higher, more.

Now that we have a way of modelling personal networks and how they change, we can turn to modelling adoption of consumer products.

Box 4.2   Simulation results: Examples of personal and social networks.

1000 agents over a world (315×315) (i.e. 99 225 patches), giving a density = about 1%	
Results over 30 runs	Examples of single runs: the lines indicate links
Social reach = 10	
Personal network: • Minimum: 0 (sd 0*) • Maximum: 9.63 (sd 0.96) Average size: 3.19 (sd 0.08) *All runs have a minimum of 0.	
Social reach = 15	
Personal network: • Minimum: 0.40 (sd 0.50) • Maximum: 7.13 (sd 0.96) Average size: 16.13 (sd 1.25)	
Social reach = 30	
Personal network: • Minimum: 13.63 (sd 1.16) • Maximum: 44.70 (sd 2.17) Average size: 28.39 (sd 0.21)	

4.3   Threshold models

The idea of consumers influencing one another is encapsulated in threshold models. In these models, a consumer's decision to purchase an item depends on how many others have purchased it. There is positive feedback system because the more other people have bought the item, the

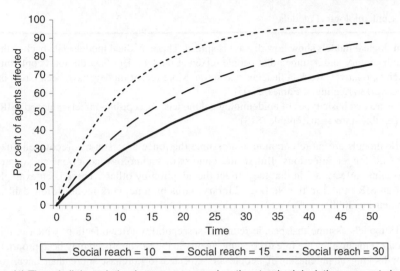

Figure 4.1   Effect of 5% of agents 'social shifting': per cent of agents for whom social circles changed over time (in composition or size). 1000 agents, 30 runs (1).

higher the perceived benefits in relation to the costs and the more likely the consumer is to buy. It could be that the item is seen as fashionable or the utility of the item may depend on joint consumption by others. Granovetter and Soong (1986) cited the example of not wanting to eat in an empty restaurant. Communication technologies fall into this category too; there is no point having a phone if no one else does. Threshold models are similar to epidemiological models, in which infections are passed from person to person, but the common epidemiological models are not necessarily suitable for studying adoption or consumption as is explained in Box 4.3. (For a wider discussion of threshold models, see Granovetter (1978) and Granovetter and Soong (1986), and for a positive feedback, see Arthur (1989).)

Different people may have different thresholds. But even those with the same threshold may adopt at different times, depending on the adoption by their personal network. Some people may have a threshold of 100% and so will never adopt. Provided their threshold is below 100%, once a person's threshold is met, they adopt. So those with low thresholds adopt when their exposure is low, and the lower the individual's threshold, the earlier the adoption. Some will have a zero threshold and will adopt irrespective of others' adoption. Bass (1969) – who produced the classic model of the timing of the initial purchase of new consumer durables – divided the buying public into two groups: 'innovators' and 'imitators'. Innovators are not influenced by others: in other words, their threshold is zero.

A threshold model may be particularly relevant in the case of an innovative product because adoption of an innovation involves risk and people look to those they know for information on costs and benefits (Valente, 1995, pp.70–71). Having studied the adoption of many innovations over many years, Rogers (2003, pp.281–282) divided adopters into five groups – innovators, early adopters, early majority, late majority and laggards:

- Innovators account for 2½% of the population. They have wide social networks, financial resources and technical knowledge, but they tend to have weak ties to wider society.

Box 4.3   Epidemiological models.

Epidemiological models show how disease is spread. These medical models date back to the nineteenth century and assumed that people mixed at random. But they do not. People mix with friends, relatives, work colleagues and so on. More recent models have been based on social networks (Keeling & Eames, 2005).

There are two basic types of epidemiological models, susceptible–infect–removed (SIR) and susceptible–infect–susceptible (SIS):

- SIR models are more common and assume that once a person has recovered, they are no longer infectious. But in the context of technology adoption, an adopter remains 'infectious' in that they affect the adoption by others. There is an example of an SIR model in the NetLogo Library: virus on a network model (Stonedahl & Wilensky, 2008).

- SIS models assume that people return to susceptibility after infection, which in this context means they are free to consume again. So the SIS approach may be appropriate for looking at purchasing if people are expected to purchase more than once, for example, to upgrade. But SIS models are not appropriate for technology adoption as a once-off decision.

- Early adopters account for 13½% of the population. They are somewhat similar to innovators but are more embedded in the society, being opinion leaders and respected role models, for whom status is likely to be important (Rogers, 2003, pp.251, 316–319).

- The early majority comprise 34% of the population. They interact frequently with their peers but are rarely opinion leaders.

- The late majority account for another 34% and are persuaded to adopt by peer pressure although they have limited resources.

- Laggards comprise the last 16% of the population and tend to interact with other laggards.

Adoption is often initially slow, then fast and finally slow again. Mathematically, this is a logistic function but is most commonly known as an S-curve. (See Chapter 10 for more on logistic functions.) Figure 4.2 imposes Rogers' analysis of adopters on this S-curve.

Agent-based models are particularly suited to threshold models because agent-based models can deal with both the local, micro – the individual and their personal network – and the global, macro, or society as a whole. To explore the characteristics of these models, we present two basic types of threshold model, which we label 'infection' and 'influence', respectively:

- In the infection models, if one member of an agent's personal network adopts, then that agent adopts.

- In the influence models, each agent has a threshold expressed as a percentage of their personal network, and if the percentage of adopters in their personal network exceeds that threshold, then that agent adopts.

But in both cases, there must be one or more agents who 'seed' the process. Following Rogers (2003, pp.281–282), these innovators are assumed to account for 2.5% of the population.

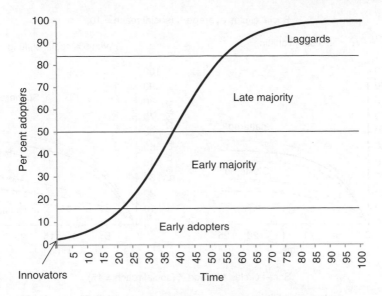

Figure 4.2   The classic S-curve of adoption.

Infection models

In the infection models, if one agent in an individual's social circle adopts, then that agent adopts. The innovators can either be scattered through the population or clustered:

- If the size of social circles average 3 – giving a network like that shown in the top row of Box 4.2 – and innovators are scattered throughout the population, adoption is much more likely to take off than if they are clustered in one or two groups. Social shifting is also important in raising adoption rates in the long run. But in none of the scenarios does adoption reach 100%: at most, it reaches 57% after 25 time periods. These scenarios are shown in the top panels of Figure 4.3.

- If the size of social circles average 7 – giving a network like that shown in the middle row of Box 4.2 – then all adopt irrespective of the distribution of innovators because there are more links in the network. The distribution of innovators only affects the speed at which 100% adoption is reached: with scattered innovators, this happens after about 10 time periods, and if innovators are clustered, about 20. But in neither case does social shifting have an effect, again because the agents are better connected. These scenarios are shown in the bottom panels of Figure 4.3.

Influence models

Unlike the infection models, in these models, each agent has a different threshold, and if the percentage of adopters in the agent's social circle exceeds that threshold, the agent adopts. The innovators are the 2.5% with the lowest thresholds. It is possible, although unlikely with large social circles, that some agents may not have anyone in their personal network. In that case, it is assumed that the agent adopts if the overall adoption rate (of the 'society') exceeds its threshold. The adoption rate depends crucially on how thresholds are distributed. Take two illustrative cases: in the first, thresholds are distributed uniformly from 1 to 100%, while in the second, they are distributed normally with a mean and standard deviation of 50. So in both cases, the average threshold is 50%.

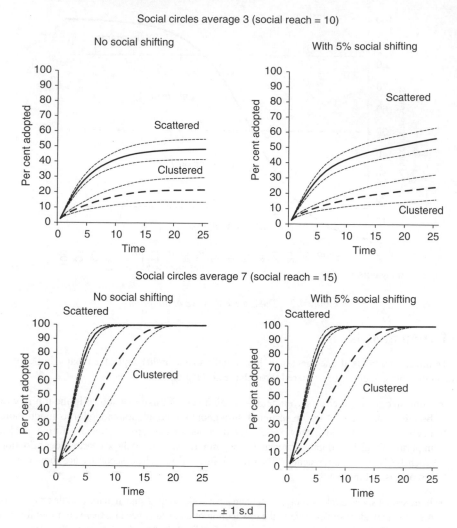

Figure 4.3   Infection model results: innovators 2.5% (1000 agents, 30 runs).

Yet as shown in Figure 4.4, the resulting adoption patterns are very different: when the thresholds are uniformly distributed, the adoption rate reaches 12% after 25 periods, but in the normally distributed case, it only reaches 3%. This is because with a normal distribution there are relatively fewer agents with low thresholds than when thresholds are uniformly distributed.

These simple models have shown that the path of take-up will vary dramatically according to the model used and the assumptions made; Table 4.1 shows that after just 10 periods, the adoption rate could vary between about 10 and 100%. This means that to predict accurately what will 'take off' and what will never become popular, it would be necessary to have a very good idea of how people are likely to be influenced. Granovetter and Soong (1986) argued that 'individual differences in sensitivity to others' behavior' means that 'unstable, oscillatory and even completely indeterminate market situations may result'. And Arthur (1989) argued that the selection of successful innovations is essentially unpredictable. So in the next section, we focus on a specific example.

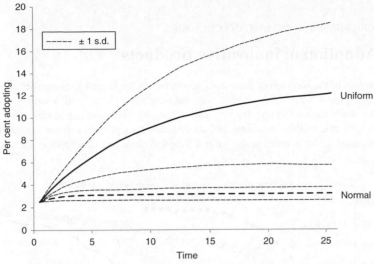

(1) In both cases, thresholds vary from 1 to 100 per cent and average 50 per cent.

Figure 4.4   Influence model results: innovators 2.5% and social circles average 28 (social reach = 30) with social shifting: thresholds distributed uniformly or normally (1) (1000 agents, 30 runs).

Table 4.1   Summary of results for threshold models: adoption rates after 10 and 25 periods.

		After	
		10 periods	25 periods
Infection models			
Social shifting	Distribution of innovators		
		Average social circle = 3	
0%			
	Scattered	42	48
	Clustered	17	26
5%			
	Scattered	43	57
	Clustered	16	25
		Average social circle = 7	
0%			
	Scattered	100	100
	Clustered	67	100
5%			
	Scattered	100	100
	Clustered	66	100
Influence models		Mean threshold: 50%	
Social shifting	Distribution of thresholds		
		Average social circle = 28	
5%			
	Normal	3	3
	Uniform	9	12

Based on Figures 4.3 and 4.4.

4.4   Adoption of innovative products

Some examples of the adoption of household appliances in the United Kingdom are shown in the top panel of Figure 4.5. For some of these, the data were not collected until adoption was already widespread, which means that only the very end of the adoption curve can be observed. For some appliances – fridges, washing machines and microwaves – adoption has reached saturation in the sense that almost all households in the United Kingdom own one (as shown in the top panel of

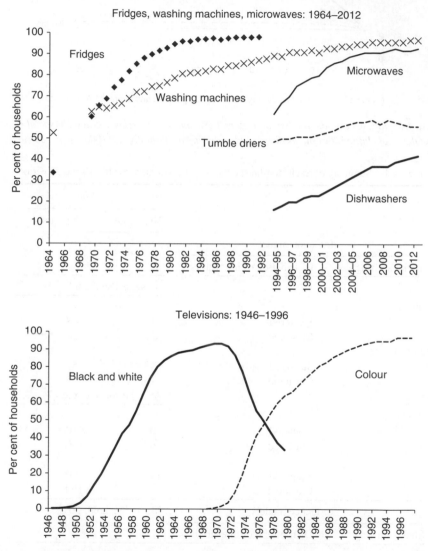

Figure 4.5   Adoption of domestic appliances in the United Kingdom (1). (1) Data not available for all years. Sources: top, adapted from Office for National Statistics (ONS) (2013); adapted from Office for National Statistics (ONS) (1996); Living in Britain (1997); Social Trends 27; (1998).

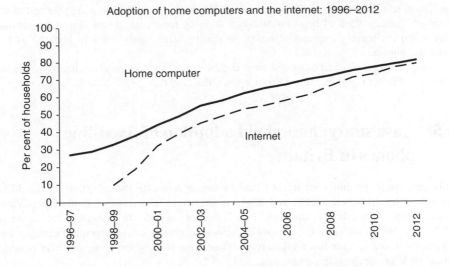

Adoption of home computers and the internet: 1996–2012

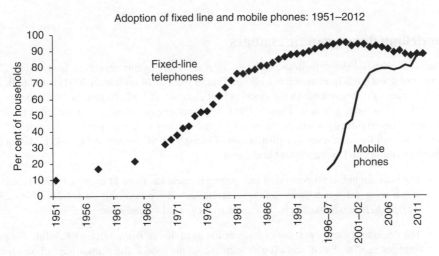

Adoption of fixed line and mobile phones: 1951–2012

Figure 4.6   Adoption of communication devices by households in the United Kingdom. Source: Marwick (1990, p.117) and adapted from Office for National Statistics (ONS) (2013).

Figure 4.5). Others – such as tumble driers and dishwashers – have remained less popular, probably due to space constraints in British houses. In contrast, televisions (TVs) – first black and white and then colour – were adopted by almost all households (as shown in the bottom panel of Figure 4.5), and now many households own several TVs.

For communication devices, adoption most nearly follows the classic S-curve of Figure 4.2. The top panel of Figure 4.6 shows how the adoption of home computers and the Internet grew together, which is hardly surprising given that initially the Internet could only be accessed with a computer. (In the future, Internet adoption is likely to be more popular than computer ownership as tablets and smartphones spread.) The bottom panel shows the spread of fixed-line and mobile phones (cell phones in the United States). In 1951, just 10% of households in the United Kingdom had phones; by the mid-1970s, half of households; and at the end of the twentieth century, 95% of households. Since then, an increasing proportion of households have relied exclusively on mobile phones, so that by 2012, 'only' 88% of households had fixed-line phones.

Adoption of phones and other consumer durables was generally much earlier in the United States (see Fischer (1992, p.22) and Bowden and Offer (1994)).

4.5   Case study: household adoption of fixed-line phones in Britain

This case study produces an agent-based model to replicate the adoption of fixed-line phones in Britain between 1951 and 2001. As becomes clear, this is a rather complicated model compared to others in the book. This is because in order to replicate what happened in the real world, all sorts of real-world factors, in particular demographic changes and changes in income, have to be taken into account. We start by explaining briefly how the model took into account these changes.

Modelling demographic changes

Fixed-line phones belong to households, so in this model agents represent households. The number of households increased from 14½ million in 1951 to 24 million in 2001. For simplicity, the total number of households in the model is kept constant, at 1000, so that, in effect, the agents resemble a longitudinal sample. However, two key demographic changes are modelled because they are likely to directly affect phone adoption: the trebling of the proportion of single person households and the more even age distribution of households (Coleman, 2000, p.78). The model reproduces these two key demographic changes:

- The increase in the proportion of one-person households from 11 to 30% by 2001, half of which were pensioner households; in the model, the proportion rises from 11 to 28% (sd 0.8), half of whom, that is, 14% (sd 0.6) were aged 60 and over.

- The decline in the proportion of households aged 40–59 from 44 to 37%, while the percentages aged under 40 and 60 plus increase; in the model, the proportion of households aged 40–59 declines from 44 to 39% (sd 0.5) in 2001, with more younger and older households.

More information on modelling demographic changes is in Appendix 4.A.

Modelling income

Over 50 years, phones became more affordable. Data on the price of phones is limited, and for simplicity, the price of phones was not included in the model. More importantly, real incomes grew. From 1951 to 2001, real GDP per head grew by 2% a year on average. This means that by 2001, real income was almost three times that in 1951. In the model, no attempt is made to reflect differences in year-on-year growth rates: it is simply assumed that incomes rise at 2% a year. (See details in Box 4.4.)

Box 4.4   Price of phones and income growth.

Price of phones

It is not straightforward to measure the price of a fixed-line phone: there is the rental charge plus the cost of the calls, which, during this period, depended on length, distance and often the time of day. However, the price of phones has been separately identified in the Retail Price Index (RPI) since 1974. Prior to that, from 1956, phones were combined with postal services. The graph below shows that the price of phones tended to follow the RPI until 1993, since when it fell sharply.

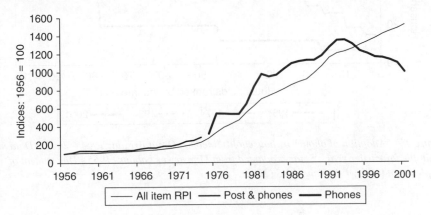

Source: adapted from ONS (2014). Data sets and reference tables; series CHAW & DOCH.

Growth in real income

This graph shows real GDP per head in the United Kingdom from 1951 to 2001, with a trend line that indicates a growth rate of 2% a year.

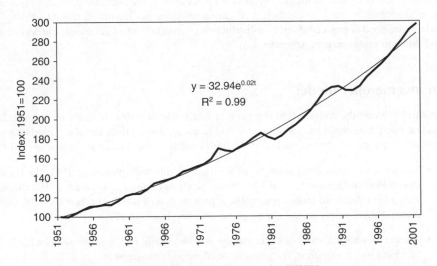

Source: adapted from Feinstein (1972), ONS (2014) (series IHXW).

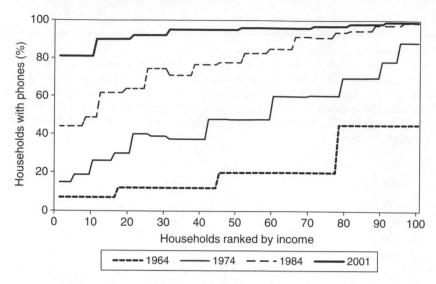

Figure 4.7   Adoption of phones by households' income, Great Britain: 1964*–2001. *Data not available for earlier years. Source: adapted from Ministry of Labour (1965), Department of Employment (1975, 1986) and ONS (2002).

The adoption of phones crept up the income scale gradually as real incomes grew, as shown in Figure 4.7. In 1964, only 7% of the poorest households had phones, but by 2001, this had reached 81%. In contrast, 45% of the richest households had phones in 1964.

The model incorporates key features of changes in the labour market over the period, such as falling economic activity rates among men of working age but higher rates for women and higher unemployment rates later in the period. As noted in Chapter 3, the overall distribution of income can be described by the Gini coefficient and in recent years has fluctuated around a third. The model is designed to produce an income distribution consistent with a Gini coefficient around this level. More information is in Appendix 4.A.

An income-only model

We start by taking the conventional approach in which adoption depends only on income. It is assumed that a household adopts if it can afford to do so, that is, if its income exceeds a given threshold. In the model, the income figure is an index number, with 1 taken as the average in 1951:

- To obtain an initial distribution of 10% of households with phones in 1951, the income threshold would have to be set at 1.85, that is, nearly twice the average income. But although such a high threshold gives a reasonable approximation of take-up in the 1950s and 1960s, it would significantly underestimate phone adoption from the 1970s.

- A lower income threshold of 1 (i.e. average income) would match adoption since the 1970s better but would significantly overestimate adoption in earlier years.

These alternatives are illustrated in Figure 4.8. This suggests that an income threshold alone could not track the observed adoption path.

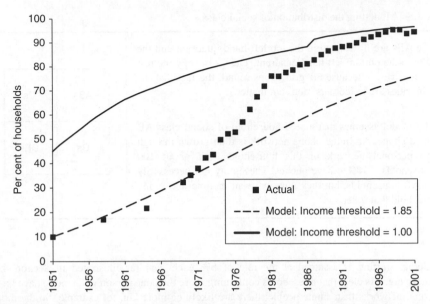

Figure 4.8   Results of the model using an income threshold only and no network effect (1000 agents, 30 runs). Source: actual – as Figure 4.6.

Modelling network effects

Although by 1958 nearly 17% of households had phones, phones were limited to the 'upper-class' ABs and 'middle-class' C1s; two thirds of the ABs had phones as did a quarter of C1s, but phones were rare among the 'lower-class' C2s, Ds and Es (Douglas & Isherwood, 1979, p.100). This is consistent with Rogers' (2003, pp.288–291) observation that those who are better educated, of higher social status and wealthy are more likely to be early adopters. By 1973, most AB households had phones, and so too did a fifth of DEs (Douglas & Isherwood, 1979, p.100). Class is defined in terms of occupational group: ABs include doctors, senior civil servants, bankers and economists, while DEs are semi-skilled and unskilled workers. The spread down the classes is reflected in the spread of phones down the income scale shown in Figure 4.7.

However, there is little point having a phone unless at least one of those in your personal network also has a phone and those in your personal network are likely to be like you: homophily – the principle that contact between similar people occurs at a higher rate than among dissimilar people – is a well-established characteristic of social networks. (See, e.g. McPherson *et al.*, 2001.) In this case study, the personal network of interest is very specific and narrow, namely, those who will influence another to adopt a phone. There is no direct evidence on this for fixed-line phones although 'AT&T research shows that half of the calls from any given residence go to only five numbers' (Fischer, 1992, pp.225–226).

To reflect the importance of class and homophily, the model groups together the upper-class ABs in one quadrant, the lower-class DEs in another and the Cs in the remaining two as illustrated in Box 4.5. As the households are distributed randomly, this will produce approximately the 25/50/25% split between ABs, Cs and DEs recorded in Census data (Casweb, 2014; General Register Office, 1952). It also ensures that each household's personal network will typically be dominated by similar others.

Box 4.5   Modelling the distribution of social class.

The ABs are distributed in the top left-hand quadrant and the DEs in the bottom left-hand quadrant. The Cs occupy the rest of the space. (Because the grid wraps round, the fact that the minorities are in 'corners' does not matter.)

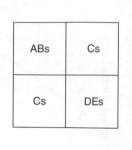

The model assumes that a seed household of social class AB has a phone. An initial phone network is then grown through the personal network of this household until about 100 households – 10% – have phones. These may not necessarily be AB households, but they must have an income above any threshold that is set.

Social shifting is assumed at the rate of 5% each year (as illustrated in Section 4.2). Furthermore, it is clear that households containing more than one person will tend to have larger personal networks than single people; there are likely be more kin, for example. So the model allows larger households to have larger networks.

As 10% of households had phones in 1951, the model starts by generating a network of phone adopters comprising 10% of households. In effect, these 10% of households are a cluster of innovators. Phones then spread through personal networks as explained in Box 4.5.

So it is now assumed that households obtain a fixed-line phone if:

• Someone else in their social circle has a phone.

• They have enough income.

The income thresholds for phones and personal network sizes were set by experimentation. The results were the following:

• The income threshold for phones was set at 0.35 (i.e. 35% of the 1951 average, set at 1). Ninety per cent of households had incomes above that level in 1951, and given real growth of 2% a year by 1968, all households had incomes above that threshold, and so income did not constrain phone adoption after 1968.

• Personal networks were modelled in the way explained earlier in this chapter, using social circles, the size of which depend on the social reach and the population density, which was about 1%. The best result was obtained with social reach for one-person households set at 8 and for multi-person households, a social reach of 12. For one-person households, this gave a personal network size ranging from 0 to 8, with an average size of 2 (sd=0.06), and for multi-person households, a personal network size ranging from 0 to 12 with an average personal network size of 4½ (sd=0.10). The networks therefore look similar that shown in the top two panels of Box 4.2.

On this basis, the model broadly replicates the adoption of phones by households from 1951 to 2001 as shown in the top panel of Figure 4.9. By comparing Figures 4.8 and 4.9, it is clear that most of the 'work' of replicating the adoption pattern is done by the social network effect. This provides a nice example of Deaton and Muellbauer's observation (noted in the Introduction to this chapter) that changes in incomes and prices alone are not sufficient to explain changes in consumption patterns.

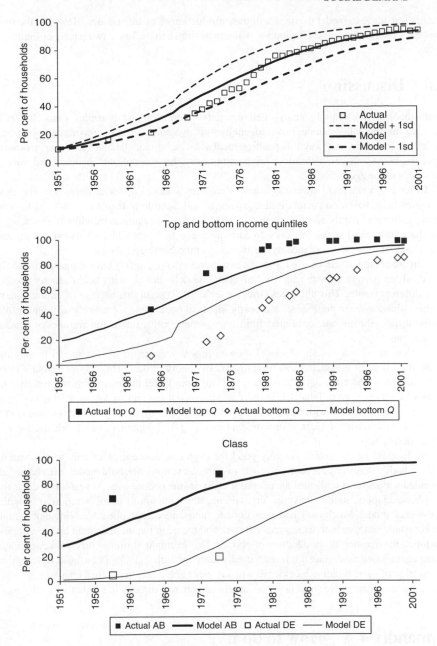

Figure 4.9   Model results compared to actual: phone adoption (1000 agents, 30 runs). Standard deviations not shown to simplify diagrams. Source: ONS (2013).

The best model slightly overestimates the adoption of phones until 1978. The model was not expected to track adoption in each year exactly as, for instance, year-on-year economic growth was assumed constant and no account was taken of the fall in the relative price of phones from 1993. Nor was the model expected to reproduce the decline in adoption rate in the last 2 years as no attempt was made to model the impact of the introduction of mobile phones. However, the model does track the income and class adoption patterns as shown in the lower two panels of Figure 4.9.

4.6   Discussion

Of this book's three central themes – heterogeneity, interaction and dynamics – this chapter has focussed on interaction although heterogeneity and dynamics are also important. Agent-based modelling is not the only way this positive feedback can be modelled, but it is a very powerful approach because it can also allow for heterogeneity, for example, in incomes and adoption thresholds of the agents.

To model interaction between consumers requires a model of social networks. The model presented here, based on social circles, is simple and flexible in that it can be used to model networks of close family and friends or wider networks of acquaintances while reproducing the key characteristics of social networks. In particular, agents do not all have networks of the same size. However, other network models are available in the NetLogo Library.

Threshold models can be used with the assumption that all agents have the same threshold – as indeed has been done here with our 'infection' model – but allowing heterogeneity produces quite different results. This illustrates Granovetter's (1978) point that because of interaction, two groups 'whose average preferences are nearly identical could generate entirely different results'. It demonstrates the importance of modelling heterogeneity rather than using averages or representative agents.

Further, the simple threshold model showed how a wide range of results can be produced unless the values of parameters can be restricted by theory or data. This echoes Arthur's (1989) discussion about the difficulty of predicting the outcomes under increasing returns, which is precisely what can be seen in Table 4.1. In this case, the increasing returns are to consumers who can obtain greater benefit the wider the ownership is spread. This increasing benefit is obvious in the case of communication devices. (For more on modelling the adoption of new products, see Watts and Gilbert (2014).)

While agent-based models are very good for exploring concepts, they can be elaborated to produce highly descriptive models. To contrast with the simple threshold model, the chapter also presented a model that replicates the adoption of fixed-line phones over 50 years. It is clear from this phone adoption model, however, that an enormous amount of detail is required to build a 'real-world' model. Much work had to be done to model adequately the underlying demographic and economic changes before the social network and the adoption models could be superimposed to address the question of the adoption of phones. This example illustrates nicely a key challenge facing agent-based modelling if it is to be used widely for policymaking or business development: the creation of basic building blocks. We will say more about this in the final chapter.

In the next chapter, we show how consumers can interact directly in another way – by barter.

Appendix 4.A   How to do it

Social circles model

Purpose: The aim of the model is to generate personal networks, that is, social circles.
Entities: Agents represent people or households.
Stochastic processes: Distribution of agents across the world and, if social shifting is used, which agents move.

Box 4.A.1   Pseudocode for the social circles model.

Create a world 315×315.
Create 1000 agents and distribute them randomly across the world.

For each agent, count the number of other agents within the distance set by the reach.

For the first run:

- If selected, for each agent, draw links between them and the other agents within the radius.

- Draw a histogram of the number of agents in each agent's social circle.

If social shifting is selected, ask agents to move and then recalculate social circles and measure changes in number or in identity of agents in each one's personal network.

Collect data.
Collect information about the minimum, average and maximum social circle sizes and print the averages over all the runs to csv file.

Initialisation:

- Choose the social reach to determine the sizes of the personal networks.

- Choose whether links are to be shown.

- Choose whether social shifting is desired and, if so, what proportion of agents move each time step and the number of time steps.

- Choose the number of runs.

Output: The sizes of the social circles – minimum, average and maximum – are recorded in a csv file. For the first run, a histogram is drawn to show the distribution of the size of personal networks, and the window shows the links (if that option is selected). If social shifting is selected, the number of agents with changed social circles is recorded.

The pseudocode is in Box 4.A.1 and a screenshot in Figure 4.A.1. For the full code, see the website: *Chapter 4 – Social Circles Model*.

Things to try using the social circles model

- Change the social reach to see the impact on the numbers in the agents' social circles.

- Examine the impact of social shifting by changing the `socialshift%`.

Advanced – requiring amending the program

- Instead of each agent having the same social reach, use different social reaches for each agent. (But remember to check that if Agent A is in Agent B's network, Agent B is also in Agent A's network!)

- Extend the model to show that the networks produced do display the desired characteristics, such as clustering.

For more on this modelling social circles, see Hamill (2010, Chapters 3 and 4) and Hamill and Gilbert (2009 or 2010).

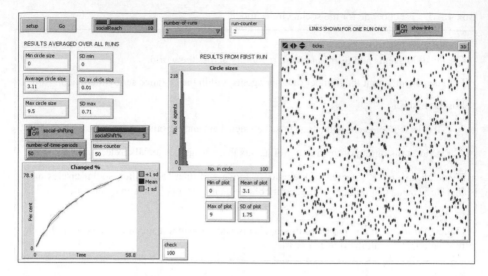

Figure 4.A.1   Screenshot for the social circles model.

Threshold model

Purpose: The aim of the model is to explore threshold models of adoption.
Entities: Agents represent people or households.
Stochastic processes: The personal networks, depending on the options used:

- The distribution of innovators

- The distribution of thresholds

- The impact of social shifting

Initialisation:

- Choose whether social shifting is required and, if so, the rate, that is, the proportion of agents who move each year.

- Choose the threshold option:

  ○ Infection model

    Choose whether the initial adopters are scattered randomly or are clustered, that is, are linked by social circles.

  ○ Influence model

    Thresholds are set randomly uniformly or distributed normally. If normally, set the mean (which will also equal the standard deviation).

- Choose the number of time periods.

- Choose the number of runs.

- Choose whether links are to be displayed.

Box 4.A.2   Pseudocode for the threshold model.

Create a world 315×315.

Create 1000 agents and distribute them randomly across the world.

For each agent, count the number of other agents within the distance set by the reach.

Determine which agents are the innovators:

- Infection

  - Innovators scattered: select agents at random.

  - Innovators clustered: grow a network of innovators from a 'seed' agent. If the network cannot be extended to generate the required number of innovators, reseed and start another network.

- Influence: heterogeneous thresholds

  - Distribute the thresholds. For the normal distribution, any thresholds greater than 100 or less than 0 are set to the mean.

  - Sort agents by threshold and select those with the lowest thresholds to be innovators.

After the first run, and if selected, carry out the social shifting, and recalculate the social circles.

Adoption spreads according to the mechanism chosen:

- Infection: if there is one adopter in the agent's social circle, the agent adopts.

- Influence: if the percentage of adopters in the agent's social circle exceeds its threshold, the agent adopts. If the agent does not have anyone in its social circle, it adopts if the overall adoption rate (of the 'society') exceeds its threshold.

Measure the number of new adopters.

Collect data.

Collect information about the minimum, average and maximum social circle sizes and print the averages over all the runs to csv file.

Outputs: The main output is the adoption curve. It is based on the average over all the runs. Data is also produced on social circle sizes and thresholds.

The pseudocode is in Box 4.A.2 and a screenshot in Figure 4.A.2. For the full code, see the website: *Chapter 4 – Threshold Model*.

Things to try using the threshold adoption model

- Explore the conditions which lead to high adoption rates.

- Try to generate the adoption curves shown in Figure 4.5 and the top panel of Figure 4.6.

  Advanced – requiring programming

- Devise different ways of allocating thresholds.

- Model the effect of broadcast media. (Hint: adapt the social effect, used in the influence option.)

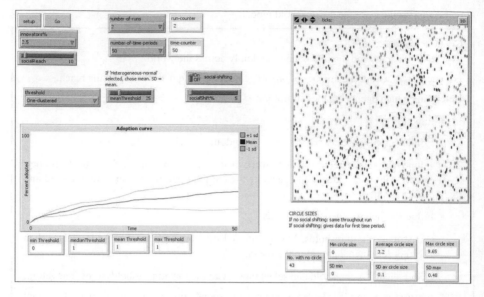

Figure 4.A.2   Screenshot of the threshold model.

Phone adoption model

Purpose: The aim of the model is to reproduce the adoption of phones in Britain, 1951–2001.

Entities: Agents are households.

Stochastic processes: Initial distributions and changes in households' characteristics, economic status and social networks.

Initialisation:

- Choose the income level above which phones are adopted.

- Choose whether a social network effect is required and, if so, choose the social reaches for multi-person and one-person households.

- Choose the rate of social shifting, that is, the proportion of households who move each year.

- Choose the rate of growth of GDP.

- Choose the number of years.

- Choose the number of runs.

- Name the file to which the results will be written.

Output: Graphs on phone adoption, demographic and economic status are drawn and the results written to a file.

The pseudocode describing the key features are summarised in Boxes 4.A.3 and 4.A.4. (More details are available in Hamill, 2010, Chapter 7.) A screenshot is in Figure 4.A.3. For the full code, see the website: *Chapter 4 – Phone Adoption*.

Box 4.A.3 Summary of whole model.

Initialisation

Create a world 315×315.

Create 1000 agents and distribute them randomly across the world.

Allocate class, household type and income:

Class: to give a 25/50/25% split by class, households in top left quadrant designated class AB; in bottom right quadrant, class DE; and others, class C. (See Box 4.5.)

Household type: one-person or multi-person; single or couple and ages. (See Box 4.A.4.)

Incomes are distributed following social class, subject to a minimum, to reproduce a Gini coefficient of about a third. (See Chapter 3.) A distribution of income is generated for each class using a normal distribution with the following means and variances:

- Class AB: mean 1.6, variance 0.6
- Class C: mean 1, variance 0.4
- Class DE: mean 0.8; variance 0.35

Allowing for:

- Second earners contributing an average of 25% of household income:
  - Initially, 25% of 'wives' under 60 work and 10% of those over 60 are assumed to have worked in the past.
- Unemployment: Initially, the rate is 0.95%.
- Early retirement: 5% of households aged 50–64.
- Half the lone parents are economically active.
- One per cent of households have long-term sickness.
- The retired have half income of workers. (Household retirees, i.e. both husband and wife.)

Select a 'seed' class AB household, and from that household, generate a phone network comprising about 10% of households built through personal networks (subject to affordability if desired).

Execution

Households age, split, combine and die. (See Box 4.A.4.)

Five per cent of households social shift each year.

Replacement households are created.

Incomes are determined:

  The proportion of second earners rises from about a half to three quarters.

    Once second earners go out to work, they are assumed to continue. On retirement, the second earner's contribution continues, reflecting a pension.

  Unemployment

    Most unemployed return to work and are replaced by newly unemployed. (Each year, 95% of those who were unemployed last year return to work, and the remaining 5% become unoccupied.) The appropriate unemployment rates are then applied again:

    1951–1970: 0.95%

    1971–1980: 2.9%

    1981–2001: 5.5%

  (See example in Box 4.A.5.)

- Retirement

    Per cent of households aged 50–64 that rises by 0.5% each year, reaching 30% by the end of the period.

    Those still working at 65 retire and their income halves.

- Growth: Incomes grow at 2% a year

Phone adoption spreads through personal networks (subject to affordability if desired): if a neighbouring household within the appropriate social reach has a phone (and if the household can afford a phone if an income threshold is applied), then that household adopts. Once adopted, the phone is kept.

  Data are collected, graphs drawn, and data sent to csv file at end of all runs.

Box 4.A.4   Demographic pseudocode.

Initialisation

Allocate ages.

> Divide population into three broad age groups and then divide each age group into narrow bands of roughly equal size. Allocate age up to 75 randomly within groups.

Allocate marital status and then divide singles between one-person households and multi-person households.

Execution

Existing households changed.

> Households age.
>
> Mortality rates applied.
>
> Widow rates applied to those 40 and over and widowed households become one-person households.
>
> Some single households under 60 combine into multi-person households.
>
> Divorce rates applied to under 60s: divorcing households split between one-person and multi-person households.

New households are created.

> Population counted and new households created to bring the total back to 1000.
>
> New households are distributed randomly and aged 25.
>
> A proportion of new households become single, and some of these singles become one-person households.

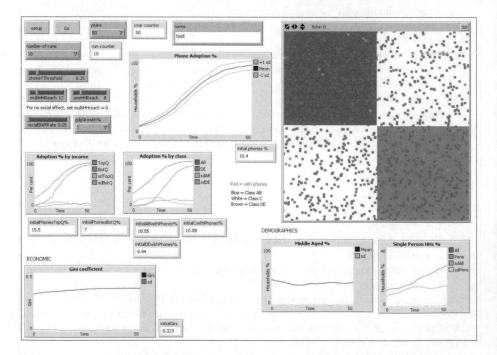

Figure 4.A.3   Screenshot of the phone adoption model.

Box 4.A.5   Example of changing income.

The income figure is an index number, with 1 taken as the average in 1951. The example is a household comprising a married couple with the husband aged 25 in class C on average income, that is, an income of 1 in 1951.

Event	Income	Calculation
1971: wife starts work and her contribution is 25%.	1.98	Given the cumulative growth rate of 2% a year, the household's income will have increased to $1 \times 1.02^{20} = 1.49$ The wife working raises the household's income to $1.49/(1-0.25) = 1.98$
1991: husband reaches 65	1.47	Income has grown at 2% a year to reach $1.98 \times 1.02^{20} = 2.94$ Retirement halves the income to 1.47
1996: husband dies	1.22	Given the cumulative growth rate of 2% a year, the income will have risen to $1.47 \times 1.02^5 = 1.63$ The income is reduced by the wife's contribution rather than the husband's as the widow will receive a pension. The income will then be $1.63 \times (1-0.25) = 1.22$
2001	1.35	Given the cumulative growth rate of 2% a year, the household income will be $1.22 \times 1.02^5 = 1.35$

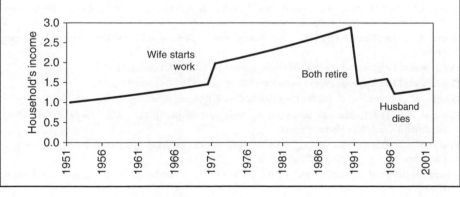

Things to try using the phone adoption model

Test the sensitivity of the results to the assumptions using the various sliders to answer questions such as the following:

- What would have happened had there been less economic growth?

- What is the effect of setting the income threshold to zero?

- What if the personal networks were bigger? Or smaller?

- Does more social shifting increase adoption?

Advanced – requiring programming

The model is essentially an infection model. Change it to an influence model, that is, requiring more than one member of a personal network to adopt before the household adopts.

References

Arthur, W.B. (1989) Competing technologies, increasing returns and lock-in by historical events. *Economic Journal*, 99, pp.116–131.

Axtell, R. (2006) Multi-Agent Systems Macro: A prospectus. In Collander, D., ed, *Post Walraisian Macroeconomics*. Cambridge: Cambridge University Press, pp.203–220.

Bass, F. (1969) A new product growth for model consumer durables. *Management Science*, 15(5) pp.215–227 (republished (2004) *Management Science*, 50(12) Supplement pp.1833–1840).

Bowden, S. & Offer, A. (1994) Household appliances and the use of time: The United States and Britain since the 1920s. *Economic History Review*, XLVLL(4), pp.725–748.

Bruggeman, J. (2008) *Social Networks*. London: Routledge.

Casweb (2014) *2001 census: Standard Area Statistics (England and Wales)* ESRC/JISC Census Programme, Census Dissemination Unit, Mimas (University of Manchester) [Online]. Available at: http://casweb. mimas.ac.uk/ [Accessed 3 January 2015].

Central Statistics Office (CSO) (1995) *Family Spending: A Report on the 1994–95 Family Expenditure Survey*. London: HMSO.

Coleman, D. (2000) Population and Family. In Halsey, A.H. & Webb, J. eds, *Twentieth Century British Social Trends*. London: Macmillan, pp.27–93.

Deaton, A. & Muellbauer, J. (1985) *Economics and Consumer Behaviour*. Cambridge: Cambridge University Press.

Department of Employment (1975) *Family Expenditure Survey 1974*. London: HMSO.

Department of Employment (1986) *Family Expenditure Survey 1984*. London: HMSO.

Douglas, M. & Isherwood, B. (1979) *The World of Goods*. London: Routledge. (Also 1996.)

Feinstein, C.H. (1972) *National Income, Expenditure and Output of the United Kingdom: 1855–1965*. Cambridge: Cambridge University Press.

Fischer, C.S. (1992) *America Calling: A Social History of the Telephone to 1940*. Berkeley: University of California Press.

General Register Office (GRO), 1952. *Census 1951: One Per Cent Sample Tables*. Part I & II. London: HMSO.

Granovetter, M. (1978) Threshold models of collective behavior. *The American Journal of Sociology*, 83(6) pp.1420–1443.

Granovetter, M. & Soong, R. (1986) Threshold models of interpersonal effects in consumer demand. *Journal of Economic Behavior and Organization*, 7, pp.83–99.

Hamill, L. (2010) *Communications, Travel and Social Networks since 1840: A Study Using Agent-based Models*. PhD thesis. University of Surrey [Online]. Available at: http://research.microsoft.com/pubs/ 145713/hamill-phd-thesis.pdf or http://www.hamill.co.uk [Accessed 3 January 2015].

Hamill, L. & Gilbert, N. (2009) *Social circles: A simple structure for agent-based social network models*. *Journal of Artificial Societies and Social Simulation*, 12(2), p.3 [Online]. Available at: http://jasss.soc. surrey.ac.uk/12/2/3.html [Accessed 3 January 2015].

Hamill, L. & Gilbert, N. (2010) Simulating large social networks in agent-based models: A social circle model. *Emergence: Complexity & Organization*, 12(4), pp.78–94.

Jackson, M. (2010) *Social and Economic Networks*. Princeton: Princeton University Press.

Keeling, M.J. & Eames, K.T.D. (2005) Networks and epidemic models. *Journal of the Royal Society: Interface*, 2, pp.295–307.

Marwick, A., 1990. *British Society since 1945*. London: Penguin.

McPherson, M., Smith-Lovin, L. & Cook, J.M. (2001) Birds of a Feather: Homophily in social networks. *Annual Review of Sociology*, 27, pp.415–444.

Ministry of Labour (1965) *Family Expenditure Survey: Report for 1964*. London: HMSO.

Office for National Statistics (ONS) (1996) *Living in Britain: Results From the 1994 General Household Survey*. London: HMSO.

Office for National Statistics (ONS) (1997) *Social Trends 27*. London: The Stationery Office.

Office for National Statistics (ONS) (1998) *Family Spending 1997–98: A Report on the 1997–98 Family Expenditure Survey*. London: The Stationery Office.

Office for National Statistics (ONS) (2002) *Family Spending: A Report on the 2000–01 Family Expenditure Survey*. London: The Stationery Office [Online]. Available at: www.ons.gov.uk/ [Accessed 3 January 2015].

Office for National Statistics (ONS) (2013) *Family spending: 2013* [Online]. Available at: www.ons.gov.uk/ [Accessed 3 January 2015].

Office for National Statistics ONS (2014) *Data sets and reference tables* [Online]. Available at: http://www.ons.gov.uk/ons/datasets-and-tables/index.html [Accessed 3 January 2015].

Rogers, E.M. (2003) *Diffusion of Innovations*. 5th Edition. New York: Free Press.

Stonedahl, F. & Wilensky, U. (2008) *NetLogo virus on a network model*. http://ccl.northwestern.edu/netlogo/models/VirusonaNetwork [Accessed 18 April 2015]. Center for Connected Learning and Computer-Based Modeling, Northwestern University, Evanston, IL.

Suitor, J. & Keeton, S. (1997) Once a friend, always a friend? Effects of homophily on women's support networks across a decade. *Social Networks*, 19, pp.51–62.

Valente, T. (1995) *Network Models of the Diffusion of Innovations*. Cresskill: Hampton Press.

Watts, C. & Gilbert, N. (2014) *Simulating Innovation: Computer-based Tools for Rethinking Innovation*. Cheltenham: Edward Elgar.

Wellman, B., Wong, R.Y., Tindall, D. & Nazer, N. (1997) A decade of network change: turnover, persistence and stability in personal communities. *Social Networks*, 19(1), pp.27–50.

Wickens, M. (2008) *Macroeconomic Theory: A Dynamic General Equilibrium Approach*. Princeton: Princeton University Press.

5

Benefits of barter

5.1 Introduction

"This is a pretty early tick, I reckon. It's the first one I've seen this year"
"Say, Huck – I'll give you my tooth for him"
"Less see it"
Tom got out a bit of paper and carefully unrolled it. Huckleberry viewed it wistfully.
The temptation was very strong. At last he said: "Is it genuwyne?"
Tom lifted his lip and showed the vacancy.
"Well, all right," said Huckleberry, "it's a trade."
Tom enclosed the tick in the percussion-cap box that had lately been the pinchbug's
prison, and the boys separated, each feeling wealthier than before.

The Adventures of Tom Sawyer, Mark Twain (1876, Chapter VI)

Mark Twain's message is clear: trade can make people feel better off even though the quantity
of goods available has not changed. This chapter looks at simple barter, the exchange of some
quantity of a good for some quantity of another good. Simple barter economies have been
described by economists since Adam Smith's *Wealth of Nations* (1776). However, Graeber
(2011) reported that anthropologists have apparently never found such economies. For example,
Diamond (2012, pp.61–75) described how trade was conducted in societies that did not use
money, where trade was as much a social as an economic activity, merging with gift-giving.
However, these are not the simple barter worlds described by Smith and those economists who
followed him. Nevertheless, there was some truth in the barter model. Sturt (1912, Chapters II,
VIII and IX) described the self-reliance of Surrey villagers and the change that came about

Agent-Based Modelling in Economics, First Edition. Lynne Hamill and Nigel Gilbert.
© 2016 John Wiley & Sons, Ltd. Published 2016 by John Wiley & Sons, Ltd.

when the loss of the open common meant that labourers who had been largely self-sufficient had instead to buy from shops:

> So the once self-supporting cottager turned into a spender of money...; and, of course, needing to spend money, he needed first to get it...To a greater or lesser extent, most were already wage-earners, though not regularly.
>
> (Sturt, 1912, Chapter IX)

Graeber argued that pure barter economies are only found where people have been accustomed to using money, but money was not available to them. That is certainly true of Tom Sawyer and Huck Finn in nineteenth-century America!

However, rather than looking at ticks and teeth, this chapter is based on what has become known as 'the Red Cross parcel problem' and is based broadly on Radford's (1945) description of what happened in a prisoner-of-war camp in the Second World War. The parcels were 'usually sent at the rate of one per man per week' and contained tins of tea, sugar, milk and meat and other basics. They also included a bar of chocolate and 50 cigarettes (Red Cross, 2015). Thus, everyone received 'a roughly equal share of essentials' and most traded so that their 'individual preferences are given expression and comfort increased' (Radford, 1945). Radford continued,

> Most trading was for food against cigarettes or other foodstuffs, but cigarettes rose from the status of a normal commodity to that of currency....Starting with simple direct barter, such as a non-smoker giving a smoker friend his cigarette issue in exchange for a chocolate ration, more complex exchanges soon became an accepted custom...A cigarette issue was worth several chocolate issues.
>
> (Radford, 1945)

The advantage of taking this scenario as the basis for a model is that the participants have no control over the total supply of goods: it was simply what rations they were given. In other words, it is an exchange economy.

The first section of this chapter models trade between just two individuals in order to tease out the essentials of the barter process. The second section introduces a model of a group, allowing agents to choose with whom they trade.

5.2   One-to-one barter

There is no money but as Radford explained, cigarettes are used instead. To avoid a divisibility problem, we assume that each chocolate bar can be divided into 50 chocolates and that neither a cigarette nor a chocolate can be divided up into smaller pieces. The price of a chocolate is the number of cigarettes exchanged for it. So if the price is 5, five cigarettes are swapped for one chocolate. If the price is 1, then there is simply a one-for-one swap. But if the price is 0.2, then five chocolates will be swapped for one cigarette.

Let us call our two individuals the Captain and the Sergeant. The Captain prefers chocolate to cigarettes, and the Sergeant would rather smoke than eat chocolate. For simplicity, we use the Cobb–Douglas utility function we introduced in Chapter 3. By asking the Captain and the Sergeant how much they would want to buy or sell at a range of prices, we can draw the Captain's demand curve and the Sergeant's supply curve and to measure utility of both. Box 5.1 gives an example and demonstrates that when demand equals supply – the market clears – the total utility of the Captain and the Sergeant taken together is maximised.

Box 5.1   Example of demand and supply.

Assumptions

Both the Captain and the Sergeant have Cobb–Douglas utility functions: $U = \text{Choc}^{\alpha}\text{Cigs}^{1-\alpha}$ where U is utility and Choc and Cigs are the rations.

Rations = 50 chocolates and 50 cigarettes

Captain's alpha = 0.9 and Sergeant's alpha = 0.1

Example of the calculations: assuming the price of chocolate = 1

As both receive the same rations, the budget is the same for both. So from Box 3.4:

Budgets = (ration of chocolate x price of chocolate) + ration of cigarettes
= (50 x 1) + 50 = 100

The optimal holding of chocolate

= alpha × budget/price of chocolate
So the Captain's optimal holding
= 0.9 × 100/1 = 90
And the Sergeant's optimal holding
= 0.1 × 100/1 = 10

They already have their rations, so

Captain's demand
= optimal holding − ration = 90 − 50 = 40
Sergeant's supply
= ration − optimal holding = 50 − 10 = 40

So demand equals supply: the market clears.

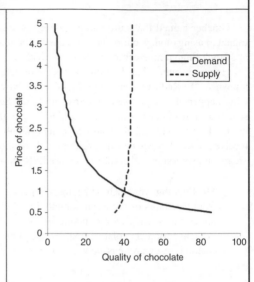

When the market clears, the joint utility is maximised. If chocolate were of a lower price – less than 1 – the Captain would want to buy more than the Sergeant is willing to supply and so less chocolate would be traded. That lower price would favour the Captain and give him a higher utility, but the Sergeant's utility would be lower. Conversely, if the price were above 1, the Sergeant would want to sell more than the Captain would want to buy and so, again, less chocolate would be traded and the joint utility would be lower. For example, if the price of chocolate were 2, then each would have a budget of 150, and the Captain would want an additional 17½, but the Sergeant would want to sell 42½, so that supply exceeds demand.

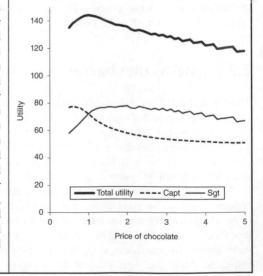

The Edgeworth Box

The standard way to examine one-to-one barter is to use an Edgeworth Box, named after the English economist Francis Edgeworth (1845–1926). An Edgeworth Box essentially combines the indifference curves of two individuals, with the size of the box being determined by the total amount of the two goods available. For the Captain and the Sergeant, the width is the total amount of chocolate available, and the height is the total quantity of cigarettes. As each receives the same ration of chocolate and cigarettes, the box is twice the chocolate ration wide and twice the cigarette ration high. The Captain's utility is measured from the bottom left-hand corner and the Sergeant's from the top right. The box is illustrated in Figure 5.1. The initial endowment is at point E, in the middle of the box: both receive R_C chocolates and R_S cigarettes. But given their preferences, indicated by the indifference curves, the utility of both can be increased by trading to a point in the white area. Recall that the further the indifference curve from the bottom left corner, the higher is the Captain's utility and the further the Sergeant's indifference curve from the top right corner, the higher is the Sergeant's utility. If they can trade so that they move to a point such as O, neither can be made better off without the other being made worse off. At point O, the Captain's and the Sergeant's indifference curves just touch but do not cross. In other words, O is a Pareto-optimal point, that is, where one agent cannot be made better off without the other being made worse off. Furthermore, both are better off than they were at point E: the Captain has moved from the indifference curve passing through E, I_C^E, to that passing through O, I_C^O, and the Sergeant from I_S^E to I_S^O. To reach this point, the Captain has given up $(R_S - O_S)$ cigarettes in return for $(O_C - R_C)$ chocolate, and the Sergeant has given up $(O_C - R_C)$ chocolate for $(R_S - O_S)$ cigarettes.

In mathematical terms, point O is one of the many points where the slopes of the Captain's and the Sergeant's indifference curves are equal, and so the marginal rates of substitution (MRSs)

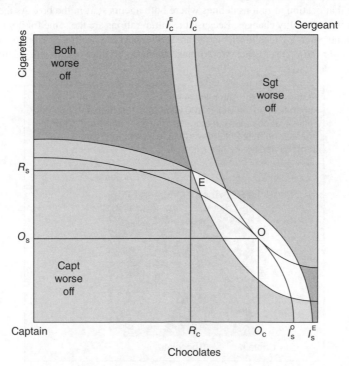

Figure 5.1   Traditional Edgeworth Box example.

of the two are also equal (see Chapter 3). These points are called Pareto optimal or Pareto efficient, and they trace out the contract curve. Those points on the contract curve that would make one or both better off but neither worse off – namely, those that fall within the white area – form the core. (For a fuller explanation of the Edgeworth Box, see textbooks such as Varian (2010, pp.583–595) or, for a more formal exposition, Cowell (2006, pp.149–157).)

Static analysis does not explore how the Captain and the Sergeant discover that setting the price to 1 will maximise their utility and clear the market. The usual workaround is to call upon an imaginary Walrasian auctioneer (which is also called the tâtonnement process). The auctioneer asks both how much they would buy or sell at given prices and they reply truthfully. The auctioneer then calculates the market-clearing price, and they trade at that price. (This process simulates perfect competition as there are no transaction costs and everyone has full information.) It is difficult to see what relationship this bears to any real-world market, and while the auctioneer's job may be trivial when there are only two agents and two commodities, it becomes very difficult when the number of agents and the number of commodities are increased. (For a full discussion of the problems with the tâtonnement process, see Axtell (2005).) Agent-based modelling, however, does allow us to explore the dynamics of trading under different trading rules.

Dynamics of the Edgeworth Box

To reproduce the Edgeworth Box in NetLogo, we draw a box to represent the total amount of chocolate and cigarettes available. We then define the utility the Captain and the Sergeant would have on each patch. The box is therefore like a chessboard in which each square represents a different combination of chocolate and cigarettes, which in turn implies different levels of utility and MRSs for the Captain and the Sergeant.

The initial allocation of rations defines where both agents start in the box. As the two agents move across it, their utility changes. Because the initial rations are the same for both agents, they start at the same point. We then block out the areas which would result in one or both being worse off and highlight those areas which would make them both better off. Figure 5.2 illustrates the

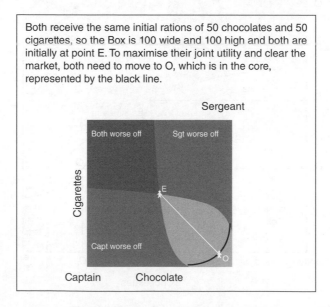

Figure 5.2   Trading with an auctioneer.

case where the Captain's alpha is 0.9 and the Sergeant's 0.1 and the rations are 50 cigarettes and 50 chocolates. The dark grey areas are those which would result in one or both being worse off. The agents will not move into these areas: they are blocked by one or both. The light grey areas show where they would both be better off. The black line, in the light grey area, is the core, that is, the section of the contract curve that is not blocked. As we demonstrated in Box 5.1, if the Captain and Sergeant swapped 40 cigarettes for 40 chocolates, the market would clear. This would be achieved by them moving to point **O**, which is in the core. (Because the quantities available are fixed, they move to the same point.) This result is therefore in line with the first theorem of welfare economics, that is, that the market-clearing equilibrium is Pareto optimal. (For further discussion, see, e.g. Varian (2010, pp.596–598).) At point **O**, both agents enjoy utility 44% higher than at the initial endowment, point **E**. This is also the point which clears the market and maximises total utility, as illustrated in Box 5.1. If there were an auctioneer to tell them what price to trade at, the Captain and the Sergeant could move immediately to point **O**, the market-clearing total utility maximising position.

However, if there are not sufficient rations to allow one of the agents to maximise its utility, the market-clearing price will not maximise joint utility, but it will give both the same increase in utility. For example, if there were a shortage of chocolate, as illustrated in Figure 5.3, the market-clearing price will yield only 95% of the maximum possible joint utility, but it does give both parties a 44% increase in utility as it did when there were sufficient rations.

But what if they have no one to tell them at what price to trade and they have to discover by negotiating? Let us start by assuming that the Captain, as the senior partner, makes the opening bid. Now the Captain would maximise his utility by 'buying' 47 chocolates for 19 cigarettes, implying a price of about 0.4 cigarettes per chocolate. This is shown as point **C** in Figure 5.3, at the top end of the core. But at that price, the Sergeant would choose to offer only 30 chocolates for 12 cigarettes (as shown by the supply curve in Box 5.1). So the Captain takes these 30 chocolates

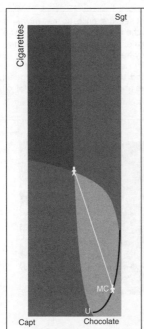

The Captain's alpha is 0.9 and the Sergeant's, 0.1.

The rations are 25 chocolates and 75 cigarettes, so the box is 50 wide and 150 high.

At the initial position, the Captain has a utility of 27.9 and the Sergeant, 67.3.

The market clearing price is 3. If the Captain trades 60 cigarettes for 20 chocolates, they move to point MC: his utility will increase by 44% to 40.3, and the Sergeant's will also increase by 44% to 97.1. This gives a joint utility of 137.4.

The joint utility could be increased by a different trade. If the Captain gave 71 cigarettes for 10 chocolates, they would move to point U, where the Sergeant's utility is 116.3 but the Captain's only 28.2. Total utility is then 144.5, more than the market-clearing trade, but clearly, such a trade offers very little to the Captain. This is because there are enough cigarettes to maximise the Sergeant's utility but not enough chocolate to maximise the Captain's.

Figure 5.3   Trading with an auctioneer when there is a shortage.

in return for 12 cigarettes (as implied by the price of 0.4). This trade would move them both nearer to point **O**, at which they would maximise their joint utility, but they can benefit from trading again. If they traded again, this time at a price called by the Sergeant to reach his maximum utility, they would move still closer to the market-clearing optimal position, **O**. In fact, their joint utility would then be 97% of what could be attained at **O**. Using this price-setting rule, they will not move again. Their path is shown in the left-hand panel of Figure 5.4.

If, on the other hand, the Sergeant called the first price, then he would offer 43 chocolates at a price of 2.5 as that would move him to point **S** in Figure 5.4 and maximise his utility. But at that price the Captain would only buy 13 chocolates for 32 cigarettes (as shown by the demand curve in Box 5.1). If the Captain were then to make an offer at his utility maximising price, there would be another trade, and they would move still closer to point **O**, increasing the utility: indeed, their joint utility would then be 99% of that which would have been achieved at the market-clearing price, **O**. This is shown in the right-hand panel of Figure 5.4.

But even this simple process assumes that the Captain and the Sergeant know the price at which their respective utilities would be maximised and are prepared to negotiate in this manner. It may, however, be that they simply haggle to reach a price. Think about what happens when you haggle at a market. The seller has asked a price and you offer something lower. What price you pay, if indeed you buy at all, will depend on how much you want it, whether you think you can buy cheaper elsewhere, your negotiating skills, how much the seller wants to sell it, the seller's skills, etc. Rather than trying to model all these factors, we simply assume that the agents agree a

Both receive the same initial rations of 50 chocolate blocks and 50 cigarettes, so the Box is 100 wide and 100 high:

E is their initial endowment.
    O is the utility maximising, market-clearing point.
    C maximises the Captain's utility.
    S maximises the Sergeant's utility.

The Captain sets first price, so they move towards C in the first trade: 12 cigarettes given for 30 chocolates. Then, the Sergeant sets the price and they trade 6 chocolates for 15 cigarettes. This leaves the Captain with 86 chocolates and 23 cigarettes and the Sergeant, 14 chocolates and 77 cigarettes. Their total joint utility is 97 % of what would be obtained at point O.	The Sergeant sets first price, so they move towards S in the first trade: 32 cigarettes given for 13 chocolates. Then, the Captain sets the price and they trade 20 chocolates for 8 cigarettes. This leaves the Captain with 83 chocolates and 10 cigarettes and the Sergeant, 17 chocolates and 90 cigarettes. Their total joint utility is 99 % of what would be obtained at point O.
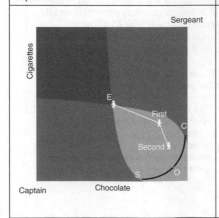	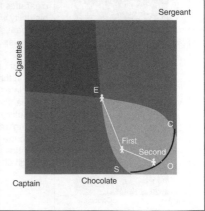

Figure 5.4   Trading in the Edgeworth Box without an auctioneer.

price that falls between their respective MRSs. This means that on average, the price will be the average of the two MRSs. For example, in the balanced case we have discussed, the Captain's initial MRS will be 9 and the Sergeant's 0.11. The pair will therefore agree a price which falls between 0.11 and 9 cigarettes for each chocolate. As each trade will change the agents' MRSs, the range of possible prices will change at each trade. We call this trading regime 'random pricing'.

Table 5.1 presents the results of running the random price-setting process 1000 times, allowing the two agents to trade up to five times. In the first round, the agents are usually able to agree a price at which they both benefit from trade. But in later rounds, this is less likely to happen because the price agreed is so close to the MRS of one of the agents that he sees no benefit in trading. Both the balanced supply and the shortage of chocolate give total initial utility of

Table 5.1   Examples of random trading.

Captain's alpha=0.9, Sergeant's alpha=0.1
1000 runs

Balanced supply

Rations				Initial MRSs	
Chocolate		50		Sgt	0.11
Cigarettes		50		Capt	9.00
Initial utility as % of max		69		Mean	4.56

After	% trading[a]	Utility as % max		Price	
	Mean	Mean	sd	Mean	sd
−1 round	91	86	8	4.2	2.3
−2 rounds	83	92	7	2.2	1.5
−3 rounds	73	95	5	1.4	1.0
−4 rounds	59	97	3	1.1	0.7
−5 rounds	46	98	2	1.0	0.6
Market-clearing price				1	

Shortage of chocolate

Rations				Initial MRSs	
Chocolate		25		Sgt	0.33
Cigarettes		75		Capt	27.00
Initial utility as % of max		66		Mean	13.7

After	% trading[a]	Utility as % max		Price	
	Mean	Mean	sd	Mean	sd
−1 round	82	87	8.3	11.5	6.3
−2 rounds	70	93	6.5	5.6	3.8
−3 rounds	63	95	5.2	3.8	2.6
−4 rounds	57	96	4.5	2.9	1.8
−5 rounds	42	97	4.5	2.4	1.4
Market-clearing price				3	

[a]Proportion of runs in which the agents traded at this round.

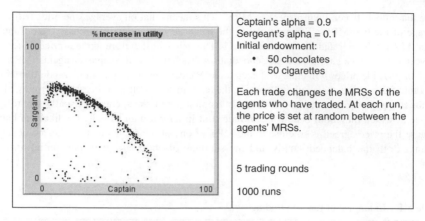

Figure 5.5   Increases in utility as a result of trade under random pricing.

around two thirds the maximum. The results show that even a single round of trading can increase the joint utility to around 80% of the maximum possible and, after five rounds of trading, this figure approaches 100%. The average price paid falls as trade progresses, tending towards the market-clearing price. Figure 5.5 shows how such trade can increase the utility of both agents: sometimes, the Captain gains more, and sometimes the Sergeant.

The two models – *Edgeworth Box Game* and *Edgeworth Box Random Model* – can be used to explore trading with different price-setting rules and different preferences with different initial allocations of rations. These models are described in Appendix 5.A.

To summarise, if there are two goods in an exchange economy and one can be bartered for the other, the agents' utilities may be increased by trade, so that 'each feels wealthier than before'. If they can discover a price that clears the market, their total utility will be maximised. Comparative statics either does not address the problem of how this point is reached or invokes some all-seeing auctioneer to coordinate trade. But the simple dynamic solutions we have explored showed that the agents can haggle their way to a position close to the market-clearing utility maximising optimum.

5.3   Red Cross parcels

Having examined how the process works for two individuals, we now turn to a group. For this, we base the model on the camp described by Radford (1945). It contained between 1200 and 2500 people, housed in separate but intercommunicating buildings, each accommodating about 200, called a 'company'. Although there was trade between companies, Radford's paper seems to suggest that trading generally took place within a company. So this model uses 200 agents to represent a company. Radford (1945) reported that initially people started by wandering around calling their offers, for instance, 'cheese for seven (cigarettes)'. But due to 'the inconveniences' of this system, it was quickly replaced by a noticeboard advertising sales and wants with contact details. 'When a deal went through, it was crossed off the board. The public and semi-permanent records of transactions led to cigarette prices being well known and thus tending to equality throughout the camp' (Radford, 1945).

In the model, each agent receives the same initial ration of chocolate and cigarettes. The agents are divided into two groups: smokers and chocolate lovers. As previously, they have Cobb–Douglas utility functions with alpha representing their preference for chocolate. The smokers are randomly allocated alphas up to 0.5 and the nonsmokers, alphas of between 0.5 and 1. So a heavy smoker will have an alpha near zero and a chocolate addict, an alpha near one.

Box 5.2   Calculation of the equilibrium price.

Both agents have Cobb–Douglas utility functions:

$$U = \text{Choc}^\alpha \text{Cigs}^{1-\alpha} \tag{5.1}$$

Following the analysis in Box 3.4, their demand for chocolate will be

$$\frac{\alpha m}{P_{\text{Choc}}} \tag{5.2}$$

where m equals their budget. Their budgets are given by their rations and the price of chocolate (as the price of cigarettes is set equal to 1) and both are issued with the same ration:

$$m = P_{\text{Choc}}\text{ChocRation} + \text{CigRation} \tag{5.3}$$

This means that the chocolate lover's demand for chocolate is

$$\frac{\alpha_\text{C}\left(P_{\text{Choc}}\text{ChocRation}_\text{C} + \text{CigRation}_\text{C}\right)}{P_{\text{Choc}}} \tag{5.4}$$

But he already holds his ration of chocolate, so his excess demand for chocolate is

$$\frac{\alpha_\text{C}\left(P_{\text{Choc}}\text{ChocRation}_\text{C} + \text{CigRation}_\text{C}\right)}{P_{\text{Choc}}} - \text{ChocRation}_\text{C} \tag{5.5}$$

Similarly, the smoker's excess demand for chocolate is

$$\frac{\alpha_\text{S}\left(P_{\text{Choc}}\text{ChocRation}_\text{S} + \text{CigRation}_\text{S}\right)}{P_{\text{Choc}}} - \text{ChocRation}_\text{S} \tag{5.6}$$

Summing (5.5) and (5.6) gives the total excess demand; setting this equal to zero and solving for P_{Choc},

$$P_{\text{Choc}} = \left(\frac{\alpha_\text{C}\text{CigRation}_\text{C} + \alpha_\text{S}\text{CigRation}_\text{S}}{(1-\alpha_\text{C})\text{ChocRation}_\text{C} + (1-\alpha_\text{S})\text{ChocRation}_\text{S}}\right) \tag{5.7}$$

But each has the same ration issued, so (5.7) becomes

$$P_{\text{Choc}} = \frac{\text{CigRation}}{\text{ChocRation}}\left(\frac{\alpha_\text{C} + \alpha_\text{S}}{(1-\alpha_\text{C}) + (1-\alpha_\text{S})}\right) \tag{5.8}$$

Based on Varian (2010, pp.594–595).

Recall that there is no money but cigarettes are used as currency so that prices in this context are the number of cigarettes exchanged for a chocolate. Furthermore, deals are only permitted in whole numbers: agents cannot trade half a cigarette or half a chocolate, for instance.

Each chocolate lover is allowed to trade with any smoker in the company. The trading price is set using one of three price-setting rules:

- The Walrasian auctioneer, as a theoretical, ideal baseline, against which we measure the performance of the other price-setting rules. Trading pairs have to decide whether or not to trade at the market-clearing price.

- The equilibrium price formula, which allows each pair of agents to calculate their optimal price, based on the analysis presented in Chapter 3, and shown in Box 5.2, with an example in Box 5.3. This means that the price at which each pair trades is determined solely by the agents' holdings and preferences.

Box 5.3   Example of trading under the equilibrium pricing regime.

Assumptions

Both the chocolate lover and the smoker receive the same initial rations of 50 chocolates and 50 cigarettes.

Chocolate lover's alpha $(\alpha_C) = 0.9$

Smoker's alpha $(\alpha_S) = 0.1$

Equilibrium price

Equation 5.8 from Box 5.3 gives an equilibrium price for chocolate:

$$\frac{\text{CigRation}}{\text{ChocRation}}\left(\frac{\alpha_C + \alpha_S}{\left(1-\alpha_C\right)+\left(1-\alpha_S\right)}\right) = \frac{50}{50}\left(\frac{0.9+0.1}{\left(1-0.9\right)+\left(1-0.1\right)}\right) = 1$$

The demand and supply of chocolate

Demand from the chocolate lover is given by Equation 5.5 in Box 5.3:

$$\frac{\alpha_C\left(P_{\text{Choc}}\text{ChocRation}_C + \text{CigRation}_C\right)}{P_{\text{Choc}}} - \text{ChocRation}_C = \frac{0.9\left(1\times 50 + 50\right)}{1} - 50 = 40$$

Supply from the smoker is given by Equation 5.6 in Box 5.1:

$$\frac{\alpha_S\left(P_{\text{Choc}}\text{ChocRation}_S + \text{CigRation}_S\right)}{P_{\text{Choc}}} - \text{ChocRation}_S = \frac{0.1\left(1\times 50 + 50\right)}{1} - 50 = 40$$

So they swap 40 chocolates for 40 cigarettes. This is the same result as the Walrasian auctioneer obtained in these circumstances, as described in Section 5.2.

- The random price-setting we introduced in Section 5.2. As with the equilibrium price-setting rule, the price will lie between the MRSs of each member of the trading pair. But the stochastic variation means that the price is not likely to be the same for two identical pairs of traders, as it is with the equilibrium price-setting rule.

To illustrate the differences between these three pricing rules, Table 5.2 shows how the initial price of chocolate will vary if the rations are 50 cigarettes and 50 chocolates:

- With the Walrasian auctioneer, the price will be 1 whatever the alphas of the trading partners.

- With the equilibrium pricing method, the price will vary between 0.3 and 3 depending on the alphas of the trading partners.

- With the random pricing mechanism, the price will vary between 0.3 and 3 when both traders have mid-range alphas for their groups but could be very high or very low if one or both of the agents have very strong preferences (i.e. very high or low alphas).

It was shown in the Edgeworth Box example that much of the potential total benefit from trading could be obtained after just five rounds. This proves to the case even when agents can now choose new trading partners after each round. Figure 5.6 shows that most of the trading, and the consequential increase in utility, occurs in the first five rounds when rations are assumed to be evenly split between chocolate and cigarettes and half the agents are smokers and half chocolate lovers. The top panel of Figure 5.6 shows the extent of trading under the three different price-setting rules. Under the auctioneer and the equilibrium price-setting rule, almost all the agents trade

Table 5.2   Initial prices under the three pricing regimes with rations of 50 cigarettes and 50 chocolates.

	Smoker's alpha[a]		Chocolate lover's alpha[b]		
			0.501	0.750	0.999
Walrasian auctioneer					
	0.001		1	1	1
	0.250		1	1	1
	0.500		1	1	1
Equilibrium					
	0.001		0.3	0.6	1.0
	0.250		0.6	1.0	1.7
	0.500		1.0	1.7	3.0
Random					
	0.001				
		Min	0.001	0.001	0.001
		Max	1.0	3.0	999.0
		Mean	0.5	1.5	499.5
	0.250				
		Min	0.3	0.3	0.3
		Max	1.0	3.0	999.0
		Mean	0.7	1.7	499.7
	0.500				
		Min	1.0	1.0	1.0
		Max	1.0	3.0	999.0
		Mean	1.0	2.0	500.0

[a]Varies between 0.001 and 0.500.
[b]Varies between 0.501 and 0.999.

in the first round and the volume of trading declines quickly thereafter. However, with the random price-setting rule, only half the agents trade in the first round although after five rounds, 90% have traded. So it is not surprising that in terms of the impact on utility, there is little to choose between the auctioneer and the agent-to-agent equilibrium trading as shown in the bottom panel of Figure 5.6. Indeed, the equilibrium price-setting rule produces more benefits than the auctioneer in the first round. This is because when the price is set by the auctioneer, each pair has to trade at that price and this may not work for some pairs of agents. In contrast under the equilibrium price-setting rule, each pair of agents is free to trade at a price that suits them. Not surprisingly, the equilibrium price-setting rule increases utility by more than the random price-setting rule if there is only one round of trading. Nevertheless, the random price-setting rule still generates an increase in total utility that is the company is 'better off' than if there had been no trading. However, the difference between the rules is reduced by subsequent trading: after five rounds of trading, the auctioneer and the equilibrium price-setting rule have increased utility by about a fifth and the random price-setting rule, by a seventh. If we take the increase in utility obtained by using the auctioneer as the measure of what would happen in an ideal system, then the equilibrium price-setting rule gives as much or more than that given by the auctioneer from the first round, while the random price-setting achieves 92% in the first round rising to 95% after five rounds.

Figure 5.7 shows examples – based on just one run – of the before-and-after demand and supply curves. This is the standard comparative statics approach. In all cases, both supply and

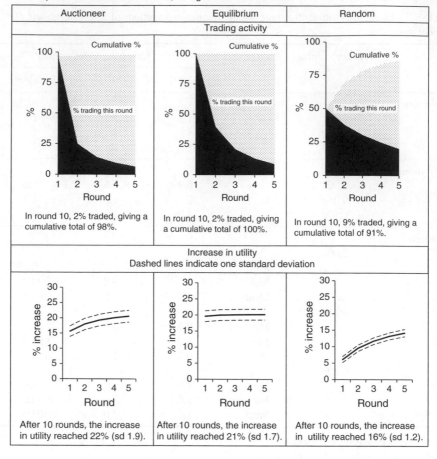

200 agents, 100 runs
Assumptions: Rations: 50 chocolates, 50 cigarettes: 50% smokers

Auctioneer	Equilibrium	Random
Trading activity		

Auctioneer
In round 10, 2% traded, giving a cumulative total of 98%.

Equilibrium
In round 10, 2% traded, giving a cumulative total of 100%.

Random
In round 10, 9% traded, giving a cumulative total of 91%.

Increase in utility
Dashed lines indicate one standard deviation

Auctioneer
After 10 rounds, the increase in utility reached 22% (sd 1.9).

Equilibrium
After 10 rounds, the increase in utility reached 21% (sd 1.7).

Random
After 10 rounds, the increase in utility reached 16% (sd 1.2).

Figure 5.6   Trading under different price-setting regimes.

200 agents, 1 run

Assumptions: Rations: 50 chocolates, 50 cigarettes: 50% smokers
Solid lines initial curves, dashed lines after 10 rounds of trading

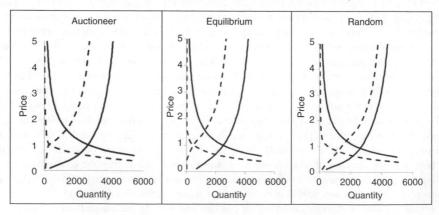

Figure 5.7   Examples of shifts in demand and supply curves.

200 agents, 100 runs

Assumptions: rations: 50 chocolates, 50 cigarettes: 50% smokers

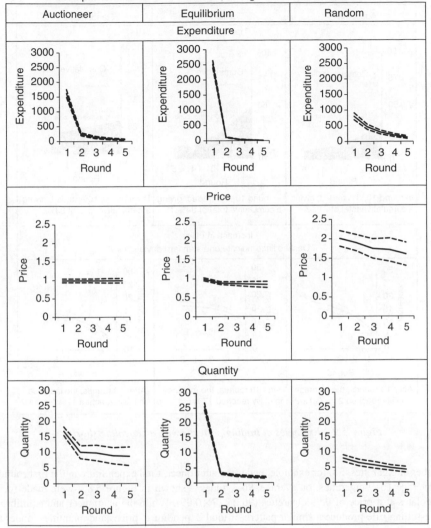

Figure 5.8   Prices and quantities traded under different price-setting regimes.
(Dashed lines indicate one standard deviation).

demand curves shift to the left, but under the auctioneer and the equilibrium price-setting rule, there is clearly little scope for more trading after 10 rounds, while there is still some scope under the random price-setting rule.

However, agent-based modelling allows us to explore the dynamics of trading by drilling down through the numbers. The first row of Figure 5.8 shows how total expenditure fell over the five rounds. By definition, this total expenditure is the product of the average price, the average quantity traded and the number of trades. Prices and expenditure are measured in terms of the

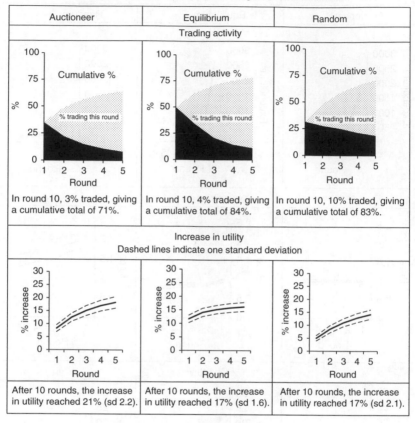

200 agents, 100 runs

Assumptions: rations: 25 chocolates, 75 cigarettes: 25% smokers

Figure 5.9   Examples of trading patterns with a chocolate shortage.

number of cigarettes. So, for example, under the auctioneer, total expenditure in the first round is on average 1619 cigarettes: on average, 96.2 trades – shown in Figure 5.8 – were made for 17 chocolates at a price of 0.99 cigarettes ($96.2 \times 17 \times 0.99$). While the auctioneer and equilibrium price-setting rule produce a similar pattern of total expenditure, prices and quantities, under the random price-setting rule, total expenditure is lower because prices are higher.

Introducing shortages

So far, we have assumed that demand and supply are evenly balanced. But Radford noted that that was rarely the case and usually there were insufficient cigarettes to satisfy everyone. Here, we take a more modern twist and ask: what if there were a high proportion of chocolate lovers and the rations of chocolate were low? As there are now more than two agents, we can model more extreme examples of shortages than in the Edgeworth Box example because we can change the proportion of smokers. If 75% of the agents are chocolate lovers but only 25 of the 100 items in the Red Cross parcel are chocolates, then there is a shortage of chocolates. In these circumstances, the market-clearing price is 5; five cigarettes will be paid for each chocolate.

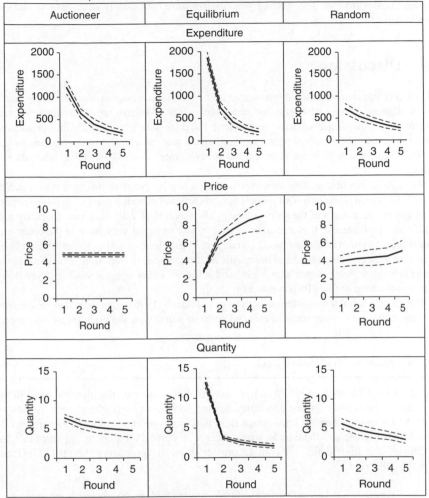

Figure 5.10   Prices and quantities traded under different price-setting regimes with a chocolate shortage. (Dashed lines indicate one standard deviation).

The top row of Figure 5.9 shows that when there is a shortage, the trading pattern does not differ significantly by price-setting rule: in fact, there is less trading under the auctioneer than when prices are set by negotiation between agents. However, the second row shows that the auctioneer still produces the greatest increase in utility. Nevertheless, the equilibrium pricing and the random pricing rules produce over 95% of the utility of the auctioneer. Overall, it shows that when there is a shortage, the outcome is less affected by the choice of price-setting rule.

However, Figure 5.10 shows that the underlying dynamics of the three price-setting processes are quite different. Under the auctioneer, the price is fixed throughout and the quantity traded gradually declines. In contrast, under the equilibrium trading system, the price rises sharply, with a consequent fall in quantity traded, consistent with an increasing shortage. Under random price setting, total expenditure falls slowly as prices rise and quantities traded fall.

5.4   Discussion

This chapter has demonstrated the power of agent-based modelling to analyse trading and has suggested some interesting results for economic theory. We have set up a simple exchange economy and allowed agents to trade under three basic price-setting rules, the Walrasian auctioneer and two rules that allow pairs of agents to negotiate the price at which to trade. We have looked at the situation in which there are sufficient resources to meet demand as well as when there is a shortage.

We have shown how trading increases welfare when people have different tastes, as Smith (1776/1861) noted repeatedly. Our models have shown that allowing pairs of agents to negotiate prices can produce much of the gain yielded by the theoretical Walrasian auctioneer. By acting in their own self-interest, they can trade in such a way as to get very close to the optimum. In other words, a system of trading based on real-world haggling, invoking Smith's invisible hand rather than Walras's theoretical and unrealistic auctioneer, can deliver similar benefits. No auctioneer is needed: Adam Smith's invisible hand achieves a near-optimal solution. (See Box 5.4 for information on Smith's invisible hand.)

This result is similar to that found by Epstein and Axtell (1996) using their *Sugarscape* model. They modelled agents who traded sugar and spice in pairs, with the price set as the geometric

Box 5.4   Adam Smith's invisible hand.

In Book IV, Chapter 2 of his *Wealth of Nations*, Smith invokes the invisible hand in the context of protecting domestic industry against foreign imports: the chapter is entitled 'Of the Restraints upon the Importation from Foreign Countries of Such Goods as Can Be Produced at Home'. At the time he wrote, there was a prohibition on the import of salt, for example, and high duties on corn to protect domestic producers. Smith (1776/1861, pp.198–199) said:

> Every individual is continually exerting himself to find out the most advantageous employment for whatever capital he can command. It is his own advantage, indeed, and not that of society, which he has in view. But the study of his own advantage naturally or rather necessarily, leads him to prefer than employment which is most advantageous to the society….By preferring the support of domestic to that of foreign industry, he intends only his own security; and by directing that industry in such a manner as its produce may be of the greatest value, he intends only his own gain, and he is in this, as in many other cases, led by an **invisible hand** to promote an end which was no part of his intention. Nor is it always the worse for the society that it was not part of it. By pursuing his own interest he frequently promotes that of the society more effectually than when he really intends to promote it.

He then went on to attack regulation. Thus, the 'invisible hand' has come to mean that it is best to allow people to pursue their own interests.

mean of the agents' MRSs (Epstein & Axtell, 1996, p.104). This rule produced prices that lie between those established by the equilibrium and random price-setting rules we have used. Epstein and Axtell (1996, p.111) commented:

> There is a sense in which this completely decentralized, distributed achievement of economic equilibrium is a *more* powerful result than is offered by general equilibrium theory, since *dynamics* of price formation are fully accounted for, and there is no recourse to a mythical auctioneer. This result harks back to Adam Smith and the classical economists whose image of markets involved no such entity.

Because agent-based modelling accommodates both heterogeneity and interaction, it is a powerful tool for modelling trading. Trading only occurs in the example we have used because agents have different tastes; that is, they are heterogeneous. Furthermore, unlike the usual comparative statics analysis, agent-based modelling facilitates the analysis of the dynamics of trade and how markets can move from one equilibrium to another. It allows us to tease out the interaction of prices and quantities and volumes of trading on total expenditure over time. It also illustrates how different micro processes can generate similar macro patterns.

This chapter has focussed on the situation in which agents have no control over the total supply of goods and can only change how they are allocated. In the next chapter, we will introduce suppliers.

Appendix 5.A   How to do it

Edgeworth Box game

Purpose: The model represents an Edgeworth Box. The aim is to select prices at which the agents can trade to move them as close as possible to their maximum utility.

Entities: There are two agents, the Captain and the Sergeant, and two goods, chocolate and cigarettes. Each agent is each given the same allocation of chocolate and cigarettes. But they have different tastes: the Captain prefers chocolate to cigarettes, and the Sergeant prefers cigarettes to chocolate. The further the Captain is from the bottom left-hand corner, the higher is his utility. The further the Sergeant is from the top right-hand corner, the higher is his utility. Their utility is represented by Cobb–Douglas utility functions, with alpha lying between 0 and 1 and representing the strength of preference for chocolate. (The higher the alpha, the stronger the preference.) The marginal rate of substitution (MRS) is as shown in Box 3.4, and so alpha cannot be 1 because the MRS would then be undefined. Unless the initial allocations happen to coincide with their preferences, the agents can increase their utility by trading.

Stochastic processes: None, unless the random price-setting mechanism is chosen.

Initialisation:

Set the alphas for the two agents:

- For the Captain, this is between 0.6 and 0.9.

- For the Sergeant, this is between 0.1 and 0.5.

Set the initial endowment of chocolate: this can be between 25 and 75. (The number of cigarettes is 100 less this number.)

Choose the price-setting mechanism:

- Market-clearing price, that is, the price at which the demand and supply curves intersect

- 'Captain's favour', the price that would maximise the Captain's utility but at which the Sergeant would be reluctant to trade

- 'Sergeant's favour', the price that would maximise the Sergeant's utility but at which the Captain would be reluctant to trade

- 'Random', the price that is set between the MRSs of the two agents

- Price chosen by you

Output: The model draws an Edgeworth Box to reflect the quantities of chocolate and cigarettes available. It then colours the box to distinguish areas:

- That are not feasible as they involve zero quantities

- Where the Captain would be worse off

- Where the Sergeant would be worse off

- Where both would be worse off

- Where both would be better off

The initial allocation is indicated, the core is drawn, and the patch on which the total utility is maximised is indicated.

The model produces a range of data on the agents' actual and potential maximum utility, MRSs and the trading and sends the plot data to a file. It also calculates the demand and supply curves for chocolate.

The pseudocode is in Box 5.A.1 and a screenshot in Figure 5.A.1. For the full code, see the website: *Chapter 5 – Edgeworth Box Game*.

Things to try using the Edgeworth Box game

- What happens when the Captain and the Sergeant do not have strong preferences? For example, if the Captain's alpha is 0.6 and the Sergeant's is 0.4?

- What happens when there are only a few chocolates? Or only a few cigarettes?

- What happens when you impose a price very close the equilibrium?

- What happens when you impose a price very far from the equilibrium?

Edgeworth Box random model

Purpose: The model is essentially the same as the game model, but it is designed to produce the results of many runs with just the random price-setting mechanism.
Entities: As for the game model.
Stochastic processes: The price is set between the MRSs of the two agents.

Box 5.A.1   Pseudocode for the Edgeworth Box game.

Draw a box that is twice the chocolate ration wide and twice the cigarette ration high.
Create two agents, called the Captain and the Sergeant.

Give both attributes to record utility, quantities of chocolate and cigarettes held, MRS, budget, optimal holding of cigarettes and offer.

Calculate the agents' initial utility.
Colour the box:

Calculate the utility that the two agents would have on each patch.

Calculate the total utility for both agents.

Calculate how much chocolate and cigarettes would have to be traded to reach that box and the implicit price.

Compare the patch utility to the agents' initial utility and colour according to whether either worse off, both worse off and both better off.

Colour the patch representing the initial allocation.

Calculate the MRSs for each agent on each patch.

Draw the contract curve:

The line should be surrounded by at least one patch where the MRS for the Captain exceeds the MRS for the Sergeant and at least one patch where the reverse is true that is the difference between the MRSs passes through zero within the patch.

Plot the three graphs showing the increase in utility and the total utility against price.

Draw demand and supply curves:

Starting with price = 0.1, ask both agents to calculate their optimal holding.

Deduct their actual holding to give excess demand for the Captain or supply for the Sergeant.

Calculated excess demand by subtracting supply from demand.

Repeat 200 times, increasing the price by 0.1 each time.

Draw demand and supply curves and calculate the market-clearing price.

Report the metrics based on rations and preferences.
Set the price according to the choice made at initialisation:

- The market-clearing price, that is, the price at which the demand and supply curves intersect

- 'Captain's favour', the price that would maximise the Captain's utility

- 'Sergeant's favour', the price that would maximise the Sergeant's utility

- 'Random', the price between the MRSs of the two agents

- Price chosen by the modeller

Agents trade:

Each agent calculates his optimal holding at the price set and compares the actual holding with the optimal holding and calculates the offer, if any, rounded appropriately so that only whole numbers are exchanged.

Agents compare offers and agree a deal on the minimum offer.

The deal is checked to ensure that neither is made worse off.

If the deal is cleared, it is done, and the agents move to a new location in the Box and their utilities recalculated.

Metrics of the deal reported and the plot data is sent to a csv file.

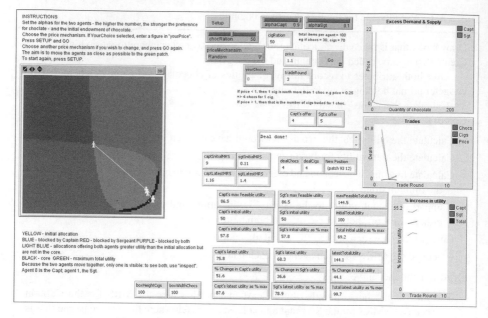

Figure 5.A.1   Screenshot of the Edgeworth Box game.

Initialisation:
Set the alphas for the two agents:

- For the Captain, this is between 0.6 and 0.9.

- For the Sergeant, this is between 0.1 and 0.5.

Set the initial endowment of chocolate: this can be between 25 and 75.
Output: The model draws an Edgeworth Box as in the game model. The results of the runs are aggregated and produced in the output box and the increase in utilities plotted.

Things to try using the Edgeworth Box random model

As for the game, try changing the alphas and the rations (Figure 5.A.2).

Red Cross parcels model

Purpose: This is a very simple trading model based on the Red Cross parcels situation as described by Radford (1945).
Entities: Two hundred agents represent the members of a company. They are divided between smokers and chocolate lovers. The agents have Cobb–Douglas utility functions in which alpha represents the strength of preference for chocolate. Each agent receives the same initial ration of the two goods, cigarettes and chocolates.
Stochastic processes:

- Allocation of preferences: smokers are allocated alphas between 0.001 and 0.5 and chocolate lovers between 0.501 and 0.999.

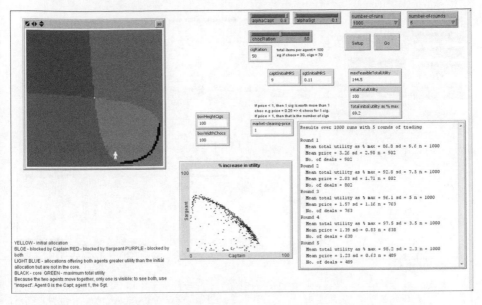

Figure 5.A.2   Screenshot of the Edgeworth Box random model.

- Choice of partners: chocolate lovers select smokers within a given distance (reach) to trade

- Price:

  ○ With the auctioneer, this will depend on the allocation of preferences.

  ○ With the other price-setting mechanisms, it will also depend on the selection of partners.

Initialisation:

There are four parameters:

- The initial number of chocolates given to each agent (The number of cigarettes is 100 less this number.)

- The percentage of smokers

- The reach – the distance which agents can search for trading partners: it must be at least 10 and a reach of 200 will give access to everyone.

- The price-setting method:

  ○ Auctioneer (based on the market-clearing price)

  ○ Equilibrium (see Box 5.2)

  ○ Random, the price that is set between the MRSs of the two agents (as in the Edgeworth Box models)

Set the number of rounds of trading and the number of runs.

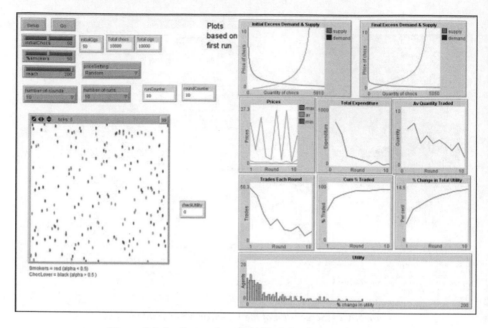

Figure 5.A.3   Screenshot of the Red Cross parcels model.

Output:

- For the first run: graphics, as shown in Figure 5.A.3, with data to a csv file.

- Mean initial and final market-clearing prices, and, for the first five plus the tenth trading rounds: average price, average quantity traded, average total expenditure, mean percentage of agents trading in this round and cumulatively, mean percentage increase in total utility after trade round. This data is sent to a csv file.

The pseudocode is in Box 5.A.2 and a screenshot in Figure 5.A.3. For the full code, see the website: *Chapter 5 – Red Cross Parcels*.

Things to try using Red Cross parcels model

Using sliders and options:

- What happens if there is an extreme shortage of chocolates? Set the initial number of chocolates to 5 and the percentage of smokers to 5.

- What happens with a very restricted reach? Set the reach to 10.

Advanced – requiring amending the program

- What happens if agents consume some of the goods between trading rounds?

- What happens if there is a new delivery of rations?

- What happens if trading costs are introduced?

Box 5.A.2   Pseudocode for the Red Cross parcels model.

Distribute 200 agents randomly within an area 141×141, with no wrapping.
Give agents attributes:

General: alpha and beta (=1 – alpha), holdings of chocolates and cigarettes, whether smoker or chocolate lover, initial and current utility and MRS

To calculate demand and supply curves: budget, optimal holding, demand, supply

For trading: identity of partner, buyer or seller, price related, optimal holding, excess demand or supply, offer, deal, expenditure, trading history

Allocate alphas to smokers of between 0.001 than 0.5; chocolate lovers, alpha greater than 0.5 and less than 1.

Draw demand and supply curves (similar to the Edgeworth Box game but over 200 agents).

Starting with price = 0.1, ask all agents to calculate their optimal holding.

Deduct their actual holding to give excess demand or supply.

Sum excess demand/supply over all agents to give a total demand and a total supply. Calculate excess demand by subtracting supply from demand.

Repeat 100 times, increasing the price by 0.1 each time.

Draw demand and supply curves and calculate the market-clearing price.

Trading

Chocolate lovers locate smokers within a distance defined by the reach as potential trading partners.

Price set:

- The market-clearing price, that is, the price at which the demand and supply curves intersect

- Equilibrium: $\text{price} = \dfrac{\text{cigarette ration}}{\text{chocolate ration}} \left(\dfrac{\text{Captain's alpha} + \text{Sergeant's alpha}}{\left(1 - \text{Captain's alpha}\right) + \left(1 - \text{Sergeant's alpha}\right)} \right)$

- 'Random', the price between the MRSs of the two agents

Offers are rounded to ensure only whole numbers are traded and the ratio of quantities gives the effective price.

Partners compare their optimal with their actual holding and decide whether or not to trade. Deal is done by adjusting holding, based on the minimum offer.

Record metrics.

Repeat drawing demand and supply.

Accumulate data at the end of each round.
At the end of the first run, draw graphics (as shown in Figure 5.A.3) and sent data to a csv file.
At the end of the final run, report results to a csv file.

References

Axtell, R. (2005) The complexity of exchange. *The Economic Journal*, 115, pp.193–210.

Cowell, F. (2006) *Microeconomics: Principles and Analysis*. Oxford: Oxford University Press.

Diamond, J. (2012) *The World Until Yesterday*. London: Penguin Books.

Epstein, J. & Axtell, R. (1996) *Growing Artificial Societies: Social Science from the Bottom Up*. Cambridge, MA: MIT Press.

Graeber, D. (2011) *Debt: The First 5,000 Years*. New York: Melville House Publishing.

Radford, R. A. (1945) The economic organisation of a P.O.W. camp. *Economica*, New Series, 12(48), pp.189–201.

Red Cross (2015) *Food Parcels in the Second World War* [Online]. Available at: http://www.redcross.org.uk/About-us/Who-we-are/Museum-and-archives/Historical-factsheets/Food-parcels [Accessed 2 January 2015].

Smith, A. (1776/1861) *Wealth of Nations*. Edinburgh: Adam Charles & Black.

Sturt, G. (1912) *Change in the Village*. New York: George H. Doran Company.

Twain, M. (1876/1884) *The Adventures of Tom Sawyer* (Online) http://www.gutenberg.org/files/74/74-h/74-h.htm#c7 [Accessed 26 May 2015].

Varian, H. (2010) *Intermediate Microeconomics*. Princeton: Princeton University Press.

6

The market

6.1 Introduction

In the previous chapter, we examined an exchange economy in which the overall supply was determined outside the model and showed how people could trade to improve welfare. This focussed on the setting of prices, given the quantity supplied. Here, we shift attention to quantities supplied, and so we introduce firms that determine how much they supply and what prices they charge.

To maximise its profit, a firm will produce until the cost of producing an extra unit – its marginal cost, including the costs of capital – equals the amount it will earn from that extra unit, its marginal revenue. By definition, the marginal revenue will be the price of that unit. So we have the rule that a firm will increase the quantity it supplies until its marginal cost equals the price it can charge. Why should a firm produce something that costs more to produce than it can be sold for? At this point, economic profit is, by definition, zero. (Of course, this definition of profit is not the same as used in company financial accounts.) For details of this analysis, see a basic economics textbook on firms such as Varian (2010) or Begg *et al.* (2011).

As in Chapter 5, we start with a very simple model to tease out the processes involved. We then move on to look at two more realistic models, one based on shops and one based on the digital world.

6.2 Cournot–Nash model

Introduction

Antoine Augustin Cournot (1801–1877) was a French mathematician who developed a model of competition focussing on quantities supplied. The simplest version takes just two firms producing identical goods – a duopoly – operating with constant marginal costs in a market with a linear

Agent-Based Modelling in Economics, First Edition. Lynne Hamill and Nigel Gilbert.
© 2016 John Wiley & Sons, Ltd. Published 2016 by John Wiley & Sons, Ltd.

demand curve. Each firm decides how much to produce according to its belief about what the other firm will produce. This decision is encapsulated in its 'reaction function', an equation that relates its own output to its belief about the output of the other firm. Plotting this function produces a reaction curve.

John Forbes Nash was awarded the Nobel Memorial Prize in Economic Sciences in 1994 for his work on game theory, and his story was the basis of the 2001 film, *A Beautiful Mind*. A Nash equilibrium is reached when each firm correctly anticipates the output of its rival and neither firm wants to make further adjustment. (A Nash equilibrium may be Pareto optimal, but it is often not as both firms may be better off if they cooperated, assuming that was permissible!) This equilibrium occurs at the point at which the reaction curves intersect. The mathematics are set out in Box 6.1. The top panel of Box 6.2 gives examples of reaction functions and a Nash equilibrium, based on the mathematics shown in Box 6.1.

A simple dynamic system, suggested by Varian (2010, pp.510–511), is that each firm adjusts its output according to what it observes the other firm is producing and each firm assumes the other will produce the same in the next period as it did in the last. An example of how this works is shown in Box 6.3.

Because both firms are adjusting simultaneously, this is cumbersome to work through by hand, and so Varian (2010, p.511) chooses to 'generally ignore the question of how the equilibrium is reached and focus only on the issue of how the firms behave in the equilibrium'. However, using an agent-based model, analysis of the dynamics holds no difficulties as will now be shown.

The agent-based model

The model has just two agents, the Red firm and the Blue firm. The user selects the parameters of the inverse demand function and the costs of each firm. This determines each firm's initial position on their respective reaction curves. The firms then follow the same process as just described: each firm assumes that the other will produce the same as it did in the last trading round. If both firms expect the other to produce at the Nash equilibrium level (of 50 units), then output will remain at that level. But if they assume the other will produce 100 units (as in the example above), it takes 10 rounds before the total output settles at the equilibrium level. This is the same result as produced by hand and is illustrated in the top pair of figures in Box 6.4.

But this all assumes that each firm does actually know how much the other produced. It is, however, easy to introduce imperfect information into the agent-based model. It can be assumed that each firm can only guess what the other firm is producing. If the error is assumed to be 1%, then instead of knowing exactly what its rival is producing, the firm assumes it is somewhere between 99 and 101% of the actual output. In this case, total output will fluctuate around the equilibrium level as shown in the middle pair of figures in Box 6.4. If the error is 10%, then the fluctuation is more obvious, as shown in the bottom pair of figures.

Box 6.4 shows only examples based on single runs. But these results are typical: Table 6.1 shows the standard deviation of total output averaged over 100 runs. The top row shows that if the two models start at the Nash equilibrium, there will be no change in total output over 100 runs. That is how it should be. The rest of the table illustrates the importance of the initial conditions and error in the information. The further the initial conditions from the Nash equilibrium and the greater the error, the greater the volatility in output.

Thus, an agent-based model derived from Cournot's classic work can be used to explore the dynamics of duopoly. Furthermore, this very simple dynamic model shows how lack of information may cause oscillations in output.

Although the simple examples used here for illustration have not taken into account differences in costs, the model, *Cournot–Nash*, allows these to be investigated. It is also possible to build in more sophisticated reaction functions. The model is described in Appendix 6.A.

Box 6.1 Cournot model and Nash equilibrium.

There are two firms: Red and Blue.
Inverse demand function expresses price as a function of quantity:

$$P = a - bQ = a - b(Q_R + Q_B) \tag{6.1}$$

where
P = price
Q = total output, Q_R = output of the Red firm; Q_B = output of the Blue firm and a and b constants

From (6.1) the revenue of Red: $R_R = PQ_R = (a - b(Q_R + Q_B))Q_R$
Thus,

$$R_R = aQ_R - bQ_RQ_B - bQ_R^2 \tag{6.2}$$

So from (6.2) marginal revenue MR for Red $= \dfrac{dR_R}{dQ_R} = a - bQ_B - 2bQ_R \tag{6.3}$

Marginal cost MC for Red is assumed to be $= C_R \tag{6.4}$

For profit maximisation, MR = MC: thus, $a - bQ_B - 2bQ_R = C_R \tag{6.5}$

Rearranging gives the reaction function for Red: $Q_R = \dfrac{a - C_R}{2b} - \dfrac{Q_B}{2} \tag{6.6}$

Similarly for Blue: $Q_B = \dfrac{a - C_B}{2b} - \dfrac{Q_R}{2} \tag{6.7}$

The Nash equilibrium is given by solving Equations 6.6 and 6.7 simultaneously to give

$$Q_R = \frac{C_R}{2b} - \frac{Q_B}{2} = \frac{a - C_R}{2b} - \frac{1}{2}\left(\frac{a - C_B}{2b} - \frac{Q_R}{2}\right)$$

which rearranging gives

$$Q_R = \frac{2}{3b}\left(\frac{a}{2} + \frac{C_B}{2} - C_R\right) \tag{6.8}$$

Thus, if costs are equal, $C_R = C_B = C$: the Nash equilibrium is given by

$$Q_R = Q_B = \left(\frac{a - c}{3b}\right) \tag{6.9}$$

Based on Begg *et al.* (2011, pp.211–212) and Varian (2010, p.510).

Box 6.2   Cournot duopoly: example of reaction functions and Nash equilibrium.

The inverse demand function is

$$P = 1500 - 10Q$$

where P = price and Q = the total quantity produced: a = 1500 and b = 10.

Reaction functions

The Red firm's reaction function is given by Equation 6.6 in Box 6.1:

$$Q_R = \frac{a - C_R}{2b} - \frac{Q_B}{2}$$

Assuming $C_R = C_B = 0$, then with a = 1500 and b = 10 and

$$Q_R = \frac{1500 - 0}{2 \times 10} - \frac{Q_B}{2} = 75 - \frac{Q_B}{2}$$

And similarly, the Blue firm's reaction function is

$$Q_B = 75 - \frac{Q_R}{2}$$

These are shown on the right.

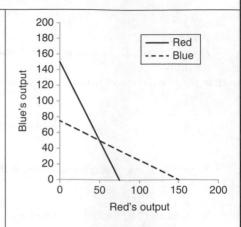

Nash equilibrium

The Nash equilibrium is at the intersection of the two curves, where both firms produce 50 units.

Assuming the marginal costs of both firms are zero, then from Equation 6.9 in Box 6.1, the equilibrium position is given by

$$Q_R = Q_B = \frac{a}{3b} = \frac{1500}{30} = 50$$

Thus, each firm produces 50 units, giving a total of 100. Using the inverse demand function, the price is 500:

$$P = 1500 - 10Q = 1500 - (10 \times 100) = 500$$

6.3   Market model

Introduction

In economics textbooks, discussion of markets starts with the model of perfect competition. The key characteristics of perfect competition are:

- Perfect information and foresight. There is no uncertainty. It is only under this condition that firms can be sure of maximising their profits.

- All firms produce identical products.

Box 6.3   Example of dynamics in the Cournot–Nash model.

The inverse demand function is

$$P = 1500 - 10Q$$

where P = price and Q = total output.

Costs are set to zero, and so from Equations 6.6 and 6.7 in Box 6.1, the reaction functions are

$$Q_R = 75 - \frac{Q_B^E}{2}$$

$$Q_B = 75 - \frac{Q_R^E}{2}$$

where Q_R and Q_B are the quantities produced and Q_R^E and Q_B^E are the expected quantities produced.

If initially each firm believes the other will produce 100 units, that is, $Q_R^E = Q_B^E = 100$, then each produces 25, as illustrated in the diagram below.

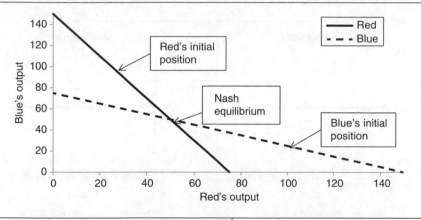

So the next round, they both assume the other will produce 25 units and each produces $(75 - 25/2) = 62.5$ units. And so on until after 10 rounds, the firms reach a Nash equilibrium with each producing 50 units, giving a total output of 100 as illustrated in the left-hand diagram (and Box 6.2).

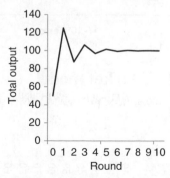

Box 6.4   Examples of the dynamics of Cournot duopolies.

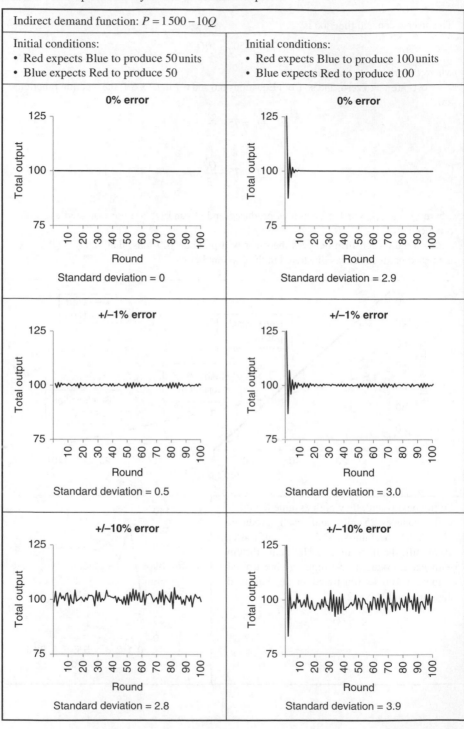

Table 6.1   Results: variation in total output.

100 runs
Based on indirect demand function: $P = 1500 - 10Q$
Starts at Nash equilibrium

Red expects Blue to produce	50
Blue expects Red to produce	50

Error	Standard deviation of total output over		
	First 10 rounds	Last 10 rounds	100 rounds
0	0	0	0
±1%	0.50	0.48	0.50
±10%	2.48	2.43	2.45

Starts away from Nash equilibrium

Red expects Blue to produce	100
Blue expects Red to produce	100

Error	Standard deviation of total output over		
	First 10 rounds	Last 10 rounds	100 rounds
0	9.43	0	2.89
±1%	9.58	0.51	2.97
±10%	9.92	2.50	3.85

- There are no barriers to entry. This means that the returns to scale must be constant or falling: there can be no increasing returns to scale. (So in the long run, average costs must be constant or rising.)

- There are a large number of firms, so no single firm can affect the price. A firm can sell all that it wishes to produce at the given price.

- The only decision a firm has to make is how much to produce.

It is difficult to find a market that meets all these conditions. The stock market is often cited as an example. Because at any one time the total supply of stocks potentially available to trade is given, it is arguably more like the exchange system discussed in the last chapter. The market for agricultural products, with many small farmers, is probably closer to perfect competition, although farmers do not enjoy perfect foresight! However, the perfect competition model can best be regarded as a kind of ideal against which to measure the performance of real markets.

The key problem with the perfect competition model is in the first assumption: perfect foresight. In that model, it is assumed that firms maximise profits and consumers maximise utility. In reality, firms can only try to maximise profits and consumers try to maximise their utility. (See, e.g. Nelson & Winter, 1982.) They may not succeed because things may not turn out as expected. Businesses have to operate under considerable uncertainty:

- Firms may not know what their competitors charge and certainly will not know what their competitors will charge in the future.

- Firms have imperfect information about their own current costs due to accounts being produced with a time lag.

- Firms will not know what their future costs will be unless they have fixed contracts with suppliers.

- Firms have little knowledge about their industry's demand curve or even their own demand curve, so they will not know how much they can sell.

Of course, experience, good management accounts and market research will provide information about what has happened in the past, but a firm can never know what will happen in the future. There is always uncertainty.

This section presents a simple, yet more realistic model, inspired by the work of Nelson and Winter (1982) and Cyert and March (1963/1992). In particular, we draw on Cyert and March's description of a department store (1963/1992, Chapter 6). There are two types of agents: shops and consumers. Shops decide how much to supply and all the shops together comprise the industry. Consumers buy from the shops. Together, consumers and shops comprise the market.

Consumers

The main focus of this chapter is on firms so we model consumers in a very simple, yet arguably realistic way. Back in 1888, Jevons observed that

> We cannot usually observe any precise and continuous variation in the wants and deeds of an individual, because the action of extraneous motives, or what would seem to be caprice, overwhelms minute tendencies. As I have already remarked, a single individual does not vary his consumption of sugar, butter, or eggs from week to week by infinitesimal amounts, according to each small change in the price. He probably continues his ordinary consumption until accident directs his attention to a rise in price, and he then, perhaps, discontinues the use of the articles altogether for a time. But the aggregate, or what is the same, the average consumption, of a large community will be found to vary continuously or nearly so. The most minute tendencies make themselves apparent in a wide average. Thus, our laws of Economics will be theoretically true in the case of individuals, and practically true in the case of large aggregates.
>
> (Jevons, 1888, Chapter IV, p.20)

In 1962, Becker returned to this point, arguing that individual rationality is not required to produce market rationality and that 'no preference system or utility function' is needed (Becker, 1962). At one extreme, households may respond to changes in opportunities, such as a price rise, quite impulsively or simply continue to spend as before but 'the fundamental theorem of traditional theory – that demand curves are negatively inclined largely results from the change in opportunities alone and is largely independent of the decision rule' (Becker, 1962). In effect, he argued that consumers simply react to budget constraints.

Following this analysis, and because we want to focus on suppliers, we have adopted a very simple model of consumers. Each consumer is allocated a 'willingness to pay' (WTP). Each round, the consumer seeks the cheapest shop that has the required item for sale, and if the price asked is less than or equal to the consumer's WTP, the consumer buys. Each consumer buys only once each round. An example of the resulting aggregate demand curve is shown in Figure 6.1. Consumers do not change from one trading round to the next.

Assumptions
1000 consumers
Each consumer is allocated a willingness to pay between 5 and 15, uniformly distributed
Each consumer buys once in the trading round

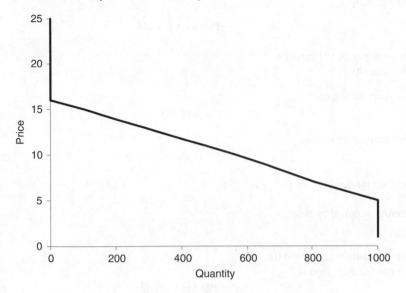

Figure 6.1   Shops: example of aggregate demand.

Shops

Like all firms, the shops have some costs that can only be changed in the longer term, for example, by moving to smaller premises, and costs that vary directly with each unit of output. A large shop with the strategy of selling large quantities cheaply in a low rent area will have a different cost structure from one that aims to sell small quantities in an expensive area. But the shop must cover its costs in order to survive. For simplicity, in this model:

- The capacity of each shop and its capacity unit costs are allocated initially, and together, they determine the shop's fixed costs.

- Variable costs are the cost per unit of buying in the goods to be sold.

The price each shop charges is determined by its variable costs plus a markup to cover its fixed costs. Drawing on the analysis provided by Nelson and Winter (1982, pp.144–146), it can be shown that for economic profit to be zero, the product of the markup and the utilisation rate must equal the cost per unit of capacity divided by the variable cost. The mathematics are given in Box 6.5.

The basic assumption is that the markup (noted by Cyert and March and still in common use) is 33%. (Close to the figure used in our village shop!) For example, if the variable cost is 7.5, the price will be 10; if the unit capacity costs are 2.5, the shop will break even if it stocks *and* sells 100 units:

$$\text{Costs} = 7.5 \times 100 + 250 = 1000$$

$$\text{Revenue} = 100 \times 10 = 1000$$

But if the shop stocks 100 units and does not sell them, it will not cover its costs and will make a loss.

Box 6.5 A shop's assumed costs and prices and profit.

Firms' costs

$$\text{Variable costs} = sQ$$

where
  s = variable cost
  Q = quantity

$$\text{Fixed costs} = \varnothing K$$

where
  ϕ = cost per unit of capacity
  K = capacity

Total costs for a shop:

$$C = sQ + \varnothing K \qquad (6.10)$$

Price charged by shop

$$P = (1 + m)s \qquad (6.11)$$

where m = markup

Quantity supplied by shop

$$Q = uK \qquad (6.12)$$

where u = utilisation rate and $0 \leq u \leq 1$
Revenue for each shop is

$$R = PQ = (1 + m)sQ \qquad (6.13)$$

Marginal revenue and marginal costs

From (6.10) and (6.12), marginal costs $\dfrac{dC}{dP} = sQ + \varnothing u$

This could be regarded as a long-term marginal cost.

From (6.13), marginal revenue $\dfrac{dR}{dQ} = (1 + m)s$

For marginal revenue to equal marginal cost: $sQ + \varnothing u = (1 + m)s$
which rearranging gives $\varnothing = msu$.

Profit
The firm's profit

$$\pi = \text{revenue} - \text{costs} = PQ - C$$

Substituting (6.10), (6.12) and (6.13) and rearranging:

$$\pi = (1 + m)sQ - (sQ + \varnothing K) = (msu - \varnothing)K$$

So if $K \neq 0$, $\pi = 0$ when $msu = \varnothing$
That is, profit is zero when the cost per unit of capacity equals the product of the markup, the variable cost and the utilisation rate. This is the point at which marginal revenue = marginal cost. Put the other way round, for profit to be zero:

$$mu = \frac{\varnothing}{s}$$

Thus, if utilisation is 100%, then the markup is the ratio of cost per unit of capacity to the variable cost. If utilisation is less than 100%, then the markup must be greater.

Each shop will supply nothing below its price but can only supply up to the limit set by its capacity. This means that each shop's supply curve is vertical up to its price, horizontal at its price and then vertical once it has sold all its stock. This contrasts with the usual textbook assumption that the higher the price, the more a firm will supply. However, when all the shops' supply curves are added together, the industry supply curve will look like those usually seen in the textbooks. A simple example is shown in Box 6.6; of course, with more shops, the industry supply curve would be much smoother!

For simplicity, the shops do not hold stocks from period to period. The time steps are quarters and the model incorporates both short-term and long-term dynamics.

In the long term – defined as every four quarters or year – shops change their capacity and the extent to which that capacity is used – the utilisation rate – according to their profit over the last year:

- If it has made a cumulative loss over the last four quarters, the shop closes.

- If it has made a cumulative positive profit (i.e. non-zero) over the last four quarters:

  - If it is operating at less than full capacity (i.e. its utilisation rate is <100%), it increases its utilisation rate.

  - If it is operating at full capacity, it increases its capacity.

At the end of every other quarter (i.e. the other three out of four), each shop may alter its utilisation, price and variable cost on the basis of its sales:

- If it has sold all its stock and its utilisation rate is less than 100%, it increases its utilisation rate.

- If it has failed to sell all its stock, it reduces its stocks for the next period, and its utilisation rate is recalculated accordingly. It also adjusts its price in line with its competitors, adjusting its markup and its variable costs if necessary. (If there are no competitors, it reduces its price anyway.)

Thus, shops can go out of business because they make a loss. However, new shops open. The UK's Office for National Statistics (ONS, 2012) reported that in 2011 the birth rate of retail companies was 10%, the same as the death rate. The model assumes that the total number of shops remains the same. Thus, if any shops die, new shops are created, using the same capacity formulation as initially. Furthermore, the ONS reported that only about half of businesses 'born' in 2006 survived for 5 years.

We created three scenarios:

- 'Perfect': all the shops have the same costs, with prices set to enable them to break even; and consumers and shops check the prices of all shops. This is therefore similar to the textbook perfect competition.

- 'Real-full search': the costs and the markups vary between shops, and thus so do prices; consequently, shops supply different quantities.

- 'Real-limited search': this is the same as the second scenario except that on average consumers and shops check the prices of only half the shops.

The initial values chosen, shown in Box 6.7, are based on the mathematics of Box 6.5. In the case of the 'perfect' scenario, the values are set at the level to give an economic profit of zero; and for the 'real' scenarios, the mean shop would have zero economic profit (i.e. if the values were set

Box 6.6   Example: shops' and industry supply curves.

Data for individual shops
Based on the analysis in Box 6.3.[a]

		Shop 1 Cheap Bulk	Shop 2	Shop 3 Small Expensive
Capacity	K	150	100	80
Unit capacity cost	ϕ	2.0	2.5	3.0
Variable	s	6	7.5	8
Markup	m	0.333	0.333	0.395
Price	P	8	10	11
Utilisation rate	u	1	1	0.95
Supply	Q	150	100	76
Profit	π	0	0	0

[a]Assuming the quantity supplied is all sold.

Shops' supply curves
Each shop only provides a certain quantity (Q) at or above its price (P).

Industry supply curve
Adding together the supply curves of the three shops gives a conventional industry supply curve in which the quantity supplied rises with price.

At a price of 8, only Shop 1 is supplying; at a price of 10, Shops 1 and 2 are both supplying; and at 12, all three are supplying

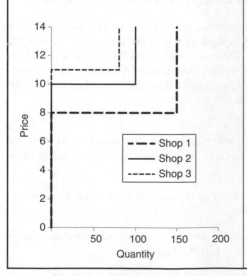

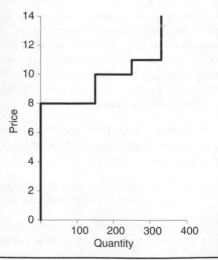

Box 6.7   Summary of shop model scenarios.

Consumers 1000 consumers WTP set randomly between 5 and 15.

Shops
Capacity, utilisation and costs
 	
    Mean capacity: demand at price = 10 divided by number of shops (set by the modeller)
 	
    Mean utilisation rate: 100%
 	
    Mean capacity unit cost: 2.5
 	
    Mean variable cost: 7.5
 	
    For the two 'real' scenarios, all normally distributed with sd set to 10% of the mean
 	
Adjustments
 	
    Utilisation rate increase: 10%
 	
    Capacity increase: 10%

at the means shown in Box 6.7). To make other assumptions would mean that the dynamic process would take a long time to settle and indeed may never settle. This is a problem with dynamic models, be they agent-based or any other type.

Results

We compared the three scenarios using 10 shops. The top row of Figure 6.2 shows that the quantity sold stays constant under the 'perfect' scenario but is lower when firms are heterogeneous ('real-full search'). If search is limited to about half the shops, then sales are lower still. So the model is consistent with the view that the further away the market is from perfect competition, the lower is the output.

The bottom row of Figure 6.2 shows that even under the 'perfect' scenario, there is some turnover among the shops: only six out of the 10 survive 5 years, which is in line with the ONS report. With heterogeneous shops, the survival rate is slightly lower: half survive the 5 years. But if search is restricted, the survival rate is still lower with three remaining after 5 years.

The model reproduces the classic result that sales are higher when there is more competition: Figure 6.3 shows that in the longer run, the more shops, the higher are sales.

6.4   Digital world model

Introduction

Neoclassical economics assume constant or falling returns to scale. This was natural in a world of manufacturing and agriculture. As production expands, people use less good resources, such as poorer quality land. However, '...the parts of the economy that are knowledge-based...are largely subject to increasing returns' (Arthur, 1990). This means that if all inputs are, say,

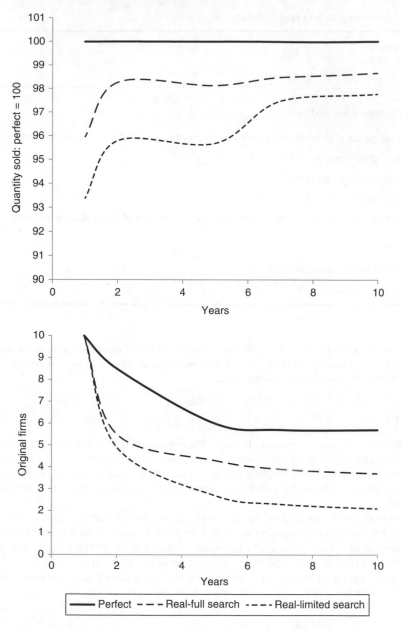

Figure 6.2   Shops model results: quantities sold and number of shops surviving, by time: industry size 10 (30 runs).

doubled, output more than doubles. And if the market for inputs meets certain conditions, long-run average costs will fall.

For a firm producing digital information – such as software, e-books or music – the capital costs are sunk: they were used to produce the digital content and cannot be redeployed to another activity as can, for example, a field or a factory. For a firm distributing digital information over the

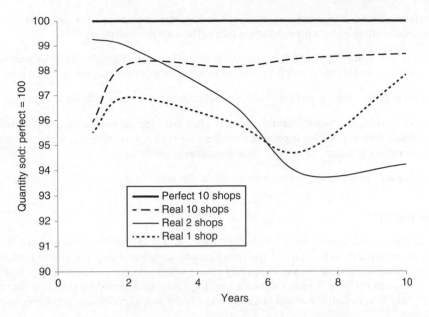

Figure 6.3   Shops model results: varying the industry size.

Internet, the constraints on supply are very different compared to, for example, a bookshop or record store on the high street or in the local mall. There are no stocks to be bought in to be resold. There may be premises to rent for the few staff needed, but these can be in low cost areas rather than in prime retail sites. Fixed costs, such as Internet access, servers and website maintenance, can be expanded easily if demand rises so capacity is not limited by, for example, space to stack books. (For more discussion, see, e.g. Shapiro & Varian (1999, pp.20–24).) This is clearly a very different situation from the shops examined in Section 6.3, which faced capacity limits and had a very different cost structure.

Prices in the digital market will reflect what consumers are willing to pay (WTP). As Shapiro and Varian (1999, pp.22–23) said, 'markets for information will not, and *cannot*, look like textbook-perfect competitive markets in which there are many suppliers offering similar products, each lacking the ability to influence prices'. The traditional model of supply therefore breaks down. In this section, we present a model of a market for a digital product.

Sellers

We take a simple extreme and assume that there are online sellers with no capacity constraints and no fixed costs. Indeed, for simplicity, it is assumed there are no costs at all. Although it would be more realistic to assume some low costs, this would add considerably to the length and complexity of the coding.

Instead of basing prices on costs, sellers are initially allocated a price based on a normal distribution with a chosen mean and standard deviation. They trade at these prices for the first round.

Sellers that fail to trade leave the industry. Those sellers that have traded look at the prices charged by others and adjust their own prices. Each seller looks at the price charged by another seller, selected at random if there are more than two sellers. If the competitor's price is lower, the seller matches that price and may undercut it. If the competitor's price is the same or higher, the seller reduces his price by a price reduction factor. There are three elements to this:

- Price-matching: a pair of sellers compare prices and the one with the higher price adopts the lower price. This alone will not allow prices to fall by more than the lowest initial price.

- Price-cutting: having price-matched, the higher priced seller undercuts the competitor.

- 'Price reduction factor': whether there is price-matching or price-cutting or not, sellers reduce their prices. This is because the sellers have to keep reducing prices in order to win customers in successive rounds, since consumers buy only once.

Examples – based on single runs – are shown in Box 6.8.

Consumers

For consumers, we again simply assume that each has a WTP, but this time it is distributed normally around a chosen mean with a chosen standard deviation. This gives a downward-sloping aggregate demand curve, and depending on the values chosen, some consumers will not buy even when the price is zero. Each consumer buys only once during the run (as in the technology adoption models discussed in Chapter 4). (In the shops model, the consumers bought each round.)

In the shops model – Section 6.3 – consumers bought from the cheapest seller. If that assumption were made in this model, and all the products were identical, the result would be trivial in that all the consumers would simply buy from the cheapest seller as the sellers have no capacity constraints. Instead, it is assumed that consumers buy from a seller selected at random. If the seller's asking price is less than or equal to the consumer's WTP, the consumer buys.

Results

We have looked at the effect of the number of sellers, the initial starting price and the price reduction strategies on the total revenue of all the sellers and the proportion of consumers who buy. As in this simple model there are no costs, maximising revenue is the same as maximising profit; and as consumers buy only once, the proportion who buy is the adoption rate. Despite its simplicity, there are many scenarios that could be examined with the model. In the examples chosen, it is assumed that the mean consumer's WTP is 100 with a standard deviation of 100, which implies that at most 84% of the consumers will buy. Sellers supply as much as is demanded at their price, so that each seller's supply curve is horizontal. This means it does not make sense to sum the individual supply curves as in the shops example in Box 6.6 because in this case supply depends on demand and there is no constraint on the quantity supplied by each seller. So instead, the supply curves for the lowest and highest priced sellers are shown. This is illustrated in Figure 6.4.

The top panel of Box 6.9 shows that, given the assumptions made, undercutting alone does not maximise either the sellers' revenue or the consumers' adoption. Furthermore, there is considerable uncertainty: the coefficient of variation is very high at around one third. In contrast, the price reduction factor produces much higher revenue and adoption with much greater certainty: the coefficient of variation is about 2%. It also shows that having more firms in the market does not result in higher revenue or adoption (and the model suggests that in fact the reverse might be the case). This apparently perverse result seems to arise because there are no capacity constraints: one seller can supply as much as 10!

Box 6.8 Price adjustment examples.

Undercutting only

- Undercutting = 10%
- Price reduction factor = 0%

Round	Seller 1	Seller 2
1	324	320
2	288	320
3	288	259
4	233	259

Round 2: Seller 2 lower: Seller 1 matches and undercuts by 10%: $320 \times 0.9 = 288$
Round 3: Seller 1 lower: Seller 2 matches and undercuts by 10%: $288 \times 0.9 = 259$
Round 4: Seller 2 lower: Seller 1 matches and undercuts by 10%: $259 \times 0.9 = 233$

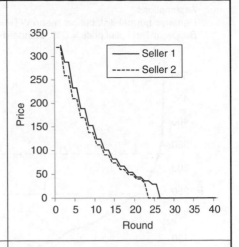

Price reduction factor only

- Undercutting = 0%
- Price reduction factor = 10%

Round	Seller 1	Seller 2
1	312	281
2	281	253
3	253	228
4	228	205

Round 2: Seller 2 lower: Seller 1 matches price. Seller 2 reduces by 10%: $281 \times 0.9 = 253$
Round 3: Seller 2 lower: Seller 1 matches price. Seller 2 reduces by 10%: $253 \times 0.9 = 228$
Round 4: Seller 2 lower: Seller 1 matches price. Seller 2 reduces by 10%: $228 \times 0.9 = 205$

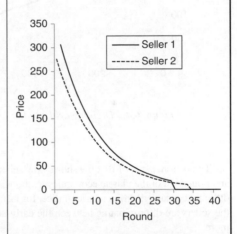

Undercutting and price reduction factors

- Undercutting = 10%
- Price reduction factor = 10%

Because price reduction and undercut factors are the same, prices converge.

Round	Seller 1	Seller 2
1	298	334
2	268	268
3	241	241
4	217	217

Round 2: Seller 2 higher: matches Seller 1 and reduces by 10%: $298 \times 0.9 = 268$. But Seller 2 also reduces by 10%: $298 \times 0.9 = 268$.
Round 3: Both reduce by 10%:
$268 \times 0.9 = 241$.

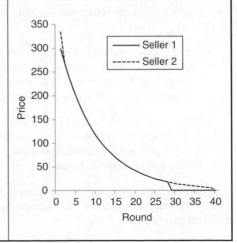

Assumptions
Demand: normal distribution: mean WTP = 100, standard deviation = 100
Supply: mean initial price = 300, standard deviation = 10% of mean. No. of sellers = 10

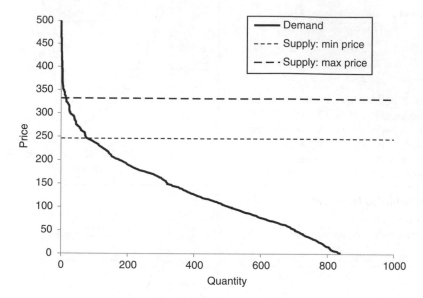

Figure 6.4   Digital world results: example of supply and demand curves.

The bottom panel of Box 6.9 shows how sellers are rewarded for starting by pricing high. This is an application of the classic economics textbook result for discriminating monopolists, who charge different consumers different prices. (See, for instance, Begg *et al.* (2011, pp.190–191).) In this case, the sellers are discriminating between the early and late adopters, the early adopters being charged more.

In the shops model, we looked at the birth and death rate of the shops. In this model, there is no replacement of sellers that fail, but we can look at how many sellers there are at a given round and how long the sellers survive. With undercutting of 10% and a price reduction factor of 10%:

- Starting with 10 sellers and an initial mean price of 100, after 10 rounds of trading, there is an 84% probability that there are between four and six sellers left in the market. If the initial mean price is 300, there is an 82% probability that there will be between six and nine. This is illustrated in the top pair of graphs in Figure 6.5.

- Again starting with 10 sellers and an initial mean price of 100, there is a 56% probability that trading will run for between 27 and 29 rounds. With an initial mean price of 300, there is a 48% probability that trading will last between 38 and 40 rounds. This is illustrated in the bottom pair of graphs in Figure 6.5.

Thus, the higher the initial price, the larger the number of sellers that survive for longer. The results illustrate why producers of digital products need to innovate by producing 'upgrades' to maintain their profits and sales!

Box 6.9 Digital world model results: revenue and adoption rate.

100 runs
Common assumptions
1000 consumers with mean WTP = 100
Standard deviation of initial price = 10% of mean
50 rounds of trading

Impact of pricing strategies
Additional assumptions: initial mean price = 300

| | 10% undercut | | 10% price reduction | | Mean *Standard deviation* Both | |
| | No price reduction | | No undercut | | 10% undercut 10% price reduction | |
Sellers	**Revenue**	**Adoption %**	**Revenue**	**Adoption %**	**Revenue**	**Adoption %**
1	Not applicable		102 403	82.4	Not applicable	
			2 716	*1.6*		
2	92 467	72.9	100 453	82.6	101 904	82.3
	24 502	*20.7*	*3 015*	*1.5*	*2 744*	*1.5*
5	83 865	62.0	99 437	82.4	101 273	82.4
	24 526	*25.8*	*2 276*	*1.5*	*2 808*	*1.4*
10	87 142	63.9	99 661	82.7	100 886	82.3
	17 471	*21.1*	*2 625*	*1.1*	*2 743*	*1.5*

Roman numbers indicate mean values and italicised numbers indicate standard deviation.

Impact of the initial price

| | | Initial mean price | |
Sellers		**100**	**300**
1	**0% undercut, 10% price reduction**		
	Revenue	67 875	102 403
	Adoption %	82.6	82.4
2	**10% undercut, 10% price reduction**		
	Revenue	67 269	101 904
	Adoption %	82.5	82.3
5	**10% undercut, 10% price reduction**		
	Revenue	66 955	101 273
	Adoption %	82.5	82.4
10	**10% undercut, 10% price reduction**		
	Revenue	66 556	100 886
	Adoption %	82.5	82.3

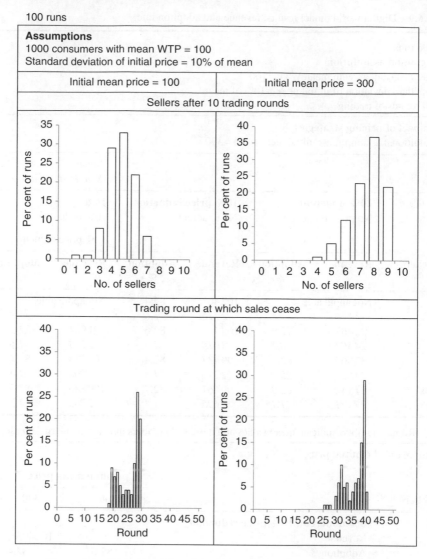

Figure 6.5   Digital world model results: life span of sellers (100 runs).

6.5   Discussion

Markets are interactively dynamic systems. Comparative statics models, comparing conditions at one point in time with those at another, can only provide a very limited view of the operation of markets. In contrast, agent-based modelling can easily handle both dynamics and interaction and can therefore provide much richer models. This chapter has presented some simple models of markets as examples.

The first model replicated the classical Cournot duopoly model: two firms interacted. Not only was the model able to track the dynamics of the relationship between two firms, but it was also able to show how the lack of exact information created oscillations in output. While the dynamics were based on a very simple idea, the model could easily be extended to accommodate more sophisticated behaviour.

The second model, based on shops, increased the number of suppliers, thus enabling more interaction between them, and introduced consumers, with whom they all interacted. The shops adjusted both their capacity and prices. Unprofitable shops went out of business and were replaced by new ones, keeping the total number unchanged. The model could reproduce the observed birth and death rate of British retailers (as the actual birth and death rates are similar). The model could also replicate perfect competition, and this was used as a baseline against which to measure the performance of alternative market structures. The results of this simple model were consistent with the view that the further away the market is from perfect competition, the lower is the output. However, it also illustrated one of the problems with agent-based modelling or, indeed, any dynamic model: how to set the initial values. If initial values are set too far away from 'reality', then the model will take a long time to reach the area of interest and may never reach it.

Finally, the digital world model was designed to highlight the differences between markets for physical products and the markets for digital information. The former are characterised by constant or falling returns to scale, while the latter are characterised by low costs and even increasing returns to scale. It was assumed, for simplicity and contrast, that there were no capacity constraints and that sellers adjusted their prices to gain market share. The analysis suggested that price undercutting can produce very variable outcomes in terms of total industry revenue and consumers' adoption. It also showed why sellers should start by pricing high and the impact of the initial price on the life of the market for the product.

It is possible to make much more complicated agent-based models of markets. A classic example is Kirman and Vriend's (2001) model of the Marseille fish market. But the models presented here have been kept deliberately simple in order to highlight the power of this modelling approach in providing an understanding of interactive dynamics. The rest of this book looks at specific markets, starting in the next chapter with the labour market.

Appendix 6.A   How to do it

The Cournot–Nash model

Purpose: To replicate Cournot's model of duopoly (as set out in Box 6.1).
Entities: There are just two agents, representing firms.
Stochastic processes: None if the firms know exactly how much the other firm produced. But if they do not know exactly, their outputs are the result of a stochastic process.
Initialisation:

- Choose parameters of inverse demand function.

- Choose the cost variables.

- Choose whether the firms have accurate information or not, and if not, how inaccurate it is.

- Choose the initial values of each firm's belief about the other's output: this can either be generated randomly or by the modeller's choice.

- Choose the number of rounds of trading and the number of runs.

Output: The model records total output at each round, and for each run, its standard deviation is calculated for the first 10 rounds, the last 10 rounds and over all rounds. After all the runs are completed, the average of these standard deviations is recorded. A set of plots is created for the first run and the results for all the runs are recoded in a csv file.

Box 6.A.1   Pseudocode for the Cournot–Nash model.

Create a world 250×250 with the origin at the bottom left corner.
Create two agents, representing two firms, Red and Blue.

Draw reaction curves:

For each firm, take expected quantities from 0 to 250 and calculate the resulting output.

Taking the results as coordinates, colour the patches red or blue according to the firm.

Calculate the Nash equilibrium quantities (based on Box 6.1).
Place the firms at their initial position on their reaction curves.
Calculate the 'distance' between the firms as measured by:

1. The difference between actual outputs and beliefs

2. The 'distance' the firms are from the Nash equilibrium

Calculate the quantity supplied for each firm in each round.
Move the agents along their reaction curves.

Collect data:

Collect price and quantity data at the end of each round.

At the end of each run, calculate the standard deviation of output for the first 10 rounds, the last 10 rounds and over all rounds.

At the end of all the runs, calculate the averages of these standard deviations.

For the first run, plot outputs and prices.

At the end of all runs, print data to a csv file.

The pseudocode is in Box 6.A.1 and a screenshot in Figure 6.A.1. For the full code, see the website: *Cournot–Nash Model*.

Things to try using the Cournot–Nash model

- There are two measures of the initial 'distance' between the two firms. The first measures the difference between expectations and total output. The second measures the difference between total output and equilibrium output: What happens when the firms start a long way apart?

- What happens when there is a large difference in the firms' costs?

Advanced – requiring amending the program:

- Change the reaction functions.

- Adapt to make the Stackelberg model in which one firm leads and the other follows. (See, e.g. Varian (2010, pp.499–504) or Begg *et al.* (2011, pp.214–215).)

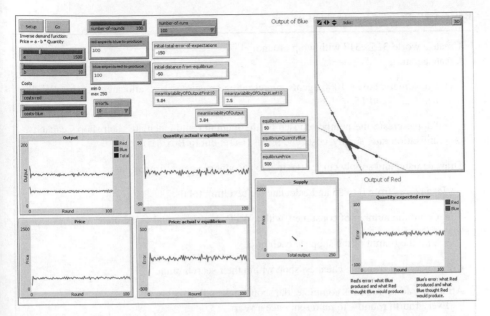

Figure 6.A.1   Screenshot for the Cournot–Nash model.

Shops model

Purpose: The aim of the model is to reproduce a market based on shops as set out in Box 6.3.
Entities: There are two types of agents: consumers and shops.
Stochastic processes:

- Consumers are located at random across the world and are allocated a 'WTP'.

- Shops are also allocated at random across the world. For all the scenarios except 'perfect', they are allocated costs and markups randomly, using a normal distribution with a given mean and a standard deviation equal to 10% of the mean.

Initialisation: Choose the scenario, the search range and the number of rounds of trading.
Output: Price, quantity, industry size and cumulative number of new shops are recorded at rounds 4, 8, 20, 28 and 40 (i.e. at the end of year 1, 2, 5, 7 and 10). For the first run, the results for all rounds are plotted. All the results, including the plots, are sent to a csv file.

The pseudocode is in Box 6.A.2 and a screenshot in Figure 6.A.2. For the full code, see the website: *Chapter 6 – Shops*.

Things to try using the shops model

Experiment with the options offered by the sliders. For example:

- What happens when the capacity costs are very low compared to the variable costs? (Change the `meanCapapcityCosts` and the `meanVariableCosts`.)

- What happens when capacity can be expanded quickly? (Change the `capacityincrease%`.)

- What happens when the initial values are set far from the zero profit values? (Use the formulae in Box 6.5 to calculate the zero profit values.)

Box 6.A.2   Pseudocode for shops model.

Create a world 315×317 with wrap-around.
Create agents:

- Consumers: create 1000 agents, representing consumers and allocate to each a 'WTP' between 5 and 15.

- Shops: create the number chosen by the modeller and calculate each shop's capacity, utilisation rate, supply, costs and prices (as set out in Box 6.5).

Draw demand and supply curves (taking no account of search limitations).

Take prices from 0 to 25 and calculate the resulting totals:

- Count the number of consumers with a WTP above or equal to the price.

- Sum the output of the shops at each price.

Consumers buy from the cheapest shop within their search range.

After the trading round is complete, the shops make adjustments.
Every fourth round – to represent once a year:

- Existing shops making a cumulative loss over the last four rounds die

- Existing shops making a profit over the last four rounds

  ○ and whose utilisation rate is less than 100%, increase their utilisation rate by 10%

  ○ and whose utilisation rate is 100%, increase their capacity by 10%

Replace any shops that have died with new shops.

In the other three rounds:

- Shops selling all their stock and operating below capacity increase their utilisation rate.

- Shops not selling all their stock reduce their supply, prices (based on comparison with competitors) and costs.

Collect data:

Collect price and quantity data plus industry size and cumulative number of new shops at the end of each round.

At the end of each run, collect data for rounds 4, 8, 20, 28 and 40. For the first run, plot data for all rounds.

At the end of all the runs, calculate the averages and standard deviations and print data to a csv file.

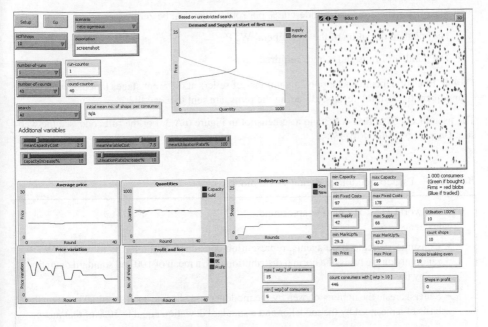

Figure 6.A.2   Screenshot of the shops model.

Advanced – requiring programming:

- Explore further the parameter space by changing the set variables such as the mean and standard deviations of capacity, capacity and variable costs and utilisation rate.
  (Change the adjustment process, e.g. change the `utilisationRateIncrease%` or the `capacityIncrease%`.)

- Use this program as the basis for other models of markets.

Digital world model

Purpose: The aim of the model is to highlight the difference between traditional markets and those for digital information. In particular, there are no capacity constraints and, for simplicity, no costs.
Entities: There are two types of agents: consumers and sellers.
Stochastic processes:

- Consumers are located at random across the world and are allocated a 'WTP' randomly from a mean of 100 and given standard deviation.

- Sellers are also distributed at random across the world and are allocated initial prices randomly, using a normal distribution with a given mean and the standard deviation set to 10% of the mean.

Initialisation:

- The number of sellers (maximum 10).

- The mean of the initial mean price.

- The price reduction % and undercut % per round: they can be zero.

- The standard deviation of the consumers' WTP.

- The number of runs and rounds required.

Output: Plots of demand and supply, the number of sellers at different stages together with prices and quantities. All the results, including the plots, are sent to a csv file.

The pseudocode is in Box 6.A.3 and a screenshot in Figure 6.A.3. For the full code, see the website: *Chapter 6 – Digital World*.

Box 6.A.3   Pseudocode for the digital world model.

Create a world 315×317 with wrap-around.
Create agents:

- Consumers: create 1000 agents, representing consumers and allocate to each a 'WTP' randomly on the basis of a normal distribution with a mean of 100 and standard deviation set by the modeller.

- Sellers: create the number chosen by the modeller and allocate each an initial price on the basis of a mean set by the modeller and a standard deviation equal to 10% of that mean.

Draw demand and supply curves at start:

Take prices from 0 to 25 and calculate the resulting totals

- Count the number of consumers with a WTP above or equal to the price.

- As the supply curves are horizontal, show two: one for the seller with the lowest price and one for the seller with the highest price.

Consumers select a seller at random and buy if its price is equal or lower than its WTP.

After the trading round is complete, the sellers adjust their prices by:

- Price-matching: a pair of sellers compare prices and the one with the higher price adopts the lower price.

- Price-cutting: having price-matched, the higher priced seller undercuts the competitor.

- 'Price reduction factor': whether there is price-matching or price-cutting or not, sellers reduce their prices. (See Box 6.8.)

Collect data:

The initial demand and supply curves are drawn at the start, and for the first run, the prices at reach round are displayed.
Total industry revenue is cumulated over the run.
At the end of rounds 1, 10, 25 and 50, data on the number of sellers, average prices and adoption rate are collected.

The round at which trading ceases is also recorded for each run.

At the end of all the runs, the average price and adoption rate at rounds 1, 10, 25 and 50 are recorded. Graphs are plotted and all data is sent to a csv file.

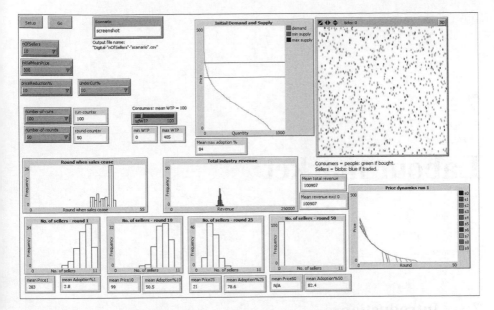

Figure 6.A.3   Screenshot of the digital world model.

Things to try using the digital world model

Experiment with the options offered by the sliders. For example:

- What happens with a very different demand curve? (Change the standard deviation of the consumers' WTP.)

- What happens when the initial mean price is set very high?

Advanced – requiring amending the program: change the price adjustment rules.

References

Arthur, B. (1990) Positive feedback in the economy. *Scientific American*, February, pp.80–85.

Becker, G. (1962) Irrational behavior and economic theory. *Journal of Political Economy*, 70(1) pp.1–13.

Begg, D., Vernasca, G., Fischer, S. & Dornbusch, R. (2011) *Economics*. Tenth Edition. London: McGraw-Hill Higher Education.

Cyert, R. & March, J. (1963/1992) *A Behavioral Theory of the Firm*. Cambridge, MA: Blackwell.

Jevons, W.S. (1888) *The Theory of Political Economy*. Third Edition. London: Macmillan & Co [Online]. Available at: http://www.econlib.org/library/YPDBooks/Jevons/jvnPECover.html [Accessed 31 January 2015].

Kirman, A. & Vriend, N. (2001) Evolving market structure: An ACE model of price dispersion and loyalty. *Journal of Economic Dynamics & Control*, 25, pp.459–502.

Nelson, R. & Winter, S. (1982) *An Evolutionary Theory of Economic Change*. Cambridge, MA: Harvard University Press.

Office for National Statistics ONS (2012) *Business Demography, 2011* [Online]. Available at: www.ons.gov. uk [Accessed 30 January 2013].

Shapiro, C. & Varian, H. (1999) *Information Rules*. Boston, MA: Harvard University Press.

Varian, H. (2010) *Intermediate Microeconomics*. Princeton, NJ: Princeton University Press.

7

Labour market

7.1 Introduction

Since the end of the Second World War, unemployment has been a prime concern of the UK Government. Its White Paper, *Employment Policy*, published in 1944 said: 'The Government accept as one of their primary aims and responsibilities, the maintenance of a high and stable level of employment after the war' (H.M. Government, 1944).

Nearly 70 years later, the Bank of England (2013) announced that it intended 'not to raise Bank Rate from its current level of 0.5% at least until the Labour Force Survey headline measure of the unemployment rate has fallen to a threshold of 7%'.

Understanding of the workings of the labour market is therefore a priority for policymakers and has been a major strand of academic work. In this chapter, we build a simple labour market model loosely based on our home town of Guildford. But first, by way of introduction, we present key features of the UK labour market.

The labour force

The United Kingdom follows conventions used throughout the European Union and by OECD to define people's labour force status. People are categorised as in employment, unemployed or economically inactive:

- Employed people do at least 1 hour a week of paid work.

- Unemployed people are not in employment and have been looking for work in the last 4 weeks and are able to start work within the next 2 weeks. It does not matter whether they are seeking full-time or part-time work or whether they are claiming social security benefits.

Agent-Based Modelling in Economics, First Edition. Lynne Hamill and Nigel Gilbert.
© 2016 John Wiley & Sons, Ltd. Published 2016 by John Wiley & Sons, Ltd.

- Economically inactive people are neither in employment nor counted as unemployed. This includes those who are students, caring for dependents, retired or unable to work due to sickness or disability.

These definitions are mutually exclusive: a given person can only have one status at a time. The numbers in each category are estimated on a quarterly basis using a survey of households, *The Labour Force Survey* (LFS). For more details, see Box 7.1.

Three key ratios – by convention incorrectly called 'rates' – are derived from these data:

- The employment rate: the percentage of all people who are in employment

- The participation rate: the percentage of all people who are economically active, that is, either in employment or unemployed

- The unemployment rate: the percentage of the economically active who are unemployed.

Box 7.2 presents recent UK labour force data on this basis.

It is, however, the unemployment rate that is the key policy variable. The unemployment rate may rise because more people become unemployed or because fewer people leave unemployment for jobs or leave the labour force. Much work has been done to identify which of these flows is the most important: see Gomes (2009) and Smith (2011) for example. Elsby *et al.* (2011) argued that

> …the leading contribution to UK unemployment cyclicality since 1975 has, in fact, been the substantial rise in rates of job loss in times of recession, accounting for approximately two-thirds of the fluctuations in the unemployment rate over each cycle. Declines in unemployed workers' job-finding prospects, while undeniably important, explain just over one-quarter of the cyclical change in unemployment in each of the recessions we examine. The remaining 10 per cent is attributed to flows involving non-participation.

Using US data, Rogerson and Shimer (2010) found that 'recessions are typically characterized by a sharp, short-lived increase in the inflow rate of workers from employment into unemployment and a large, prolonged decline in the outflow rate of workers from unemployment into employment'. In short, a lot of people get fired and few get hired.

Box 7.1 The Labour Force Survey (LFS).

The LFS is a major survey of households designed to produce estimates of employment, unemployment, economic inactivity and other labour market data on a quarterly basis. A nationally representative sample of approximately 100 000 people aged 16 and over is interviewed in each 3-month period. Because it is based on quarters, rather than months, for reason of costs, some short-term changes in labour market status will not be recorded. For example, if someone moves from employment to unemployment and then back into employment within the quarter, their unemployment spell will be missed.

The ONS publishes figures for rolling 3-month average time periods. For example, the ONS estimated that there were 2.625 million unemployed in January to March 2012. There had been 2.671 million unemployed in the previous quarter, October to December 2011; and so the ONS reported that unemployment had fallen 45 000 on the previous quarter.

Sources: Clegg (2012a & 2012b), ONS (2013c).

Box 7.2   Employment, participation and unemployment rates: 2013, Q2, United Kingdom.

			Millions
Economically active			
	In employment	29.98	
	Unemployed	2.51	
Total economically active			32.49
Economically inactive			
	Students	2.31	
	Looking after family/home	2.24	
	Long-term sick	2.05	
	Retired	1.37	
	Others	1.03	
Total economically inactive			8.99
Total population aged 16–64			41.48

Employment rate

$$\frac{\text{In employment}}{\text{Total population}} \times 100 = \frac{29.98}{41.48} \times 100 = 72.3\%$$

Participation rate

$$\frac{\text{Economically active}}{\text{Total population}} \times 100 = \frac{32.49}{41.48} \times 100 = 78.3\%$$

Unemployment rate

$$\frac{\text{Unemployed}}{\text{Economically active}} \times 100 = \frac{2.51}{32.49} \times 100 = 7.7\%$$

Note that these rates are based on the population aged 16–64. Rates based on all people aged 16 and over will differ.

Source: from ONS (2013a).

Figure 7.1 confirms these views. The top part of Figure 7.1 shows unemployment in the United Kingdom since 2001. Until 2008, around 1½ million people were unemployed at any one time, and as shown in the lower part of the figure, the gross inflows to and outflows from unemployment were some 700 to 800 thousand each quarter. Then in the third quarter of 2008, the gross inflow into unemployment rose sharply, and this was not matched by an increase in outflow until a year later. The level of unemployment has since been around 2½ million with the gross inflow and outflow between 900 thousand and 1 million each quarter. Thus, at the macro level, the total number unemployed may appear to change little, because the inflows are similar to the outflows, while at the micro level, large changes are occurring: many workers are becoming unemployed, while many unemployed are, at the same time,

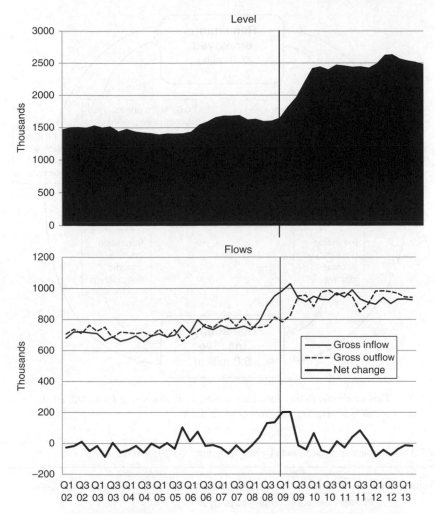

Figure 7.1   Unemployment level and the unemployment flows in the United Kingdom:
2001–2013. Source: from ONS (2013c).

finding work. This means that to understand the labour market, it is necessary to examine the flows into and out of work.

Figure 7.2 illustrates the flows in the UK labour market between the first and second quarters of 2013. (See Box 7.1 for an explanation of how these flows are measured.) One third of those who were unemployed in the first quarter had left unemployment in the second quarter, either for work or to become inactive. The probabilities of moving between the three possible states of economic activity are called hazard rates. Examples are shown in Box 7.3. Figure 7.3 shows the hazard rates of moving between the three basic employment states in the United Kingdom from the start of the series in 2001.

These examples are based on data from the UK LFS and reflect the changes between one quarter and the next as explained in Box 7.1. But the LFS does not record all the changes. First, as noted in Box 7.1, changes within a quarter will be missed (ONS, 2013c). US data miss fewer

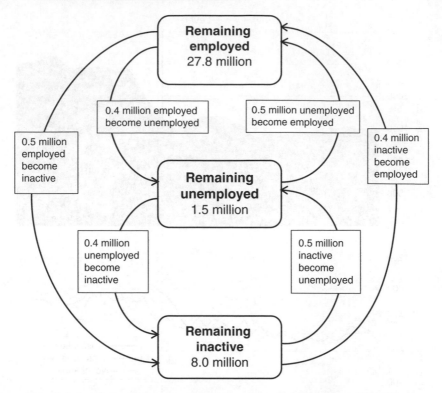

Figure 7.2   Labour market flows in the United Kingdom: comparing Q1 to Q2, 2013 (see Box 7.1 for definitions). Source: from ONS (2013c).

Box 7.3   Examples of hazard rates, United Kingdom: Q1 2013 to Q2 2103.

$$\frac{\text{Number of people who moved from employment to unemployment}}{\text{Number of people employed in Q1 2013}}$$

$$= \frac{404 \text{ thousand}}{28.7 \text{ million}} = 1.4\%$$

$$\frac{\text{Number of people who moved from unemployment to employment}}{\text{Number of people unemployed in Q1 2013}}$$

$$= \frac{545 \text{ thousand}}{2.5 \text{ million}} = 21.8\%$$

Source: from ONS (2013c).

such shifts because it is based on month-to-month changes. (See Box 7.4 for more information on the differences between UK and US data.) Second, it does not allow for those who move directly from one job to another without becoming unemployed. Using LFS data between 1996 and 2007, Gomes (2009) estimated that on average 2.9% of those in employment changed jobs directly each quarter; over the same period, 1.3% became unemployed.

Probability of leaving employment

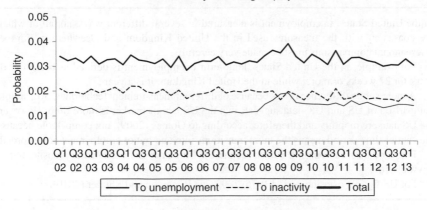

Probability of leaving unemployment

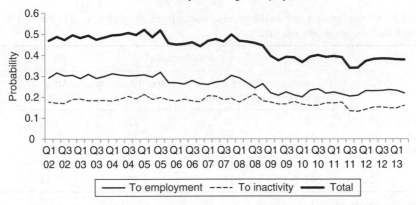

Probability of leaving inactivity

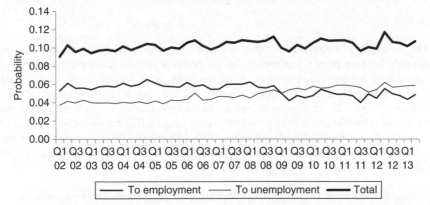

Figure 7.3   Hazard rates, United Kingdom: 2001–2013. Source: from ONS (2013c).

Box 7.4   The US labour market.

In the United States, unemployment is measured in several different ways, not all of which are consistent with the measures used in the United Kingdom and elsewhere in Europe. International comparisons must be made very carefully.

For example, in the United States, long-term unemployment is defined as being out of work for 27 weeks or more, while in the United Kingdom, it is a year.

A more subtle difference arises because of different measurement techniques. So a simple comparison of US and UK data suggests that the US labour market is more fluid. However, the US data are monthly and therefore, according to Gomes (2009), not comparable because the shorter time period means the more transitions into and out of employment are recorded.

For more information on US data, see the US Bureau of Labor Statistics website: http://www.bls.gov.

For US figures over the period 1976–2009, see Rogerson and Shimer (2010).

Table 7.1   Unemployment rate and duration of unemployment by age: April to June 2013, United Kingdom, seasonally adjusted.

	Percentages				
	Rate	Up to 6 months	Over 6 and up to 12 months	Over 12 and up to 24 months	All over 24 months	All
16–17	38.1	70	18	12	[a]	100
18–24	19.2	51	16	18	14	100
25–49	6.0	43	18	18	22	100
50+	4.7	38	16	18	27	100
All	**7.8**	**47**	**17**	**17**	**19**	**100**

Source: from ONS (2013d).
[a] By definition, those under 18 cannot be unemployed for over 2 years.

The probability of becoming unemployed and once unemployed of returning to work varies significantly between people. For instance, in the first part of 2013, unemployed people had a 38% chance of leaving unemployment, either for work or to become economically inactive (as shown in Figure 7.3). Yet, if all the unemployed had such a high probability of leaving unemployment, only 2% of a given cohort would be continuously unemployed over 2 years. (The maths are $(1-0.38)$ raised to the power 8 which equals 0.02.) But in the second quarter of 2013, one in five of those unemployed in the United Kingdom (19%) had been continuously unemployed for over 2 years (Table 7.1). The longer someone is unemployed, the less likely they are to get a job. The ONS (2013c) reported that

> Over the year from April-June 2012 to April-June 2013, if one had been unemployed for less than three months one was 3.2 times more likely to move from unemployment into employment compared with someone who has been unemployed for over two years, and 1.9 times more likely compared with someone who has been unemployed for between six and 12 months.

Other indicators of the heterogeneity of the unemployed include:

- Younger workers are more likely to be unemployed. The unemployment rate is much higher for younger workers than for older workers (Table 7.1); in the year to June 2013, workers under 25 were three times more likely to become unemployed than older workers (ONS, 2013c).

- Employment history matters. Those who have experienced recent unemployment are more likely to become unemployed again. The ONS (2013c) reported that

> Between April-June 2012 and April-June 2013, one was 8.5 times more likely to move from employment into unemployment if one had been employed for less than six months compared with someone who has been employed for between 5 and 10 years.

Furthermore, those who are unemployed at one point in time were more likely to have been unemployed previously and are likely to remain unemployed for longer.

  - Those with recent employment are less likely to become unemployed: in 2007, the probability of an employed person becoming unemployed was 10% if they had been unemployed in the previous period but only 6% if inactive and 1% if employed (Gomes, 2009).

  - Those with recent employment who do become unemployed are more likely to find another job. 'The job-finding rate is 46% if two quarters earlier the person was employed, 23% if the person was inactive and 18.6% if the person was unemployed' (Gomes, 2009).

- Qualifications and job skills are also important.

However, gender is less so: 'The employment hazard rates for men and women have followed fairly similar patterns to one another' although the hazard rates are higher for men. For example, from 'the second quarter of 2008 to the second quarter of 2013 the average unemployment hazard rate for men was 1.9% compared with 1.4% for women' (ONS, 2013c).

Employers

Employers are highly heterogeneous too. In particular, there are a few very large employers and many small employers. Axtell (2001) observed that in the United States, the probability that a firm is larger than a given size is inversely proportional to that size, for example, one in a million firms will employ more than 1 million people. Mathematically, this is known as a power law distribution. (For more on power laws, see Box 7.5.)

Simple analysis suggests that the same holds for the United Kingdom. At the start of 2013, the Department for Business and Skills (BIS, 2013) estimated there were almost 5 million organisations in the United Kingdom, all but about 90 thousand in the private sector. They employed 31 million people. However, 3.9 million, or nearly 80%, were one person businesses. Yet 40% of people were employed in large organisations with 500 or more employees. (Details are shown in the top panel of Box 7.6.) The National Health Service is the largest employer in the United Kingdom with 'more than 1.6 million people' (NHS, 2015). The supermarket firm, Tesco, is thought to be the largest private employer in the United Kingdom, with 'over 310 000' employees (Tesco, 2014). Plotting this data on logarithmic scale produces the straight line that is a characteristic of power law distributions and an exponent of −1, as shown in the bottom panel of Box 7.6.

The average size of all organisations is 21 in the United Kingdom. But, as shown in Box 7.6, only about 2% of organisations have 20 or more people: the majority of firms have less than five.

Box 7.5   Power law distributions.

A power law distribution is said to exist if 'the probability of measuring a particular value of some quantity varies inversely as a power of that value' (Newman, 2005). Power law distributions are observed in many contexts, although often only over the higher values. In economics, it has been long established that the distribution of wealth follows a power law distribution.

Example: imagine there are 1000 agents, with some item distributed between them very inequitably so that the majority of agents have only 1 item, but a few agents have significantly more, as shown in the table. The graph plots the data on a logarithmic scale giving the straight line that is characteristic of a power law distribution. The line has an exponent of -1.

Number of items	Number of agents with that number of items	Total number of items
1000	1	1000
500	2	1000
150	8	1200
10	90	900
1	899	899
Total	1000	4999

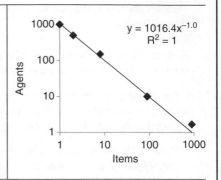

If the exponent is less than 2, 'the mean is not a well-defined quantity, because it can vary enormously from one measurement to the next, and indeed can become arbitrarily large' (Newman, 2005). While the average can be calculated from any given sample, it may vary considerably between samples. This can be illustrated with the example above. If all 1000 agents are included, then the average number of items per agent is 5. If the agent with 1000 items is excluded, the average over the remaining 999 drops to 4. And if the top three agents are excluded, the average drops to 3.

When the exponent is -1, the distribution is often said to follow Zipf's law. But strictly, Zipf's law applies to ranked data. For example, the event with the highest probability occurs twice as often as the event with the next highest probability and three times as often as the third ranking item and so on.

For more on power law distributions, see Newman (2005).

What then is a 'representative firm'? The skewness of the distribution casts doubt on Marshall's assertion (1890/1920, Book IV, Chapter XIII.9) that

> ...a representative firm is in a sense an average firm. But there are many ways in which the term "average" might be interpreted in connection with a business. And a Representative firm is that particular sort of average firm, at which we need to look in order to see how far the economies, internal and external, of production on a large scale have extended generally in the industry and country in question. We cannot see this by looking at one or two firms taken at random: but we can see it fairly well by selecting, after a broad survey, a firm, whether in private or joint-stock management (or better still, more than one), that represents, to the best of our judgment, this particular average.

It also casts doubt on the validity of using a representative firm in modern models.

Box 7.6 UK organisations by size: 2013.

Size	Organisations		Total employment		Average employment[a]
	Number	*Per cent*	Thousand	*Per cent*	
1[b]	3 877 795	*77.8*	4 421	*14*	1
2–4	614 985	*12.3*	1 839	*6*	3
5–9	244 635	*4.9*	1 679	*5*	7
10–19	130 715	*2.6*	1 806	*6*	14
20–49	70 950	*1.4*	2 157	*7*	30
50–99	22 840	*0.5*	1 579	*5*	69
100–199	11 020	*0.2*	1 540	*5*	140
200–249	2 260	*0.04534*	503	*2*	223
250–499	4 290	*0.08607*	1 484	*5*	346
500–300 000	4 593	*0.09215*	12 522	*40*	2 726
Tesco	1	*0.00002*	300	*1*	310 000
NHS	1	*0.00002*	1 500	*5*	1 500 000
Total	**4 984 085**	*100*	**31 340**	*100*	**21**

[a] Employment divided by number of organisations.
[b] Includes self-employed owner-managers.

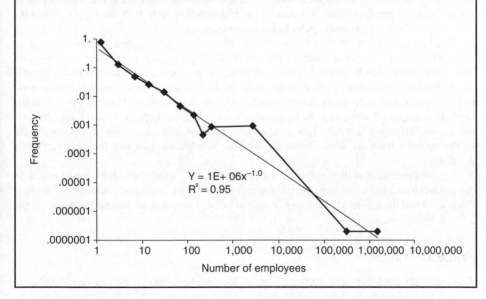

Sources: based on data from Department for Business and Skills (2013: Table 2 – whole economy), NHS Confederation (2014) and Tesco (2014).

We noted in Chapter 6 that about 10% of retailers go out of business and are replaced each year. While the proportions vary between industry groups, as some sectors grow and others decline, this is also broadly true for all businesses. So while the macro picture of the number of employers may appear constant, once again, there is a great deal of change at the micro level.

Summary

To sum up, while the labour market may appear fairly stable at the macro level, there is much activity at the micro level. Many people move between employment, unemployment and inactivity even though the total number in each group changes little. Firms close and are replaced by new ones. Both labour and organisations are highly heterogeneous. There is no 'average employer', and it is tempting to say there is no 'average worker' either. The importance of dynamics and heterogeneity suggest agent-based modelling may provide insights into the labour market.

7.2   A simple labour market model

The labour market is dynamic and there is great diversity among the participants, both workers and employers. To capture this diversity in full, very large-scale agent-based models are being built. For example, Guerrero and Axtell (2013) built a model of the Finnish labour market with a 'one-to-one scale with the Finnish labor force', that is, 2.5 million agents. And Axtell is currently working on a model of the US labour market comprising over 100 million agents and drawing on 'three dozen' data sources (Axtell, 2013). Such models are beyond the scope of this book.

So in this section, we present a simple labour market model, using 1000 agents and 100 employers, as used by the French WORKSIM model (Lewkovicz et al., 2009). However, rather than addressing a particular policy issue, as Lewkovicz et al. do, our model aims simply to capture the essential features of the labour market, making minimal assumptions. It illustrates the basic dynamics and shows how small imbalances due to heterogeneity in both the supply of and the demand for labour can generate cycles in unemployment.

To add some realism, where possible, this simple model is broadly based on our home town of Guildford. Box 7.7 provides information about the labour supply and demand in Guildford. To keep the model simple, many details – such as that many workers commute out of Guildford – are overlooked. In this model, agents either work full-time or are unemployed. This is in contrast to the classic micro textbook treatments which focus on the number of hours worked, with the implicit assumption that workers can choose their hours. (See, e.g. Begg et al. (2011, pp.230–234) and Varian (2010, pp.174–178).) This standard assumption is rather surprising given the evidence to the contrary (such as Tam, 2010), and so this simplification of our model seems quite justifiable.

We build the model in three stages. In the first stage, we establish the distribution of wages. In the second, we model job search, matching employers with vacancies and unemployed workers. Finally, we add the labour market flows described in the 'Introduction', basing the model on our home town of Guildford.

Stage 1: Wages

There are 100 employers and 1000 employees. Workers are either employed or unemployed. Those who become inactive drop out of the model and are replaced by new workers joining the labour force. So there are always 1000 workers and 1000 jobs.

As we have noted, workers are heterogeneous in many respects. In this model, we assume that this heterogeneity is entirely reflected in their wages. The distribution of wages is based on that of full-time workers in Guildford (see Box 7.8). We built a model to generate a log-normal distribution with a mean normalised to 100. (See Appendix 7.A for details.) Figure 7.4 shows an example of the wage distribution based on this method that best meets the stylised facts set out in Box 7.8.

Box 7.7   Guildford: labour supply.

Guildford is a town of about 150 000 inhabitants about 30 miles to the south-west of London. Some 70 000 or nearly 80% of the working age population are economically active.

Economic activity in Guildford (October 2012 to September 2013)

Economically active		77.1%
In employment		69.8%
Employees	55.7%	
Self-employed	13.3%	
Unemployed		5.8%

While as many as half the workers travel out of Guildford to work – 1 in 8 commuting to London, which is a 35 minute train journey – others come from the surrounding area to work in Guildford.

Thirty per cent of the employee jobs were in 'public admin., education and health' in 2012. In comparison with the rest of the United Kingdom, a higher than average proportion of workers is in the higher occupational groups: 38% are managers, directors, senior officials or in professional occupations. One third of the employees are part-timers.

There are about 6 500 employers and some 65 000 in employment so each employer on average employs about 10 people. However, the three largest employers – the university, the hospital and the local government – together account for about 13% of employees. Combining data from various sources suggests that the power law distribution noted in Box 7.6 for the whole of the United Kingdom applies locally too, although possibly with a slightly higher exponent because there are no very large employers.

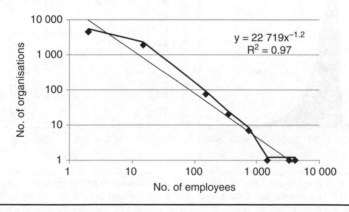

$$y = 22\ 719x^{-1.2}$$
$$R^2 = 0.97$$

Sources: from ONS (2014), Guildford Borough Council (2009, pp.8–9), University of Surrey (2013, p.26), Royal Surrey County Hospital (2013, p.26).

Stage 2: Job search

On average, each employer has 10 employees, to reflect the observed average in Guildford, but the size of employers is distributed according to a power distribution of about (minus) one, as shown in Box 7.9.

Box 7.8   Distribution of wages in the Guildford and Aldershot travel-to-work area, 2012.

In 2012, the average gross weekly pay of full-time workers was £624 per week. But about 60% earned less than this average. The median was lower, £505, or about 80% of the average. In other words, half of workers earned less than 80% of the average wage. Only workers in the top decile earned more than around twice average pay as shown in the bottom line of the table below.

Percentiles	Pay £ per week	As % of average pay
Bottom decile	125	20
Lower quintile	238	40
Middle quintile	419	67
Median	505	80
Upper quintile	606	100
Top quintile	875	140
Top decile	1181	190

Source: adapted from ONS (2013b).

1000 agents. 100 runs.

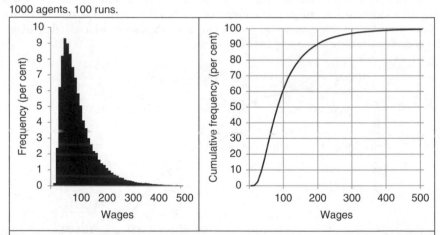

The average wage is set equal to 100 and standard deviation of the log-normal distribution is set to 0.7.This distribution is consistent with the observed distribution shown in Box 7.8: 64% of workers have wages below the average and the top decile – the top 10 per cent of workers – earned more than twice the average wage. (The plots show only 99.6% of workers because 0.4% have wages more than 5 times the average and are therefore off the end of the plot.)

Figure 7.4   Results of model: an example of the distribution of wages generated by the model.

Box 7.9   Guildford: labour demand.

Model assumptions

Number of employers	Average no. of employees per employer	Total employees	*Per cent of employers*	*Per cent of employees*
1	100	100	*2*	*20*
1	97	97		
3	50	150	*3*	*15*
4	30	120	*4*	*12*
27	15	405	*27*	*41*
64	2	128	*64*	*13*
100	10.0	1000	*100*	*100*

So we now have workers to whom wages have been allocated and employers who want a given number of workers. All the workers are allocated at random to employers, so that there is no unemployment. The modeller selects the number of job-seekers – workers looking to find another job – and the extent of wage flexibility. There are always 100 employers and 1000 workers. The number of job-seekers also equals the number of vacancies. This simplifying assumption means that there is no cyclical unemployment, but as we shall show, frictional and structural unemployment can arise. (See Box 7.10 for information on the types of unemployment.) Note that job-seekers are not counted as unemployed until they have been through the job search procedure and failed to find work. This means that workers can move from one job to another without being unemployed.

The employers want to fill their vacancies and the job-seekers want a new job. How can they be brought together in the model? Job search can be initiated in two ways: by employers with vacancies or by job-seeking workers. In this simple example, we have adopted an employer-led process: employers in effect advertise their vacancies at the same wage that they paid to the worker who left the job. The reasons for choosing this approach are essentially technical: the programming is somewhat simpler and it is easier to add employer preferences, such as favouring those who have been unemployed for a shorter time.

Employers do not adjust the wages they offer and workers have to take what is offered or remain unemployed. Workers are 'price-takers', that is, they have to accept the wage offered and cannot negotiate. However, workers can only accept wages within a given range of their past wage.

Box 7.10   Types of unemployment.

Three types of unemployment are generally recognised:

- Frictional unemployment. Workers may leave their jobs voluntarily in order to find something 'better'. This is called frictional unemployment and is seen as a sign of a healthy economy with a mobile workforce. It explains why there is always unemployment, even when vacancies exist.

- Structural unemployment arises when workers' skills do not match the job opportunities.

- Cyclical unemployment or demand-deficient unemployment arises when output is below full capacity, that is, unemployment is due to a general fall in demand.

For more, see Begg *et al.* (2011, pp.531–533).

The extent of this wage flexibility is set by the modeller specifying the maximum wage increase and the maximum wage decrease any job-seeker can accept. This chosen wage bracket is the same for all workers. So, for example, if both are set at 0%, there is no wage flexibility and the worker can only accept a job at exactly the same pay as they received in their previous job. But if both are set at 10%, then workers can accept jobs offering wages between 90 and 110% of their last wage. There may be many reasons why workers would take a job paying a lower wage than they previously earned: a lower paid job may be preferred because it is closer to home, reducing travel costs, or is better work in some sense. Setting the maximum wage decrease to zero could be regarded as analogous to the 'wage stickiness' that is a key feature of 'new Keynesian' models, which refers to the failure of wages to fall so that the labour market clears and all seeking work obtain it.

The process starts with the employer with the highest paid vacancy looking at all the workers seeking jobs within the wage range in which that vacancy lies. The employer then selects the worker whose last wage was the highest, on the basis that this is the only indicator of quality available to the employer. But the employer pays the wage offered, not the previous wage the worker received. Depending on circumstances, this could be more or less than the worker's previous wage. Then the next-best paid vacancy is filled and so on. Considering the highest paid first may seem an odd assumption. However, given the shape of the wage distribution – as illustrated in Figure 7.4 – the highest paid workers will have a smaller selection of jobs to choose from than lower paid workers, and so to maximise the chances of the top paid finding jobs, they are considered first. Other assumptions could be made. Because the model notionally reflects the labour market in a single town, any worker can take a job with any employer except their last one, thus ensuring that job-seekers do not simply return to their last employer.

The details are in Appendix 7.A, together with some suggestions about how to verify a model with such complicated interaction.

The model repeats the process 100 times, each time with a new set of data, and then reports the averages over the 100 runs. Despite the simplicity of the model, the results are rather interesting.

A selection of results are shown in the top panel of Figure 7.5: a high rate of unemployment is associated with small changes in the mean wages of those who move to new jobs. Further investigation shows that when there is no downward flexibility of wages permitted:

- The relationship between the maximum wage increase permitted, set by the modeller, and the resulting increase in mean wages of those who move to new jobs follows a semi-logarithmic relationship, as shown in the left middle panel.

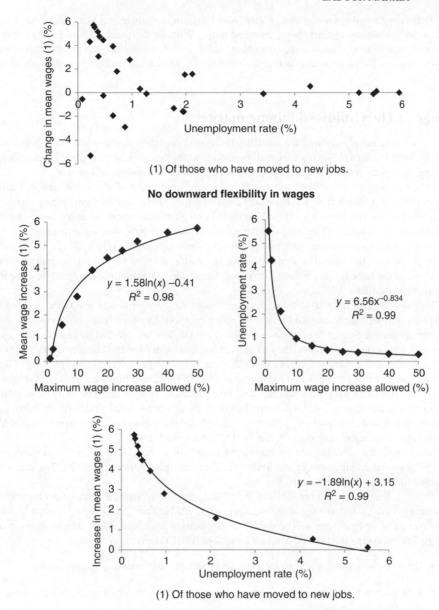

Figure 7.5   Results from the job search model.

- The relationship between the maximum wage increase permitted, set by the modeller, and the resulting unemployment rate follows a power law relationship, as shown in the right middle panel.

- The relationship between the unemployment rate and the observed changes in the mean wages of those who move to new jobs follows a semi-logarithmic distribution, as shown in the bottom panel.

These results make sense in that greater wage flexibility results in less unemployment. Thus, the model is validated against theory in broad terms. Whether the precise relationships implied between wage flexibility and unemployment are valid is another question. The point of this model is to understand the basic process before incorporating it into a more realistic model, to which we now turn.

Stage 3: The Guildford labour market

So far, we have simply allowed the modeller to decide how many workers become job-seekers, thus creating vacancies. Now, we extend the model so that vacancies are created by employers closing or workers retiring or quitting. The time period used is a quarter of a year.

When employers close, they are replaced by new employers of the same size and offer wages drawn at random from the log-normal distribution. These may be significantly different from those of the employer who closed, so there is no guarantee that those made redundant by the closing employers will be able to take jobs with the new employers. Consistent with the observed 'business demographics', two employers 'die' each quarter (ONS, 2012). Only small employers die as the mortality rate falls with increasing size, and it would be unrealistic to allow one of the three major employers to close. The resulting unemployment could be regarded as structural (see Box 7.10).

Workers are aged from 20 to 59. This range is used for simplicity as in reality those going to university will start work later and many will retire later too. Age is included only to ensure that workers do not live forever. When workers retire at age 60, they are replaced by new workers aged 20 who are allocated a wage level they expect drawn at random from the log-normal distribution. (This does mean that there is a chance that a 20-year-old could get a very high wage but it avoids the need to make more complicated assumptions about the profile of lifetime earnings.) So, again, there is no guarantee the retired workers will be replaced by similar workers. Only those in the labour force are explicitly modelled. Retired workers do not appear in the model. As the initial age of workers is distributed randomly between 20 and 59 and three quarters, and workers retire at 60, on average, 6 will retire each quarter, that is, 0.6% of the workforce.

To allow for the other reasons for leaving the labour force, the modeller sets two percentages: for moving from employment to inactivity and from unemployment to inactivity. These can be disabled by setting the rates to zero.

Due to heterogeneity, the demand and supply may not always match as imbalances may occur as retiring workers and closing employers are replaced. However, there is no change in total labour demand or total supply. The model is summarised by a simplified activity diagram in Figure 7.6. Following the Unified Markup Language (UML) conventions:

- The workers' states are shown by a rounded rectangle, for example, unemployed.

- A decision is shown by a diamond with the options labelled, for example, to seek work or leave the labour force.

- An activity is shown by a narrower, more rounded rectangle, for example, entering the labour force.

- A transition is shown by an arrow, for example, employed leave labour market.

(For more on the use of UML in agent-based modelling, see Bersini, 2012.)

At the start of the quarter, some of the employed leave their jobs voluntarily to seek other work, some are made redundant due to employers closing, and some become inactive due to

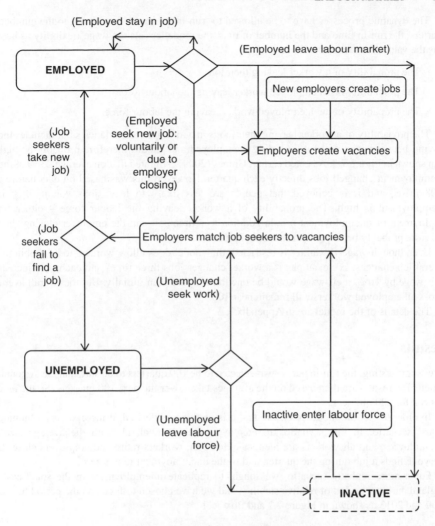

(Employed stay in job)

EMPLOYED

(Employed leave labour market)

New employers create jobs

(Job seekers take new job)

(Employed seek new job: voluntarily or due to employer closing)

Employers create vacancies

(Job seekers fail to find a job)

Employers match job seekers to vacancies

(Unemployed seek work)

UNEMPLOYED

Inactive enter labour force

(Unemployed leave labour force)

INACTIVE

Figure 7.6   Simple labour market model.

retirement or for some other reason. Those unemployed already decide whether to seek work or leave the labour force. All those leaving the labour force – from employment or unemployment – leave the model and are replaced by new workers, who are seeking work. New employers replace those who have gone out of business and they create vacancies. Other employers create vacancies to replace those who have left. So total labour supply equals total labour demand. Employers then fill their vacancies from the job-seekers, as described earlier. When this matching process is complete, some job-seekers will have found new jobs, but others will be unemployed. As before, job-seekers are not counted as unemployed until the matching process is complete and they have failed to find a new job. This means that, as in the LFS flow data, a move from employment to unemployment and back into employment within the quarter will not appear in the unemployment statistics.

The dynamic processes have to be allowed to 'run-in' to settle. In addition to the number of quarters, the run-in time and the number of runs, the modeller sets the wage flexibility as before plus the value of three probabilities:

- The probability of a worker leaving their job
- The probability of an employed worker leaving the labour force
- The probability of an unemployed worker leaving the labour force.

The probability of a worker leaving their job is in addition to redundancies but includes those moving between jobs without becoming unemployed and should therefore probably be higher than shown in Figure 7.3. As noted earlier, Gomes (2009) estimated that on average 2.9% of those in employment changed jobs directly each quarter. However, this was based on data before the 2008 crisis, and it is believed that people are less likely to leave jobs voluntarily when unemployment is high. The probability of a worker leaving the labour force – either from employment or unemployment – is in addition to retirement, and the employer closing should therefore probably be lower than shown in Figure 7.3.

Even though wage flexibility is restricted, this model does allow workers to be mobile over several job changes. For example, if a worker changes jobs three times and each time increases their wage by 10%, their wage would be one third higher than initially. But the overall average across all employed workers will remain near 100.

The details of the model are in Appendix 7.A.

Results

After some testing, the run-in period was selected to be 100 quarters to be sure that the system has settled. The results are then based on the averages taken over the next 100 quarters. So the model was run for 200 quarters.

In order to test the model to ensure that it is working as desired, it incorporates a 'homogeneous' scenario. In this scenario, all employers are identical, all with the average size of 10 employees, and all workers are identical. However, workers retire and employers close. But everyone finds a job during the quarter, and so the unemployment rate is zero.

For a more realistic scenario, we sought to replicate unemployment in the south-east of England during a period of relative stability, and we have chosen to focus on the period between 2009 and 2013 as shown in Figure 7.7 and Box 7.11.

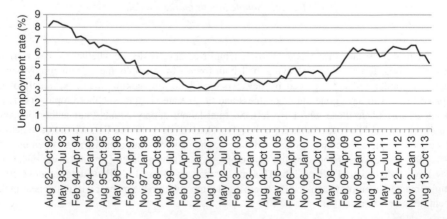

Figure 7.7   Unemployment rate in south-east England: 1992–2013. Source: from ONS (2014).

Box 7.11   Unemployment data since 2009.

Unemployment rate (%): south-east England[a] – May 2009 to October 2013

No. of quarters	21
Average	6.1
Maximum	6.6
Minimum	5.2
Range	1.4

[a] Not available for Guildford.
Source: From ONS (2014).

Hazard rates per quarter (%): United Kingdom[a] – Q2 2009 to Q2 2013

			Average/*standard deviation*		
			From		
	Employment		**Unemployment**		**Inactivity**
To					
Employment			22.2	*(1.2)*	4.8	*(0.4)*
Unemployment	1.5	*(0.1)*			5.7	*(0.3)*
Inactivity	1.8	*(0.2)*	15.9	*(1.4)*		

Source: from ONS (2013c).
[a] Not available for Guildford or south-east England.

An example of key results over 30 runs, with the underlying assumptions, is shown in Table 7.2. The greater the wage flexibility, the lower is the rate of unemployment, the lower the proportion of unemployed who are long-term unemployed, and the greater the probability of moving from unemployment into work. That is all as would be expected. But, in this model, the fewer workers who leave their job, the higher the rate of unemployment. This is because there is less activity in the job market and thus fewer job opportunities and less likelihood of finding a suitable job. The results for limited wage flexibility combined with 2–3% leaving employment seem to be closest to the observations in Box 7.11: an unemployment rate of about 6% and an unemployment to employment hazard rate of about a fifth. But the model produces a lower proportion of long-term unemployed than observed.

7.3   Discussion

We have presented a simple model in order to illustrate the key dynamic processes underlying the labour market. Nevertheless, the explicit assumptions required are many:

- Demand and supply, in terms of the number of jobs and the number of workers, are fixed and initially balanced so that there is full employment.
- Wages are distributed log-normally to reflect the distribution observed in the Guildford area.

Table 7.2   Results from the simple labour market model.

Assumptions
- % of employed workers leaving the labour force per quarter = 2
- % of unemployed workers leaving the labour force per quarter = 1.5

Key results (over 30 runs)

	Per cent of employees leaving jobs[a]				Mean (sd)
	1	2	3	4	5
Wage flexibility: max wage increase: 5%, max wage reduction: 0%					
Unemployment rate (%)	5.98 (0.35)	5.84 (0.29)	5.49 (0.38)	5.49 (0.21)	5.46 (0.32)
% of unemployed long term	23.46 (1.17)	21.77 (1.19)	20.16 (1.08)	18.98 (1.32)	17.91 (1.30)
Hazard rate: U to E%	18.14 (0.92)	19.91 (0.89)	21.90 (0.99)	23.04 (1.14)	24.63 (1.28)
Wage flexibility: max wage increase: 10%, max wage reduction: 10%					
Unemployment rate (%)	2.31 (0.21)	2.16 (0.20)	2.0 (0.21)	1.85 (0.20)	1.77 (0.22)
% of unemployed long term	13.01 (2.89)	12.09 (2.94)	11.31 (2.36)	11.99 (3.14)	11.73 (2.52)
Hazard rate: U to E%	34.98 (3.19)	38.1 (3.33)	40.68 (3.24)	41.72 (4.21)	43.41 (3.81)

[a] In addition to retiring and due to employers closing.

- The distribution of the size of employers is determined by a power law distribution with an exponent of -1, reflecting the distribution observed in the Guildford area.

- The 'death rate' of employers is two per quarter, selected randomly.

- Workers are evenly distributed between the ages of 20 and 60, and those aged 60 retire and are replaced by workers aged 20.

- Other than for retirement and as a result of the 'death' of employers, workers are selected at random to leave their jobs.

- Job search is initiated by employers, who fill the best paid jobs first.

- Employers do not change their wage offers.

- Workers are only differentiated by their wage in the job search process.

- Workers accept the wages offered.

In addition, there are implicit assumptions. For instance:

- The fact that workers can choose not to work implies that they have some means of support, either private resources or government benefits.

- The labour market is isolated so that workers have to find jobs within it.

- There is no cyclical unemployment.

The modeller sets the values of just five parameters:

- The probability of leaving employment to seek a new job

- The probabilities of leaving employment or unemployment for inactivity

- The extent of wage flexibility: the maximum wage increase and the maximum wage reduction allowed

Neither employers nor workers are explicitly optimising. Employers are simply trying to maintain their desired labour force and workers to obtain a wage within the specified range. Yet despite this simplicity, it is possible to replicate the kind of unemployment seen in Guildford and south-east England in recent years. Furthermore, examination of example runs shows (Figure 7.8) that the unemployment rate fluctuates too, in a way that suggests cycles even though there is no change in the total number of workers demanded. These fluctuations are not the 'cyclical unemployment' that results from changes in demand, but cyclical unemployment in the sense of 'occurring in cycles'. The unemployment observed is frictional and structural and entirely due to mismatch, to heterogeneity.

Of course, the results of the model do not match the observations very closely because this is a simple model. The workers only differ in one characteristic, namely, wages. There is no allowance for age, gender, education or time spent unemployed. In particular, given that the model did not take into account that the long-term unemployed are less likely to return to work than others, it is hardly surprising that the model underestimates the proportion of unemployed who are long-term unemployed. Adding such characteristics would complicate the model immensely and require many more assumptions. The purpose here was to create the simplest model that could reflect the basic dynamics of the labour market.

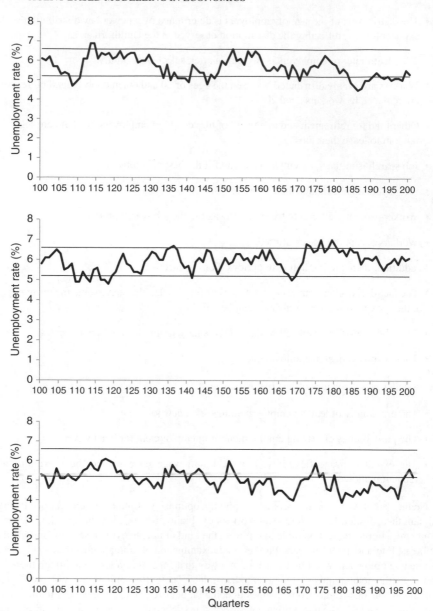

Figure 7.8   Results: examples of the unemployment rate (%) based on maximum wage increase of 5% (as illustrated in Box 7.11). (Thin lines show the observed range of unemployment rates (see Box 7.11).)

It could be said that the model has produced a straight line with some random variation and that a much simpler model would match the data just as well. But a simpler model would not be emulating the complicated flows that comprise the labour market. Think of a swan – black or white – gliding across a lake. The turbulence created by its paddling is not visible, but without understanding the dynamics of the paddling, you would not be able to understand how the swan is able to glide.

Despite our aim to 'keep it simple', the programming has been quite complicated and illustrates just how much detail is required to model the labour market. It is vital to establish what the model is actually doing. This is not just a matter of verification and validation but also assessing properly the implications of taking different approaches to modelling any given economic activity. It is not sufficient simply to say 'we can match these observations'. There are usually many ways a given set of observations can be matched. We have shown in Figure 7.5 how the simple approach we have taken to modelling job search results in a specific set of relationships between wage increases and the unemployment rate. The power law and semi-logarithmic relationships between unemployment and wage flexibility were not programmed in but emerged from the behavioural rules used. These relationships may or may not be acceptable or realistic. But they need to be explored before the model is used to answer bigger questions. This is an important lesson for agent-based modellers who are understandably so keen to do exciting policy-orientated work that they neglect to explore and understand the modelling of basic economic processes. Building blocks that are based on agreed assumptions and have been fully tested and understood need to be created so that those using them for policy analysis can be clear on what exactly their models are doing.

Returning to the three main themes of the book, even this simple model demonstrates the importance of modelling heterogeneity, dynamics and interaction:

- Both employers and workers are highly diverse. This heterogeneity causes a mismatching that results in unemployment.

- The labour market is highly dynamic: there are large flows into and out of work and into and out of the labour force.

- Like any market, buyers (in this case, employers) and sellers (in this case, workers) interact.

Again, we have shown how the micro and macro can be brought together effectively using agent-based modelling. This is especially important in the labour market, because relative stability is observed at the macro level despite a great deal of activity at the micro level. In contrast, traditional textbooks separate micro and macro (e.g. Begg *et al.*, Chapters 10 & 23).

To sum up, again, we have demonstrated the importance of modelling heterogeneity, dynamics and direct interaction and how agent-based modelling can bring together the micro and macro.

Appendix 7.A   How to do it

Wage distribution model

Purpose: The aim of the model is to produce a log-normal wage distribution.
Entities: Agents represent people.
Stochastic processes: Random allocation of wages using a log-normal distribution.
Outputs: Results are displayed on the screen and printed to a csv file.

The pseudocode is in Box 7.A.1 and a screenshot in Figure 7.A.1. For the full code, see the website: *Chapter 7 – Wage Distribution Model*.

Things to try using the wage distribution model

Use the slider to generate different distributions.

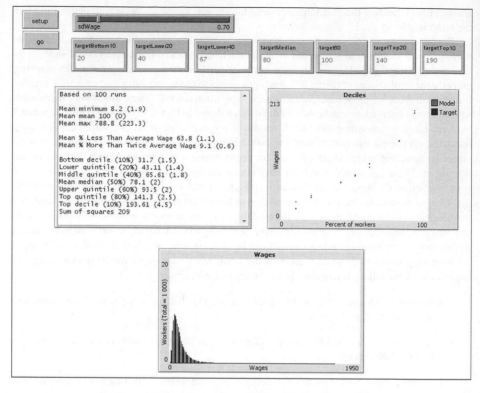

Figure 7.A.1   Screenshot of wage distribution model.

Box 7.A.1   Pseudocode for the wage distribution model.

Create 1000 workers.

Repeat 100 times:

    Allocate wages.

    Allocate a wage drawn randomly from a log-normal distribution to workers.

    Calculate the average wage and normalise it to 100.

    Recalculate workers' wages.

Data collection:

    Record the key points on the wage distribution: bottom decile, bottom 20%, bottom 40%, median, bottom 60%, bottom 80% and top decile.

    For each, calculate the cumulative difference squared from the target (to measure goodness of fit).

    Collect the data for each run.

Take the averages over the 100 runs.

Plot the wage distribution for all runs.

Plot the results of the model against the target over 100 runs.

Send the output to a csv file.

Job search model

Purpose: The aim is to model job search.

Entities: There are two types of agents: employers and workers.

Stochastic processes: Wage distribution, allocation of workers to employers and selection of job-seekers.

Initialisation: The modeller selects the number of job-seekers and the extent of wage flexibility (by specifying the maximum wage increase and the maximum wage decrease any job-seeker can accept).

Outputs: Results are shown on the interface and sent to a csv file.

The pseudocode is in Box 7.A.2. There is some very complicated programming involved in this job search model, so how can we be sure that it is working as we intended? Box 7.A.3 explains how the model has been verified. Figure 7.A.2 shows a screenshot. For the full code, see the website: *Chapter – Job Search Model*.

Things to try using the job search model

Use the sliders to examine the effect of different levels of wage flexibility.

Advanced – requiring amending the program:

- What is the effect of not starting with the highest paid vacancies or job-seekers?

- Devise different job search mechanisms.

Box 7.A.2   Pseudocode for the job search model.

Create a world 315×315.

Create 1000 agents to represent workers and 100 to represent employers and distribute them randomly across the world.

For each run:

    Allocate a wage to each worker.

    Allocate a firm size to each employer.

    Allocate workers to employers.

    Select the required number of workers to seek new jobs.

    The employers of the job-seekers create vacancies.

Vacancies are filled, starting with the best paid and working down the wage distribution. Employers fill their vacancies with the highest paid eligible worker.

Verification checks are carried out (see Box 7.A.4).

Data from each run is collected.

Means over all the runs are calculated and shown on the screen and printed to a csv file.

Box 7.A.3   Notes on verification of the job search model.

To test that the model is working as intended, it includes a range of checks at both the micro and macro level:

At the micro level:
Workers

- Do any job-seekers receive wage increases outside the specified range? If so, then the wage restrictions have not been modelled correctly.

- Have any workers been re-employed by their last employer? This is not supposed to happen as if it did all the job-seekers could simply slot back into the jobs they have just left.

Employers

- Does the sum of the number of employees and the number of vacancies equal the employer's size? Are there any employers for whom the sum of their unfilled vacancies and new recruits not equal their total initial vacancies? If not, then the recruitment process has not been modelled correctly.

At the macro level:

- Do the total vacancies equal the total number of workers with no employers? If not, there is an error because the overall demand for labour is set to equal the overall supply.

- Do the total new recruits equal the total number of workers who have found jobs? If not, then the recruitment process has not been modelled correctly.

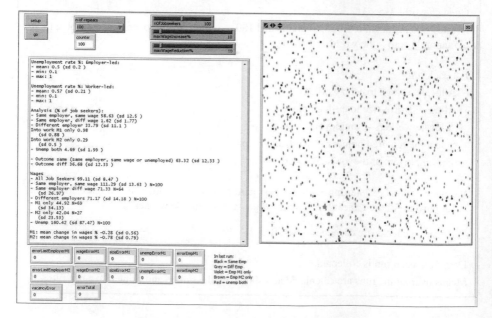

Figure 7.A.2   Screenshot of job search model.

Box 7.A.4   Pseudocode for the Guildford labour market model.

Create a world 315×315.

For each run:

Create 1000 agents to represent workers and 100 to represent employers and distribute them randomly across the world.

Workers are allocated:

- A wage – see wage distribution model above.

- An age, distributed evenly between 20 and 59.75.

Allocate a firm size to each employer.
Allocate workers to employers.

Dynamics:

Clear past records as appropriate.
  Employers 'die' making their workers redundant.
  New employers are created with vacancies at wages selected from the log-normal distribution. Workers age and retire if aged 60 and are replaced by 20-year-olds.
  Workers leave their job to seek new jobs: number set by slider.
  Workers leave the labour force: numbers set by sliders.
  All those who leave the labour force are replaced by new workers, who are allocated a wage at random from the log-normal distribution.
  Employers create vacancies to replace the workers who have left, offering the same wage as paid to those who have left.
  Employers fill vacancies, as in the job search model.

Data collection at the end of the quarter:

- The unemployment rate and various flows are measured.

- The overall wage level is also monitored.

- Averages are collected.

Data from each run is collected.

When all runs are completed, means over all the runs are calculated and shown on the screen and printed to a csv file.

Guildford labour market model

Purpose: A simple labour market model based on Guildford.
Entities: There are two types of agents: employers and workers.
Stochastic processes: Wage distribution, the age distribution, allocation of workers to employers and selection of job-seekers and selection of workers to leave the labour force.

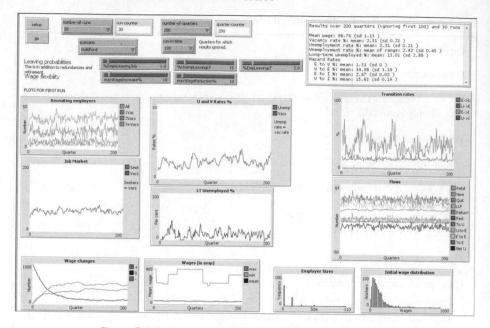

Figure 7.A.3   Screenshot of Guildford labour market model.

Initialisation:

- Wage flexibility as in the job search model

- The probability of a worker leaving their job in addition to redundancies but including those moving between jobs without becoming unemployed

- The probability of an employed worker leaving the labour force in addition to retirement

- The probability of an unemployed worker leaving the labour force in addition to retirement

- The number of quarters and the run-in time

- The number of runs

Outputs: Results are shown on the interface and sent to a csv file. Plots for the first run are sent to another csv file.

The pseudocode is in Box 7.A.4 and a screenshot in Figure 7.A.3. For the full code, see the website: *Chapter 7 – Guildford Labour Market Model*.

Things to try using the Guildford labour market model

Use the sliders to examine the effect of different levels of wage flexibility and flows.
    Advanced – requiring amending the program:

- Allow employers to give preference to job-seekers who have only recently left their jobs and discriminate against the long-term unemployed.

- Make the probabilities of leaving a job dependent on age.

- Add education.

- Replace the employer-led job search mechanism with the worker-led mechanism.

- Allow workers to search for jobs before giving notice, that is, so that there is a time lag in the creation of vacancies.

References

Axtell, R.L. (2001) Zipf distribution of U.S. firm sizes. *Science*, 293(5536), pp.1818–1820.

Axtell, R.L. (2013) *Endogenous Firms and Their Dynamics*. Presented at ESRC Conference on Diversity in Macroeconomics: New Perspectives from Agent-based Computational, Complexity and Behavioural Economics 24–25 February 2014, University of Essex [Online]. Available at: http://www.acefinmod.com/docs/ESRC/Axtell-Firms.pdf [Accessed 28 December 2014].

Bank of England (2013) *Forward Guidance* (7 August) [Online]. Available at: http://www.bankofengland.co.uk/monetarypolicy/pages/forwardguidance.aspx [Accessed 3 January 2015].

Begg, D., Vernasca, G., Fischer, S. & Dornbusch, R. (2011) *Economics*. Tenth Edition. London: McGraw-Hill Higher Education.

Bersini, H. (2012) UML for ABM. *Journal of Artificial Societies and Social Simulation*, 15(1), 9 [Online]. Available at: http://jasss.soc.surrey.ac.uk/15/1/9.html [Accessed 3 January 2015].

Clegg, R. (2012a) *Interpreting Labour Market Statistics*. Office for National Statistics [Online]. Available at: http://www.ons.gov.uk [Accessed 17 July 2014].

Clegg, R. (2012b) *Guide to Labour Market Statistics*. Office for National Statistics [Online]. Available at: http://www.ons.gov.uk [Accessed 17 July 2014].

Department for Business and Skills (BIS) (2013) *Business Population estimates for the UK and Regions 2013. Additional tables* [Online]. Available at: https://www.gov.uk/government/collections/business-population-estimates [Accessed 3 January 2015].

Elsby, M., Smith, J. & Wadsworth, J. (2011) The role of worker flows in the dynamics and distribution of UK unemployment. *Oxford Review of Economic Policy*, 27(2), pp.338–363.

Gomes, P. (2009) *Labour Market Flows: Facts from the United Kingdom*. Working Paper, 367. London: Bank of England [Online]. Available at: http://www.bankofengland.co.uk/research/Documents/workingpapers/2009/wp367.pdf [Accessed 3 January 2015].

Guerrero, O.A. & Axtell, R.L. (2013) Employment growth through labor flow networks. *PLoS One*, 8(5), e60808 [Online]. Available at http://www.plosone.org/article/info%3Adoi%2F10.1371%2Fjournal.pone.0060808 [Accessed 3 January 2015].

Guildford Borough Council (2009) *Guildford Economic Development Study*. Prepared for the Guildford Borough Council and Guildford Business Forum, Department of Economics of the University of Surrey [Online]. Available at: http://www.guildford.gov.uk/CHttpHandler.ashx?id=5581&p=0 [Accessed 3 January 2015].

H.M. Government (1944) *Employment Policy*. Ministry of Reconstruction. Cmnd, 6527. London: HMSO.

Lewkovicz, Z., Domingue, D. & Kant, J.D. (2009) An agent-based simulation of the French labour market: Studying age discrimination. *The 6th Conference of the European Social Simulation Association*, Guildford [Online]. Available at: http://www-desir.lip6.fr/~sma-site/seminaires/Exposes/ZL_DD_JDK.pdf [Accessed 3 January 2015].

Marshall, A. (1890/1920) *Principles of Economics*. London: Macmillan & Co. Ltd. [Online]. Available at: http://www.econlib.org/library/Marshall/marP27.html#IV.XIII.9 [Accessed 3 January 2015].

Newman, M.E.J. (2005) Power laws, Pareto distributions and Zipf's law. *Contemporary Physics*, 46(5), 323–351 [Online]. Available at: http://arxiv.org/pdf/cond-mat/0412004.pdf [Accessed 3 January 2015].

NHS (2015) *NHS in England* [Online]. Available at: http://www.nhs.uk/NHSEngland/thenhs/about/Pages/overview.aspx [Accessed 23 March 2015].

Office for National Statistics (ONS) (2012) *Business Demography, 2011*. [Online] Available at www.ons.gov. uk [Accessed 30 January 2013].

Office for National Statistics (ONS) (2013a) *Labour Market Statistics, August 2013* [Online]. Available at: http://www.ons.gov.uk/ons/rel/lms/labour-market-statistics/august-2013/statistical-bulletin.html [Accessed 3 January 2015].

Office for National Statistics (ONS) (2013b) *Annual Survey of Hours and Earnings* [Online]. Available at: http://www.ons.gov.uk/ons/rel/ashe/annual-survey-of-hours-and-earnings/index.html [Accessed 19 March 2013].

Office for National Statistics (ONS) (2013c) *Full Report: Moving between Unemployment and Employment* 7 November [Online]. Available at: http://www.ons.gov.uk [Accessed 26 March 2013].

Office for National Statistics (ONS) (2013d) *UNEM01: Unemployment by age and duration* [Online]. Available at: http://www.ons.gov.uk [Accessed 22 September 2013].

Office for National Statistics (ONS) (2014) *NOMIS: Official Labour Market Statistics* [Online]. Available at: http://www.nomisweb.co.uk/ [Accessed 26 March 2013].

Rogerson, R. & Shimer, R. (2010) *Search in Macroeconomic Models of the Labor Market*. Working Paper, 15901. Cambridge, MA: National Bureau of Economic Research [Online]. Available at: http://www.nber. org/papers/w15901 [Accessed 24 September 2013].

Royal Surrey County Hospital NHS Foundation Trust (2013) *Annual Report and Accounts for the period 1 April 2012 to 31 March 2013* [Online]. Available at: http://www.royalsurrey.nhs.uk/ [Accessed 11 March 2014].

Smith, J.C. (2011) The ins and outs of unemployment. *The Economic Journal*, 121, 402–444.

Tam, H. (2010) Characteristics of the underemployed and the overemployed in the UK. *Economic & Labour Market Review*, 4(7), 8–20.

Tesco (2014) *Tesco UK – About Us* [Online]. Available at: http://www.tescoplc.com/index.asp?pageid=282 [Accessed 3 January 2015].

University of Surrey (2013) *University of Surrey Financial Statements 2012–13* [Online]. Available at: http:// www.surrey.ac.uk/about/.../university_of_surrey_accounts_2012-13.pdf [Accessed 11 March 2014].

Varian, H. (2010) *Intermediate Microeconomics*. Princeton: Princeton University Press.

8

International trade

8.1 Introduction

'The archaeological record demonstrates that our Ice Age ancestors were already trading tens of thousands of years ago Cro-Magnon sites…contain Baltic amber and Mediterranean seashells transported thousands of miles inland' (Diamond, 2012, p.60). Today, international trade is vital to the health of the world economy. Exports accounted for 29% of the GDP of the OECD countries in 2012; and for the United Kingdom, it was 32%. But there is great variation between countries, as shown in Table 8.1. At one extreme, the United States and Japan are relatively closed economies with low levels of international trade, while at the other extreme, the Netherlands and Belgium are very open economies.

The study of international trade is a vast area exploring why countries trade and how is it managed. In this chapter, we focus on exchange rates and, in particular, the UK pound, the US dollar and the euro. We start with a brief introduction. (For more introductory level explanations, see Begg *et al.* (2011); for more advanced material, see Feenstra and Taylor (2011); and for particular reference to the Eurozone, see Baldwin and Wyplosz (2012).)

Definition of exchange rates

An exchange rate is the price of one currency in units of another currency. We start by explaining how nominal exchange rates are expressed and how effective and real exchange rates are calculated.

Nominal exchange rates

The term 'exchange rate' means the rate at which a given pair of currencies is exchanged. An exchange rate can be expressed in one of two ways, as illustrated in Box 8.1. It is essential to be clear which rate is being used at any one time. The shorthand convention adopted in this chapter is that, for example, €/£ means the number of euros that can be bought for £1. This is the exchange rate that people use when they travel.

Agent-Based Modelling in Economics, First Edition. Lynne Hamill and Nigel Gilbert.
© 2016 John Wiley & Sons, Ltd. Published 2016 by John Wiley & Sons, Ltd.

Table 8.1   International imports and exports in goods and services as per cent of GDP (2012).

	Imports	Exports
United States	17	14
Japan	17	15
Greece	32	27
China	25	27
United Kingdom	34	32
Switzerland	42	52
Germany	46	52
Netherlands	80	88
Belgium	85	86
Eurozone	43	46
All EU	43	45
OECD	30	29

Source: based on OECD (2014a).

Box 8.1   Definition of exchange rates.

Let us take the exchange rate between the euro (€) and the British pound (£):

- The international value of domestic currency is the quantity of foreign currency per unit of domestic currency: for example, for a UK resident, it is €1.3/£.

- The domestic price of foreign exchange is the quantity of domestic currency per unit of foreign currency: for example, for a UK resident, it is £1/€1.3 or £0.77/€.

Examples:

- The United Kingdom imports a car from, say, Germany, that costs €30000.

  The exchange rate is the UK domestic price of foreign exchange: £0.77/€.

  The cost of the car in the United Kingdom is €30000×0.77=£23100.

- Germany imports a car from the United Kingdom that costs £23100.

  The exchange rate is the international value of the United Kingdom's currency: €1.3/£.

  The cost of the car in Germany is £23100×1.3=€30 000.

(For more details, see Begg *et al.* (2011, pp.549–550) and Feenstra and Taylor (2011, pp.422–425).)

Effective exchange rates

However, for economic analysis, the exchange rate between one pair of currencies provides limited information because countries trade with many others. The effective exchange rate takes this into account. It is the average based on a basket of exchange rates in which each rate is weighted according to the extent to which the pair of countries trade. It is therefore a measure of the overall purchasing power of a currency. Of course, trading patterns change over time, and so the effective exchange rate will vary according to which weights are used. (For more on effective exchange rates, see Begg *et al.* (2011, pp.551–552) and the Bank of England (2014).)

Real exchange rates

So far, we have discussed nominal exchange rates. In contrast, the real exchange rate compares the price of a basket of goods and services in two countries by expressing them in the same currency. It is determined by prices in each of the countries and the nominal exchange rate. If a country's real exchange rate falls, that country becomes more competitive because its goods are cheaper to buyers in the other country. That can come about if prices fall in the exporting country, if prices rise in its trading partner or if the nominal exchange rate falls. For the real exchange rates to be constant if prices rise in a country, the exchange rate must fall so that its currency buys less foreign currency. Box 8.2 shows an example.

Box 8.2   Calculation of real exchange rate.

The real exchange rate is defined as

$$\frac{\text{Home prices} \times \text{international value nominal exchange rate}}{\text{Foreign prices}}$$

Assume that a basket of goods that costs £100 in the United Kingdom costs €125 in the Eurozone and that the international exchange rate is €1.3/£.

Expressed in euros, the real exchange rate is

$$\frac{\text{Price of UK basket in €}}{\text{Price of Eurozone basket in €}} = \frac{£100 \times 1.3}{€125} = 1.04$$

Or expressed in UK pounds, the real exchange rate is:

$$\frac{\text{Price of UK basket in £}}{\text{Price of Eurozone basket in £}} = \frac{£100}{€125 \times 0.77} = 1.04$$

If prices in the United Kingdom rose by 10% and nothing else changed, then the real exchange rate would rise by almost 10%, making the United Kingdom less competitive:

$$\frac{£110 \times 1.3}{€125} = 1.14$$

The nominal exchange rate needs to fall by almost 10% to €1.18/£ to restore the real exchange rate:

$$\frac{£110 \times 1.18}{€125} = 1.04$$

Such a change in the nominal exchange rate would represent a depreciation in the pound, improving the United Kingdom's balance of trade by reducing the cost of UK products in the Eurozone and making United Kingdom's imports from the Eurozone more expensive.

(For more, see Begg *et al.* (2011, pp.556–557) or Feenstra and Taylor (2011, pp.462–463).)

Purchasing power parity

If the real exchange rate exceeds one, the currency is said to be 'overvalued', as shown in the example in Box 8.2; when it is less than one, 'undervalued'. When the real exchange rate equals one, there is said to be purchasing power parity (PPP). In other words, there is said to be PPP when the price of a basket of goods in one country is the same as in another when expressed in a common currency. Mathematically, there is PPP when the nominal exchange rate between two currencies equals the ratio of prices in the two countries. The principle of PPP proposes that prices in trading countries tend to converge over time due to market forces. Box 8.3 explains further and provides an example.

The concept of PPP is regarded as useful because if prices are to converge, then the real exchange rate should move towards 1, and this expectation can be used to forecast future exchange rates. However, evidence suggests that in the short run real exchange rates are very variable. This is illustrated in Box 8.4. In the short run, the difference between relative price levels and exchange rates can differ by 20% or more. There are many reasons for this discrepancy: for example, not all goods are traded, there are transport costs, and it can take time for contracted prices to adjust. Convergence to PPP is very slow, at 15% a year (Feenstra & Taylor, 2011, pp.466–468; Rogoff, 1996).

Interest rate parity

In the same way that trading tends to equalise prices across countries, free movement of capital tends to equalise interest rates. With the free movement of capital, investors will seek to put their money where the return is best. If one country has a higher interest rate than another, funds will flow into the country with the higher interest rate, causing the exchange rate to appreciate. Once the exchange rate has risen so high that it is expected to depreciate sufficiently over the term of the investment to offset the gain from the higher interest rate, interest rate parity will have been reached and the capital flows will stop. So when investors consider putting their money in another currency, they must also take into account the possibility of changes in the exchange rate. For example, if an investor could earn 4% in another country and only 2% in their own country, then they will move their funds provided that they did not expect to lose their gain from the higher interest rate through a change in the exchange rate. The market will ensure that interest rate parity is quickly established. (For more, see Baldwin and Wyplosz (2012, p.363) and Begg *et al.* (2011, pp.561–562).)

Box 8.3 Purchasing power parity.

$$\text{Real exchange rate} = \frac{\text{Home prices} \times \text{international value nominal exchange rate}}{\text{Foreign prices}}$$

Setting the real exchange rate to 1 and rearranging gives

$$\text{International value nominal exchange rate} = \frac{\text{Foreign prices}}{\text{Home prices}}$$

For example, if a basket of goods costs £100 in the United Kingdom and €120 in the Eurozone, then there would be PPP if the international value nominal exchange rate of UK pounds was 1.2. This is known as the PPP exchange rate.

(For more, see Begg *et al.*, 2011, p.557.)

Box 8.4   Comparative price levels.

The table shows a selection of OECD estimates of comparative price levels (CPLs) on a monthly basis to provide measures of differences in price levels between countries. CPLs are defined as the ratios of PPPs for private final consumption expenditure to exchange rates. Each column shows the number of specified monetary units needed in each of the countries listed to buy the same representative basket of consumer goods and services. In each case, the representative basket costs a hundred units in the country whose currency is specified.

Examples of comparative price levels, September 2014

Country/currency	Germany	Greece	Netherlands	United Kingdom	United States
	EUR	EUR	EUR	GBP	USD
Germany	100	114	93	83	106
Greece	87	100	81	73	92
Netherlands	108	123	100	90	114
United Kingdom	120	137	111	100	127
United States	95	108	88	79	100

Source: based on OECD (2014b).

Comparison of prices in the United Kingdom and the United States

The column for the United Kingdom shows 79 for the United States, meaning that you would spend £79 in the United States to buy a basket of goods and services that would costs £100 in the United Kingdom. Conversely, the column headed United States shows that a basket of goods in the United States costing $100 would cost $127 in the United Kingdom. This implies that for PPP, the exchange rate should be $1.27 per £. In fact, the average daily spot price during that month was $1.63 per £ (Bank of England, 2014).

Comparison of Eurozone prices

The column for the United Kingdom shows 83 for Germany, meaning that you would spend £83 in Germany to buy a basket of goods and services that would costs £100 in the United Kingdom. Conversely, a basket of goods in Germany costing €100 would cost €120 in the United Kingdom. This implies that for PPP, the exchange rate should be €120/£. In fact, the average daily spot price during that month was €1.2678/£ (Bank of England, 2014), fairly close to the PPP exchange rate.

But for Greece, the position is quite different: you would spend £73 in Greece to buy a basket of goods and services that would cost £100 in the United Kingdom, implying a PPP exchange rate of €1.37/£. But being in the Eurozone, Greece has the same exchange rate as Germany, €1.2678/£.

While prices in Greece are clearly lower than in Germany, prices in the Netherlands are higher: a basket costing €100 in the Netherlands would cost only €93 in Germany and €81 in Greece. Despite all three countries – Germany, Greece and the Netherlands – being in the Eurozone, prices differ markedly.

Exchange rate regimes

Exchange rates are determined by the intersection of supply and demand for currencies. How that works depends on which exchange rate regime is being used. Exchange rate policy options are summarised by what has become known as 'the Trilemma'. For financial stability, a government can choose two, and only two, of the following three options:

- Fix the exchange rate.

- Set the interest rate.

- Permit free movement of capital.

If a government tries to have all three, a financial crisis ensues such as happened in the United Kingdom in 1992. The UK government tried to have a semi-fixed exchange rate – by committing the pound to the exchange rate mechanism (ERM), a precursor of the euro – and set its own interest rates and allow capital to move freely. This proved unsustainable and the United Kingdom had to leave the ERM.

Currently, in 2014, the United Kingdom, the Eurozone and the United States allow their exchange rates to float and permit free movement of capital. This, briefly, is how it works. A firm in the United Kingdom wants to import, say, a car from Germany, and the German exporter will want to be paid in euros, so the United Kingdom firm has to exchange pounds for euros, that is, to buy euros. Conversely, a German firm wanting to import, say, machinery from the United Kingdom exchanges euros for pounds, that is, buys pounds. However, as there is free movement of capital, the demand and supply of currency are not only affected by trade but also by financial flows. Investors seek the best returns globally. So if, for example, a UK investor wants to buy US treasury bonds, the investor will buy US dollars in exchange for UK pounds, increasing the demand for US dollars. Thus, the demand for a currency will be determined by those wishing to buy from the country or invest in it, and the supply by those in the country who want to buy goods from or invest abroad. Buyers and sellers are brought together in the foreign exchange market, which is 'one of the largest and most liquid markets in the world'. The market sets 'spot' prices (or 'fixes') to establish the relative value of two currencies. Forty per cent of the global foreign exchange trading takes place in London (FCA, 2014).

With a floating exchange rate, any deficit in the current account will be offset by capital movements on the financial account, as it is in the United Kingdom (see Box 8.5). If a country has a trade deficit, it can balance its books by its central bank raising interest rates to attract an inflow of capital. To summarise, with floating exchange rate and capital mobility, the country's central bank fixes its interest rate and the exchange rate is established by the market. However, in 2014, interest rates are close to zero in many countries, including the United Kingdom, the Eurozone and the United States, and have been since 2008 in order to stimulate their economies and so cannot be used as a policy instrument to manage exchange rates. (For more on these issues, see Feenstra and Taylor, 2011, pp.519–521 & 687–691.)

In the past, fixed exchange rates were more usual in Western economies. Up to the First World War and again at times in the 1920s and early 1930s, many countries were on the Gold Standard. Under the Gold Standard, the values of currencies were expressed in terms of gold. There were no restrictions on the movement of capital, and the central banks had no freedom to adjust the money supply – and thus determine their interest rates – because money had to be backed by gold.

After the Second World War, the Gold Standard was replaced by the Bretton Woods arrangements that lasted until the early 1970s. Exchange rates were fixed, although subject to

Box 8.5   The UK balance of payments.

The balance of payments account has three parts:

- Current account: exports and imports of goods and services and returns on foreign investment

- Capital account: the transfer of fixed assets, intangibles (such as patents) and certain other items

- Financial account: sales and purchases of stocks and share and other financial assets (ONS, 2014a).

By definition, under floating exchange rates, the balance of payments must balance. In the United Kingdom, the capital account is small and the deficit on the current account is offset by the surplus on the financial account. In other words, the United Kingdom imported more than it exported and paid by selling financial assets.

An important aspect to note is that the balance on the current account actually represents a small difference between two very large numbers: in 2013, the UK exports of goods and services were worth £511 billion and its imports £543 billion, both representing around a third of GDP as shown in Table 8.1. Thus, the trade balance, being the difference between these two figures, was −£32 billion, just 1.8% of GDP. The rest of the current account balance, −£40 billion, was accounted for by items such as net investment income.

The United Kingdom's balance of payments for 2013

		£ million
Current balance		
Exports of goods and services	511 275	
Imports of goods and services	543 375	
Balance of trade		−32 100
Other changes		−40 295
Current account		−72 395
Capital balance		530
Financial account		62 592
Net errors and omissions		9 273
Total		0

Source: from ONS (2014b).

occasional revaluations or devaluations. If exchange rates are fixed and free movement of capital is allowed, the country's interest rate will be determined by the market as investors seek the best returns globally. Because countries wanted fixed exchange rates and to be able to set their own interest rates, under the Bretton Woods arrangements, capital mobility was severely restricted. Central banks had to buy or sell their currency to ensure that the markets cleared.

While the currency of the Eurozone as a whole floats, the situation of individual states in the Eurozone is different because their exchange rate is fixed. A Eurozone country has to accept

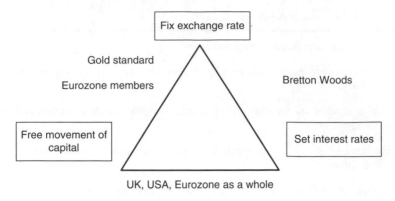

Figure 8.1   The Trilemma.

whatever value is established in the market by the floating euro, and this is determined by what is happening in all the other Eurozone countries. The European Central Bank sets the interest rate for the Eurozone as a whole and capital can flow freely. Eurozone countries are therefore left with only fiscal policy – public spending and taxation – to manage their economies.

The three options and the various systems that have been used are summarised in Figure 8.1. (For more on exchange rate regimes and the Trilemma, see Begg *et al.* (2011, Chapter 29) and Feenstra and Taylor (2011, pp.540–544), and for specific reference to the Eurozone, see Baldwin and Wyplosz (2012, pp.361–363 & 380–381).)

The experience of the British pound, the US dollar and the euro

Floating exchange rates fluctuate, especially in the short term, when the underlying fundamentals have little influence (Cheung *et al.*, 2004; Feenstra & Taylor, 2011, pp.530). Figure 8.2 shows how the exchange rates between the UK pounds and the euro and the US dollar, respectively, have fluctuated. The top panel shows how the average annual spot rates have fluctuated since 1999:

- The €/£ exchange rate has fallen from around 1.6 to around 1.2. This drop is said to be a depreciation of the pound against the euro (but an appreciation of the euro) and means that UK goods are cheaper in the Eurozone, but Eurozone goods – and holidays – are more expensive for UK residents.

- The US$/£ exchange rate has varied between 1.44 and 2.00.

However, there is considerable fluctuation within years too, as shown in the bottom panel of Figure 8.2: in 2013, the euro varied from 5% above to 3% below the annual average, while the US dollar exchange rate varied from 5% above to 6% below the annual average.

As previously explained, an effective exchange rate is based on a weighted basket of currencies. As calculated by the Bank of England, the United Kingdom's effective exchange rate fell by about a fifth between 2007 and 2013, reflecting the fall in the UK pound against the euro and US dollar shown in the top panel of Figure 8.2. (The euro currently has a weight of 46.2, and the US dollar 17.5 out of a total of 100.) Effective exchange rates for the pound, euro and US dollar are illustrated in Figure 8.3. The effective rates for both the UK pound and the US dollar have fallen, while that for the euro has increased.

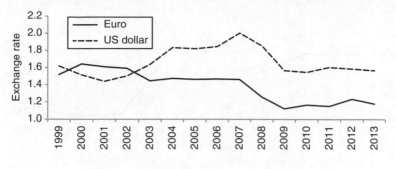

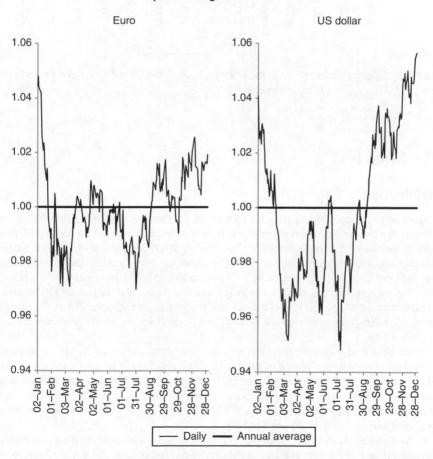

Figure 8.2   Fluctuations in the exchange rates of UK pounds. Source: from Bank of England (2014).

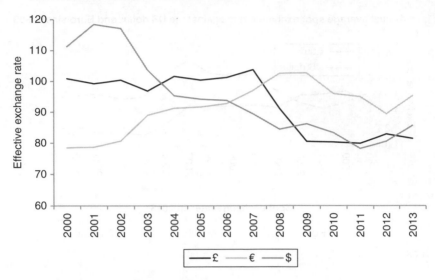

Figure 8.3   Effective exchange rates: the United Kingdom, the United States and Eurozone, 2000–2013. Source: from Bank of England (2014).

8.2   Models

Introduction

All agent-based macroeconomic models of which we are aware have assumed that the economy is closed – that is there is no international trade. For example, this is the case for both the EURACE model encompassing the whole of the EU (Dawid *et al.*, 2012) and Salle *et al.*'s (2013) NetLogo macroeconomic model. Agent-based modelling has, however, been used to explore certain aspects of international trade. For instance, Gulden (2013) produced a NetLogo model of two economies interacting, focussing on comparative advantage, and De Grauwe and Kaltwasser (2012) used an agent-based model to simulate the behaviour of individual foreign exchange traders. De Grauwe's work (2012 & 2014) has suggested that instability and even chaos are readily generated in models of exchange rates.

Yet textbook analysis mostly focusses on comparative statics, assuming the system snaps from one equilibrium to another. (See, e.g. Begg *et al.* (2011, pp.571–573) and Feenstra and Taylor (2011, pp.665–687).) The arguments presented are qualitative rather than quantitative, telling 'stories'. For example, the 'story' told about a country with a fixed exchange rate, no capital mobility and a balance of trade deficit goes like this: raise interest rates to reduce output and imports and thus restore the balance of trade.

We have chosen to take a very simple approach to explore some of the underlying dynamics. We focus on the long-term fundamentals, rather than day-to-day fluctuations. Begg *et al.* (2011, pp.567) asserted that, in the long run, the current account determines exchange rates. We take an even narrower view and focus on the balance of trade. For simplicity, we do not include interest rates or capital flows in our model because, as noted previously, interest rates in the developed countries are currently being used to stimulate economic activity rather than manage the exchange rates.

In most agent-based models, time is measured in specific periods, such as quarters or years. In this model, the dynamic processes take place in stages. No time period is specified.

Assumptions

There are just two agents, one representing the Home country and the other the rest of the world, or 'World' for short. The exchange rate therefore represents the effective exchange rate as described earlier. Following the convention used earlier in the chapter, the exchange rate means the number of units of World currency exchanged for each unit of Home currency.

In this model, the price of exports is determined by prices in the Home country, and prices in the Home country do not affect the overall price level in the World. This is a simplifying assumption because the markets for some products are global and the prices are not set by a single country. Oil is the obvious example: what can happen to the exchange rate of oil-producing countries when the oil price falls was illustrated by the dramatic fall of the Russian rouble in 2014?

The Home country can be set to represent one of five countries:

- The United Kingdom, which is a fairly open economy with a floating exchange rate

- The United States, which also has a floating exchange rate but is a relatively closed economy

- A 'strong' Eurozone country, based on Germany, which is a fairly open economy with a fixed exchange rate and a balance of trade surplus

- A 'weak' Eurozone country, based on Greece, which has a similar degree of openness to the United Kingdom but a larger negative trade balance (as a proportion of GDP) and a fixed exchange rate

- An 'open' Eurozone country, based on the Netherlands, which has a balance of trade surplus and a fixed exchange rate.

The assumptions and initial calculated values are set out in Table 8.2. Box 8.6 explains how initial exchange rates are calculated from these data. For the Eurozone countries, the exchange rate is calculated for the Eurozone as a whole in the same way as it is for the United Kingdom and United States with their floating exchange rates. This rate is then applied to the three Eurozone countries irrespective of their individual circumstances.

Four scenarios are specified:

- Inflation (or deflation)

- The effect of a depreciation (or appreciation)

- An exogenous change in demand for exports

- A change in fiscal policy

The modeller can choose the size of the change and the import and the export price elasticities. All the results quoted in the following are based on changes of 10% and price elasticities of −1. There is no stochastic element in this model. It is purely deterministic and so there is no need for multiple runs.

Table 8.2   Model assumptions and initial values.

	United Kingdom	United States	Eurozone	Eurozone countries		
				Strong	Weak	Open
Exchange rate regime	Floating	Floating	Floating	Fixed	Fixed	Fixed
Output (Y)	100	100	100	100	100	100
Export share (X)[a]	32	14	46	52	27	85
Import share (M)[a]	34	17	43	46	32	80
Government spending (G)	50	50	50	50	50	50
Private domestic demand ($(C+I)$)[b]	52	63	n.a.	44	55	45
Home-produced prices[c]	1.2	0.8	n.a.	1.0	0.8	1.1
Home prices index[d]	1.18	0.78	n.a.	1.03	0.87	1.08
Exchange rate[e]	0.885	1.518	0.935	0.935	0.935	0.935
Real exchange rate	1.040	1.178	n.a.	0.965	0.828	1.006
Balance of trade	−0.2	0	n.a.	2.8	−12.6	7.9

n.a., not applicable.
[a] Based on Table 8.1.
[b] Calculated on the standard national accounting convention: $Y = (C+I) + G + (X-M)$ where Y, GDP; C, consumption; I, investment; G, government; X, exports; and M, imports.
[c] Based on Box 8.4. World prices standardised to 1.
[d] Weighted average of home price of imports and prices of home-produced output.
[e] Calculated as shown in Box 8.6.

Inflation

We start by examining what happens if a country's rate of inflation is higher than that of its trading partners. If Home prices rise faster than World prices, the impact on trade will depend on whether the exchange rate is floating or fixed.

If it is floating and there is no 'stickiness' in the adjustment of prices or the nominal exchange rate, the exchange rate will depreciate so that the World price of exports does not change. But this depreciation will increase the price of imports at Home. The effect on the balance of trade and prices at Home will depend on the price elasticity of imports. Assuming it is −1, so that expenditure remains the same despite the price rise, then the quantity of imports will fall, the balance of trade will improve, and output will rise. So for floating exchange rates:

- Stage 1: Export prices and exchange rate adjust.

- Stage 2: Import prices rise.

For a worked example based on the United Kingdom, see Box 8.7.

However, in a Eurozone country, the exchange rate will not adjust in response to inflation in an individual country. Instead, the increase in export prices is passed on to the rest of the world and results in a reduction in demand. So for Eurozone countries:

- Stage 1: Export prices rise.

- Stage 2: Export volumes fall.

Box 8.6 Determination of exchange rates in the model.

Nominal exchange rate

Demand for Home's currency = value of Home's exports:

$$= Q_H^X \times P_H^X$$

where Q_H^X = volume of Home's exports and P_H^X = price of Home's exports.

Supply of Home's currency = value of Home's imports:

$$= Q_H^M \times P_H^M$$

where Q_H^M = volume of Home's imports and P_H^M = price of Home's imports.

But the price of imports depends on the exchange rate and world prices, that is,

$$P_H^M = \frac{P_W}{E_{W/H}}$$

where P_W = world prices and $E_{W/H}$ is the nominal exchange rate expressed as number of units of world currency exchanged for one unit of Home currency.

To balance, $Q_H^X \times P_H^X = Q_H^M \times \dfrac{P_W}{E_{W/H}}$.

So

$$E_{W/H} = \frac{Q_H^M \times P_W}{Q_H^X \times P_H^X} = \frac{\text{value of Home's imports at World prices}}{\text{value of Home's exports at Home prices}}$$

Example: The United Kingdom (from Table 8.2)

- Volume of imports: $Q_H^M = 34$

- World prices: $P_W = 1$

- Volume of exports: $Q_H^X = 32$

- Home prices: $P_H^X = P_H = 1.2$ (where P_H = Home domestic prices)

Nominal exchange rate

$$E_{W/H} = \frac{Q_H^M \times P_W}{Q_H^X \times P_H^X} = \frac{34 \times 1}{32 \times 1.2} = 0.885$$

Real exchange rate

The price level will be

$$\big(\text{Price of imports} \times \text{import share}\big) + \big(\text{price of home produced} \times (1 - \text{import share})\big)$$

$$= \left(\frac{1}{0.885} \times 0.34\right) + \big(1.2 \times 0.66\big) = 1.18$$

So the real exchange rate is

$$\frac{\text{Price of Home basket in World currency}}{\text{Price of World basket in World currency}} = \frac{P_H \times E_{W/H}}{P_W} = \frac{1.18 \times 0.885}{1.00} = 1.04$$

UK balance of trade

- Imports: $Q_H^M \times \left(P_W \times \dfrac{1}{E_{W/H}}\right) = 34 \times \left(1 \times \dfrac{1}{0.885}\right) = 38.4$

- Exports: $Q_H^X \times P_H^X = 32 \times 1.2 = 38.4$

Balance = exports − imports = 38.4 − 38.4 = 0

Box 8.7   Effect of inflation with floating exchange rate.

Initial position

Taking the example from Box 8.6 based on the United Kingdom:

- Volume of imports: $Q_H^M = 34$

- World prices: $P_W = 1$

- Volume of exports: $Q_H^X = 32$

- Home prices: $P_H^X = P_H = 1.2$ (where P_H = Home prices)

Nominal exchange rate:

$$E_{W/H} = \frac{Q_H^M \times P_W}{Q_H^X \times P_H^X} = \frac{34 \times 1}{32 \times 1.2} = 0.885$$

The world price of Home's exports is

$$P_H^X \times E_{W/H} = 1.2 \times 0.885 = 1.06$$

And so the price of imports at Home is

$$P_H^M = \frac{P_W}{E_{W/H}} = \frac{1}{0.885} = 1.13$$

Prices rise and exchange rate falls...

If Home prices rise by 10% and export prices rise by 10%, then

$$P_H^X = P_H = 1.2 \times 1.1 = 1.32$$

and if all are passed through and the nominal exchange rate adjusts fully, then

$$E_{W/H} = \frac{Q_H^M \times P_W}{Q_H^X \times P_H^X} = \frac{34 \times 1}{32 \times 1.32} = 0.805$$

This is a depreciation that keeps the world price of Home's exports the same as previously:

$$P_H^X \times E_{W/H} = 1.32 \times 0.805 = 1.06$$

The volume of sales to the World is therefore not affected, and so earnings from exports will rise in terms of the Home country's currency: $Q_H^X \times P_H^X = 32 \times 1.32 = 42.24$.

...raising import prices

But imports will now cost 10% more at Home:

$$P_H^M = \frac{P_W}{E_{W/H}} = \frac{1}{0.805} = 1.242$$

(*Continued*)

Box 8.7   (*Continued*)

What happens to the balance of trade depends on how Home's demand for imports changes as a result of this price rise. If the price elasticity for imports is −1, then the Home country's volume of imports would fall to 90% of what it was previously, and the cost of imports becomes

$$Q_H^M \times \frac{P_W}{E_{W/H}} = (34 \times 0.90) \times \left(\frac{1}{0.805}\right) = 38.01$$

And the balance of trade would be +4.2.

...raising the real exchange rate
The price level will rise from 1.2 to 1.29:

$$(\text{Price of imports} \times \text{import share}) + (\text{price of home proded} \times (1 - \text{import share}))$$
$$= (1.13 \times 1.1 \times 0.34) + (1.2 \times 1.1 \times 0.66) = 1.29.$$

And so the real exchange rate is restored to 1.04:

$$\frac{\text{Price of Home basket in World currency}}{\text{Price of World basket in World currency}} = \frac{P_H \times E_{W/H}}{P_W} = \frac{1.29 \times 0.805}{1.00} = 1.04$$

...and, assuming nothing else changes, raising GDP because imports fall

$$Y = D + G + (X - M) = 52 + 50 + 32 - 30.6 = 103.4$$

(See note (b) to Table 8.2.)

The results for all five countries are shown in Table 8.3. Comparing the experiences of the floating and Eurozone countries, there are two consistent differences:

- In the countries with floating rates, the nominal exchange rates fall so that the real exchange rates are unchanged. In the Eurozone countries, there is no change in the nominal exchange rates and the real exchange rates rise, implying they are less competitive.

- GDP rises in the countries with floating exchange rates because the volume of exports is maintained by the drop in the nominal exchange rate, which also reduces imports. However, in the Eurozone countries, output falls as exports fall and as there is no change in imports. (Note b to Table 8.2 explains.) Eventually, the fall in exports will, in turn, reduce imports and the inflationary pressures, but a fuller model is needed to accommodate these effects. Of course, if the inflation is endemic across the Eurozone, the exchange rate will change in a similar way as it has for the United Kingdom and United States.

Within the Eurozone, experience varies according to the extent the economy depends on exports: the higher the export share, the greater the drop in output and the greater the rise in prices.

Figure 8.4 illustrates the dynamics for the United Kingdom.

This analysis assumes that full adjustment happens quickly. In practice, that may not be the case and this is explored further in the next scenario.

Table 8.3 Results: Inflation scenario – a 10% increase in prices.

Assumptions

| Import price elasticity | −1 |
| Export price elasticity | −1 |

	United Kingdom	United States	Eurozone countries		
			Strong	**Weak**	**Open**
Balance of trade					
Initial	−0.2	0	2.8	−12.6	7.9
Final	4.2	1.2	8.0	−10.5	17.3
% change in					
Exchange rate	−9	−9	0	0	0
Real exchange rate	0	0	5	6	2
Prices	10.0	10.0	5.2	6.2	2.0
Output[a]	3.4	1.7	−5.2	−2.7	−8.4

[a] Assuming nothing else changes.

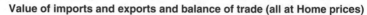

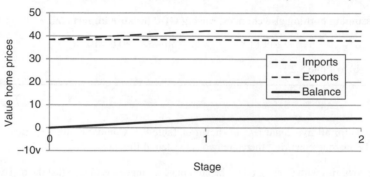

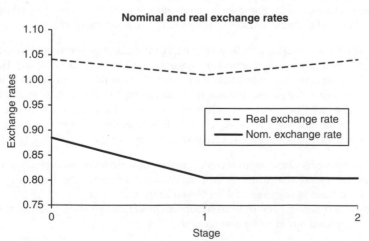

Figure 8.4 Results: dynamics of the effect of a 10% increase in prices in the United Kingdom. (Based on data in Table 8.3).

Depreciation

Under fixed exchange rates, step depreciations – often called devaluations – are sometimes allowed to improve the balance of trade by reducing the price of exports, thus boosting demand for them. In the United Kingdom, this happened most notably in 1967, under the Bretton Woods exchange rate regime. The Prime Minister Harold Wilson told the nation on television:

> From now on the pound abroad is worth 14 per cent or so less in terms of other currencies. That doesn't mean of course that the pound here in Britain, in your pocket or purse or bank, has been devalued.

Nevertheless, if the price of imports rises, demand for imports will fall. Back in 1967, this was to be avoided by people 'buying British' and the government controlling prices and incomes. That was the theory.

But in practice, the story is not quite so straightforward. The initial change in the trade balance may be the opposite to that desired, and an effect emerges that is known as the J-curve. It arises because there are time lags or prices are 'sticky' or because the changes are simply not passed on at all. For instance, import prices may not change by as much as the change in the exchange rate. For example, a 2005 study found that a 10% depreciation resulted in a 4% rise in retail prices over 1 year. This may be due to existing contracts, but it may also be due to the fact that a portion of the price of an imported good will reflect costs incurred between the port at which it arrives and the shop at which it is sold. Likewise, the drop in export prices may not be passed on in full. Evidence suggests some of the 14% devaluation of the UK pound in 1967 allowed exporters to increase their profit margin rather than reduce prices. If the quantities of imports and exports respond slowly to the change in the exchange rate, the trade deficit may actually worsen because the demand for exports does not rise and the demand for imports does not fall (Begg *et al.*, 2011, pp.580–581; Feenstra & Taylor, 2011, pp.660).

To model this, we assume the adjustment takes place in three stages:

- Stage 1: Import prices rise by half the amount expected as a result of the fall in the exchange rate, but there are no other changes. This rise in price with no fall in demand results in the trade balance worsening.

- Stage 2: Export prices rise and export volumes adjust but to only half the extent indicated by the price elasticity. The demand for imports falls in response to the price rise in Stage 1. The trade balance improves.

- Stage 3: Import prices rise to fully reflect the depreciation in the exchange rate, and the demand for imports falls. The demand for exports adjusts fully; and the trade balance now shows the full benefit of the depreciation.

Box 8.8 shows the results for the weak Eurozone country demonstrating the J-curve. The rise in prices offsets the fall in the exchange rate, so the real exchange rate is unchanged, but the demand for imports is boosted and the balance of trade improves.

Exogenous drop in demand for exports

In the inflation scenario, we saw how demand for exports could drop as a result of prices in the Home country rising. But the demand for a country's exports may also drop for all sorts of other reasons: for instance, tastes may change or another country may become more competitive and

Box 8.8   Results: Effect of a 10% depreciation on the weak Eurozone country.

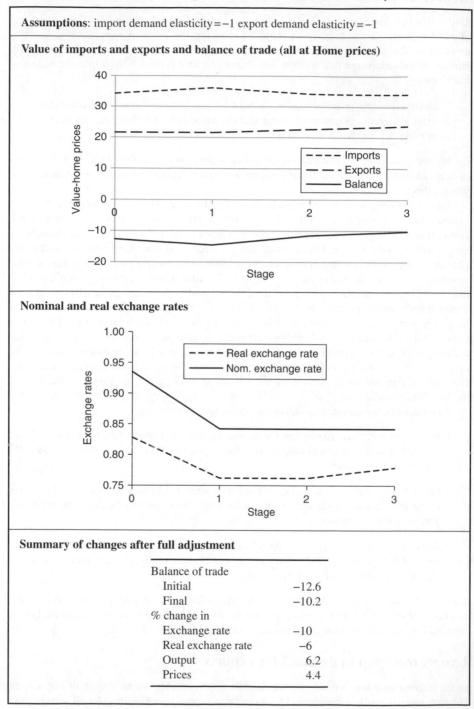

Assumptions: import demand elasticity $=-1$ export demand elasticity $=-1$

Value of imports and exports and balance of trade (all at Home prices)

Nominal and real exchange rates

Summary of changes after full adjustment

Balance of trade	
Initial	−12.6
Final	−10.2
% change in	
Exchange rate	−10
Real exchange rate	−6
Output	6.2
Prices	4.4

Table 8.4   Results: Effect of exogenous 10% drop in demand.

Assumptions		
Import price elasticity	−1	
Export price elasticity	−1	
	United Kingdom	**United States**
Balance of trade		
Initial	−0.2	0
Final	−7.3	−2.1
% change in		
Exchange rate	11	11
Real exchange rate	7	10
Prices	−3.3	−1.4
Output[a]	−10.0	−4.5

[a] Assuming nothing else changes.

gain market share. Here, we examine the effect of an exogenous drop in the demand for the Home country's exports.

If there is an exogenous drop in the demand for exports and the exchange rate is fixed, the result is that the balance of trade deteriorates, affecting output. That will in turn reduce the demand for imports, which will help to restore output and the balance of trade. It also depends on how the country's policy makers react; for example, do they reduce taxation to stimulate home demand? A full macroeconomic model is needed to examine these issues.

Here, we confine our examination to countries with a floating exchange rate. There are three stages:

- Stage 1: There is an exogenous drop in the demand for exports. Nothing else changes and the balance of trade worsens.

- Stage 2: The floating exchange rate adjusts. The demand for the Home currency falls because of the reduction in exports, but the Home country's demand for World currency has not changed. As a result, the exchange rate rises. (This may seem counter-intuitive. Demand for the Home currency has fallen, and therefore, so surely should its price? However, the exchange rate is expressed as the amount of World currency per unit of Home currency. If it were expressed as the amount of Home currency per unit of World currency, it would have fallen as the World wants less of Home's currency.) This brings the balance of trade back into balance.

- Stage 3: The rise in the exchange rate reduces the cost of imports, which boosts demand for them. This causes the balance of trade to move into deficit again.

Table 8.4 shows results for both the United Kingdom and United States; and Figure 8.5 illustrates the dynamics for the United Kingdom. In practice, these changes are likely to happen simultaneously to some extent, and the changes in the exchange rate will be ameliorated by capital flows.

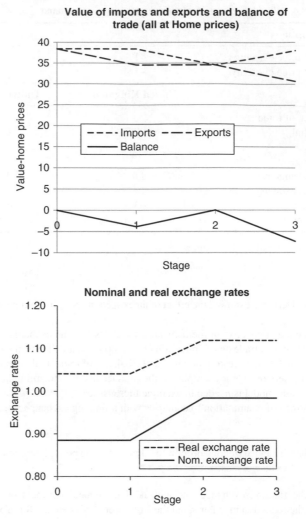

Figure 8.5   Results: dynamics of effect of exogenous 10% drop in demand in the United Kingdom. (Based on data in Table 8.4).

Fiscal change

We noted in the introduction that the only policy lever available to Eurozone countries was fiscal policy and that at present even in countries with floating exchange rates, the use of monetary policy is limited. So in this last scenario, we examine the possible impact of fiscal policy.

The importance of the government in the economy will determine the impact of changes in fiscal policy: the bigger the government's share, the larger the impact. OECD (2013) data show that in 2011 general government expenditure was about 50% of GDP in the United Kingdom, Germany, the Netherlands and Greece but nearer 40% in the United States. The impact on output is calculated as the product of the percentage fiscal change and the government expenditure as a percentage of GDP. It is assumed that any change in government expenditure does not affect

Table 8.5   Results: Fiscal policy scenario – 10% cut in government expenditure.

Assumptions		
Import price elasticity	−1	
Export price elasticity	−1	

	United Kingdom	United States
Balance of trade		
Initial	−0.2	0
Final	3.9	0.9
% change in		
Exchange rate	−5	−4
Real exchange rate	−3	−3
Prices	1.7	0.6
Output[a]	0	−2.1

[a]Assuming no other changes.

taxation; in other words, it only affects the government's borrowing requirement. So, for example, if there is a 10% reduction in government expenditure and government expenditure accounts for half of GDP, then output falls by 5%. It is assumed that the marginal propensity to import is the same as the average and that the government's propensity to import is the same for the country as a whole, that is, the initial share of imports. So, for example, if the share of imports were about one third, a 5% drop in output would reduce imports by 1.6% of output. For countries with a fixed exchange rate, that is the end of the first round effect: the cut in government expenditure would reduce demand for imports.

But for countries with floating rates, the change in imports will change the exchange rate, which will in turn change the prices of imports and exports and thus the demand for them. To sum up:

- Stage 1: The change in government expenditure changes output, which changes the demand for imports and the floating exchange rate.

- Stage 2: The change in the exchange rate will affect the demand for imports and exports.

Table 8.5 shows a set of results for the two countries with floating rates for a 10% cut in government expenditure: the balance of trade improves; and Figure 8.6 illustrates the dynamics for the United Kingdom.

8.3   Discussion

The theory of international trade is well developed but relies largely on comparative statics and qualitative descriptions. As this chapter has indicated, international trade is difficult to model, and this no doubt explains why modellers tend to confine themselves to closed economies. There also appears to be a dearth of data on reactions to shocks to trade and the impact of policy changes on trade.

So the model produced has been designed to do no more than allow an exploration of the different exchange rate regimes in countries with different circumstances. In that sense, it could be said to allow for heterogeneity. It uses simple dynamic processes and there are no stochastic

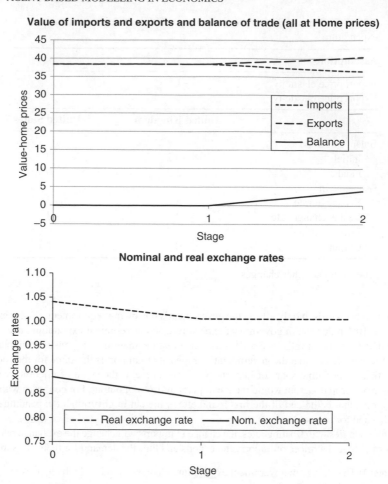

Figure 8.6   Results: dynamics of the effect of a 10% cut in taxes in the United Kingdom. (Based on data in Table 8.5).

variations. The interactions are between the Home country and the rest of the world. But the key feature is the dynamics. Of course, other assumptions could have been made about the dynamic processes. But the important message is that this way of modelling does provide a useful way to explore these processes. Furthermore, even this simple model highlights the difference between a country with a floating exchange rate and one belonging to the Eurozone, illustrating the problems a Eurozone country faces if its circumstances deviate from the majority of other Eurozone countries.

It also demonstrates just how difficult it is to model an open economy because there are so many interactions between different parts of the economy and so many uncertainties about the timing of the resulting changes. Our simple and limited model may provide the basis for more sophisticated work, and there are many suggestions as to what might be done in the 'Things to try' section. Those wishing to take this further would do well to consult de Grauwe's (2014) *Exchange Rates and Global Financial Policies.*

Appendix 8.A   How to do it

International trade model

Purpose: To permit the exploration of the dynamics underlying changes in exchange rates and the balance of trade.

Entities: Two agents representing countries: Home and rest of the World. There are five types of Home country.

Stochastic processes: None.

Box 8.A.1   Pseudo-code for the International trade model.

Create world 41×41.
Create 2 breeds – Home and World – and create one agent of each.

Set initial conditions

Specify the data for each country and the Eurozone (as shown in Table 8.2).

Calculate the exchange rates for the United Kingdom, United States and Eurozone as a whole (as illustrated in Box 8.8).

Allocate the Eurozone exchange rate to the Eurozone countries.

Calculate the real exchange rate, price index and trade balance.

For the inflation scenario

For floating rates:

Stage 1: Export prices and exchange rate adjust (as illustrated in Box 8.7).

Stage 2: Import prices rise.

For Eurozone rates:

Stage 1: Export prices rise.

Stage 2: Export volumes fall.

Recalculate the price index, output, real exchange rate and balance of trade.

For the depreciation scenario

Stage 1: Import prices partly change.

Stage 2: Export prices and volumes change.

Stage 3: Full adjustment.

For the exogenous export change scenario

Stage 1: Volume of exports changes.

Stage 2: Exchange rate changes: no volume changes.

Stage 3: Volumes change.

For the fiscal policy scenario

Stage 1: Volume of imports and exchange rate change.

Stage 2: Demand for imports and exports changes.

Output stage-by-stage results to the screen and plot the graphs.
    At the end print, summary information and the plots to a csv file.

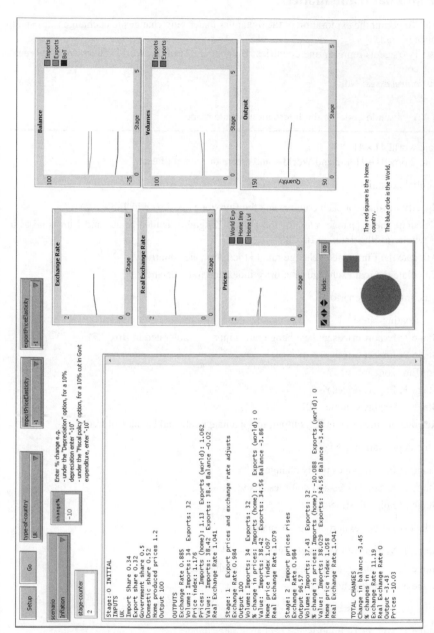

Figure 8.A.1   Screenshot for the International Trade model.

Initialisation: Select type of country, the scenario to be investigated, the percentage change and import and export price elasticities.

Output: Data on balance of trade and its components, exchange rate, prices and total output. This is shown on-screen and plotted, with the data shown sent to a csv file.

The pseudo-code is in Box 8.A.1 and a screen shot in Figure 8.A.1. For the full code, see the website: *Chapter 8 – International Trade Model.*

Things to try using the International Trade model

Explore the effect on the different types of changes on different countries, with different import and export price elasticities.

Advanced – requiring amending the program:

- Amend the characteristics of the countries.

- Extend the model to take into account financial transactions and monetary policy.

- Change the dynamics, adding more stages, for example, to allow prices to be affected by the output gap; see how the exchange rate might move towards PPP.

- Allow some export prices to be determined by global markets.

References

Baldwin, R.E. & Wyplosz, C. (2012) *The Economics of European Integration*. Fourth Edition. Maidenhead: McGraw-Hill Education.

Bank of England (2014) *Statistical interactive database* [Online]. Available at: http://www.bankofengland. co.uk. For effective exchange rates http://www.bankofengland.co.uk/statistics/pages/iadb/notesiadb/ Effective_exc.aspx [Accessed 16 November 2014].

Begg, D., Vernasca, G., Fischer, S. & Dornbusch, R. (2011) *Economics*. Tenth Edition. London: McGraw-Hill Higher Education.

Cheung, Y.-W., Chinn, M.D. & Marsh, I.W. (2004) How do UK-based foreign exchange dealers think their market operates? *International Journal of Finance and Economics*, 9, pp.289–306.

Dawid, H., Gemkow, S., Harting, P., van der Hoog, S. & Neugart, M. (2012) *The Eurace@Unibi model: An agent-based macroeconomic model for economic policy analysis* [Online]. Available at: http://www.wiwi. uni-bielefeld.de/lehrbereiche/vwl/etace/Eurace_Unibi/ [Accessed 3 February 2015].

De Grauwe, P. (2014) *Exchange Rates and Global Financial Policies*. Singapore: World Scientific Publishing [Online]. Available at: http://www.worldscientific.com/worldscibooks/10.1142/8832 [Accessed 5 February 2015].

De Grauwe, P. & Kaltwasser, P. (2012) Animal spirits in the foreign exchange market. *Economic Dynamics & Control*, 36, pp.1176–1192.

Diamond, J. (2012) *The World Until Yesterday*. London: Penguin.

Financial Conduct Authority CA (2014) *FCA fines five banks £1.1 billion for FX failings and announces industry-wide remediation programme*, London [Online]. Available at: http://www.fca.org.uk/news/ fca-fines-five-banks-for-fx-failings [Accessed 3 January 2015].

Feenstra, R.C. & Taylor, A.M. (2011) *International Economics*. Second Edition. New York: Worth.

Gulden, T.R. (2013) Agent-based modeling as a tool for trade and development theory. *Journal of Artificial Societies and Social Simulation*, 16(2) [Online]. Available at: http://jasss.soc.surrey.ac.uk/16/2/1.html [Accessed 12 October 2014].

Organisation for Economic Co-operation and Development (OECD) (2013) Total General Government Expenditure. In *National Accounts at a Glance 2013*. Paris: OECD Publishing [Online]. Available at: http://www.oecd-ilibrary.org/economics/national-accounts-at-a-glance-2013/total-general-government-expenditure_na_glance-2013-table55-en [Accessed 28 November 2014].

Organisation for Economic Co-operation and Development (OECD) (2014a) Share of international trade in GDP in OECD. In *OECD Factbook 2014: Economic, Environmental and Social Statistics*. Paris: OECD Publishing [Online]. Available at: http://www.oecd-ilibrary.org/economics/oecd-factbook-2014. factbook-2014-en [Accessed 14 October 2014].

Organisation for Economic Co-operation and Development (OECD) (2014b) *Monthly comparative price levels* [Online]. Available at: https://stats.oecd.org/Index.aspx?DataSetCode=CPLinOECD.Stat http:// stats.oecd.org/ [Accessed 9 November 2014].

Office for National Statistics (ONS) (2014a) *An introduction to the United Kingdom balance of payments* [Online]. Available at: www.ons.gov.uk [Accessed 14 October 2014].

Office for National Statistics (ONS) (2014b) *Statistical bulletin: Balance of payments, Q2 2014*. [Online]. Available at: www.ons.gov.uk [Accessed 28 November 2014].

Rogoff, K. (1996) The purchasing power parity puzzle. *Journal of Economic Literature*, 34(2), pp.647–668.

Salle, I., Yıldızoğlu, M. & Sénégas, M.-A. (2013) Inflation targeting in a learning economy: An ABM perspective. *Economic Modelling*, 34, pp.114–128.

9

Banking

9.1 Introduction

Banks are part of almost everyone's lives in the United Kingdom: people use banks for everyday transactions, to hold their savings and to lend them money as indicated by the stylised facts in Box 9.1. Banking is based on a powerful mechanism, fractional reserve banking, which is the focus of this chapter.

Fractional reserve banking

Fractional reserve banking allows banks to make money or, rather, create credit. Banks do this by 'exploiting the fact that money left on deposit could profitably be lent out to borrowers' (Ferguson, 2008, p.49). This is not new. It can be traced back to the founding of the Swedish Riksbank in 1656 and was described by Adam Smith in the eighteenth century (1776/1861, Book II, Chapter II).

Fractional reserve banking works like this. The bank needs to hold a percentage of the sum deposited with it to meet day-to-day demand for cash withdrawals. This percentage is called the reserve ratio. If the reserve ratio is 10%, then the bank can lend out 90% of its deposits. So if a bank takes in £1000, then it is free to lend out £900. This means that there is now £1900. The recipient of the loan uses that £900 to buy something. The money is then passed to a retailer, who puts it in the bank. The bank then has another £900 deposited and can lend out a further £810 (being 90% of £900). The total money in circulation is now £2710 (being £1000 plus £900 plus £810). A fourth round adds a further £729, bringing the total to £3439. And so it continues, with less being lent out at each round. After about 50 rounds, there is less than £5 to lend out. But by then, the original £1000 has grown to almost £10 000. The bank deposit multiplier, which records the ratio of the total loaned out to the initial loan, is 10. This is illustrated in the figures in the top row of Box 9.2, with the mathematics in the bottom row. To sum up, as a result of fractional

Agent-Based Modelling in Economics, First Edition. Lynne Hamill and Nigel Gilbert.
© 2016 John Wiley & Sons, Ltd. Published 2016 by John Wiley & Sons, Ltd.

Box 9.1   Stylised facts about borrowing, savings and banking by households in Great Britain.

Almost all households have a bank account.
Only 2% of adults 'lived in households without access to a current or basic bank account, or savings account' in 2008/2009 (HM Treasury, 2010).

The distribution of savings is highly skewed:

- A third of households had no savings at all.

- 40% had savings of less than £10000.

- About 20 had savings of £20000 or more.

(Data for 2010–2011: ONS, 2012, pp.37–38)

Debt (in 2008/2010)

- A quarter of households had a mortgage on their main residence, on average £92000 (ONS, 2011, p.18).

- Half of households had non-property related debt: on average £7000 (ONS, 2012, pp.13–15).

---

reserve banking with a reserve ratio of 10%, an initial £1000 can be increased to £10000 (assuming that there is a demand for these loans). (For more on this, see, e.g. Begg *et al.*, 2011, p.424.)

However, this standard textbook calculation takes no account of partial repayments of the loan before the end of the term, as is common with mortgages, for example (Mallet, 2011). If part of the loan is repaid each month, then those repayments can be lent out again. The dynamics are then quite different. For example, if a loan is made for 3 years, or 36 months, and there is no interest, 1/36 of the loan will be repaid every month. To illustrate the effect of this on the bank deposit multiplier, let us go back to the example previously and assume that each round takes 1 month. The bank lends out £900 in Month 1. In Month 2, the borrower spends the loan, and so the £900 is deposited back in the bank. But the borrower repays £25. This means that in Month 2, the bank not only has £810 to lend out, as described earlier in the textbook example, but also the £25 repaid; so the bank can lend £835. The next month, this £835 is deposited, and so the bank can lend 90% of £835, that is, £751. In addition, it receives another £25 repaid from the first loan of £900 and £23 from the second loan of £835. So the bank can lend out £799 instead of just £729 in the textbook example. And this continues: the figures for the first year are shown in Table 9.1.

The original money is being repaid and lent out again and again and again. The repayments made each month look small, but their cumulative effect is significant. Instead of the process becoming exhausted after 50 months with no new money being loaned out, now after 4 months, the amount of new loans starts to increase. The total lent out reaches almost £10000 after 11 months and continues to rise. And this means that the bank deposit multiplier can, if there are no other constraints, rise well above the 10 in the textbook version and continue rising. As Figure 9.1 shows, after about 2½ years, the multiplier has risen to 100.

Obviously, a short-term loan is repaid faster than with a long-term loan. Many bank loans will be for longer than the 3 years assumed, and so the compounding effect of repayments will be

Box 9.2 The bank deposit multiplier.

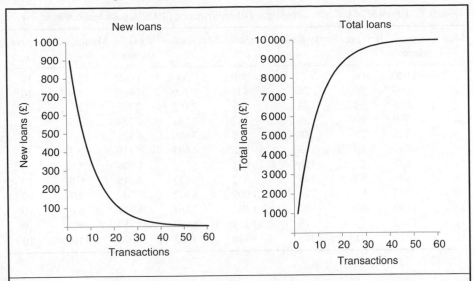

Assume the banking system has deposits, D_0, and a reserve ratio of ρ, then it will loan, l_1,

$$l_1 = (1-\rho) D_0 \tag{9.1}$$

This results in an increase in deposits by the amount lent so the new deposits total

$$D_1 = l_1 + D_0 = (1-\rho) D_0 + D_0 = (1+(1-\rho)) D_0 \tag{9.2}$$

The next round, it can lend

$$\begin{aligned} l_2 &= (1-\rho) D_1 = (1-\rho) \left[1 + (1-\rho) \right] D_0 \\ &= \left[1 + (1-\rho) + (1-\rho)^2 \right] D_0 \end{aligned} \tag{9.3}$$

and so on. The total loans, L, over t periods is given by

$$L = \sum_{i=0}^{t} l_i = \sum_{i=0}^{t} (1-\rho)^i D_0 \tag{9.4}$$

This is a geometric series and so in the limit as $t \to \infty$, total loans, L, are

$$L = \frac{D_0}{\rho} \tag{9.5}$$

The multiplier, M, the ratio of total loans, L, to original deposits, D_0, is given by

$$M = \frac{L}{D_0} = \frac{1}{\rho} \tag{9.6}$$

Example
If $\rho = 8\%$, then, from (9.6), the multiplier

$$M = \frac{1}{0.08} = 12.5$$

Table 9.1   Example of the cumulative power of repayments: £1000 deposit lent out over 3 years.

Month	New deposit	Reserve	Repayments	New loans	Total loans	Total deposits	Multiplier	Reserve ratio (%)
1	1000	100		900	900	1000	1.0	10
2	900	90	25	835	1710	1900	1.9	10
3	835	84	48	799	2462	2735	2.7	10
4	799	80	68	787	3181	3534	3.5	10
5	787	79	88	797	3889	4321	4.3	10
6	797	80	108	825	4607	5119	5.1	10
7	825	83	128	871	5350	5944	5.9	10
8	871	87	149	932	6133	6815	6.8	10
9	932	93	170	1009	6972	7747	7.7	10
10	1009	101	194	1102	7881	8757	8.8	10
11	1102	110	219	1211	8873	9859	9.9	10
12	1211	121	246	1336	9963	11070	11.1	10

much less. For instance, if the loan were a 25-year mortgage, the repayments would be only 1/300 of the sum lent each month (instead of 1/36). For this mortgage, it would take 18 months for the bank deposit multiplier to approach 10 and nearly 10 years for it to reach 100. The effect of the length of loan on new loans and on the bank deposit multiplier is illustrated in Figure 9.1.

All these calculations implicitly assume that there is a demand for all the bank wishes to lend (and as Box 9.1 shows, British households do seem to have a high propensity to borrow) and that the regulations permit lending on this scale, about which we shall say more later in this chapter. Furthermore, the calculations do not take into account the effect of interest payments.

The textbook example in effect represents an interest-only loan with zero interest which is repaid at the end of the term. The repayment process just described also assumes no interest payments. If interest is paid, the dynamics of the process are changed again. By convention, loans to households are usually repaid in equal monthly instalments. In the early years of long-term loans, the repayments largely comprise of interest, and most of the amount borrowed is not repaid until later. This is illustrated in Box 9.3. The longer the term of the loan, the slower the money will be recycled and the lower the bank deposit multiplier will be, all other things being equal. However, the effect of interest repayments on the multiplier process depends on who eventually receives the interest and what they do with it.

If the high multipliers shown in Figure 9.1 seem implausible, note that before the financial crisis, the bank deposit multiplier in the UK was around 90! But by 2010, it had fallen to about 14 due to the drying up of bank lending (Begg et al., 2011, p.433). What these calculations underline is the importance of modelling full dynamic processes and the potential power of fractional reserve banking to create money.

Banking crises and the regulation of banks

Because the fractional reserve system implies gearing – sometimes called leveraging – the system is inherently unstable: a small, unfavourable change can cause a bank to fail. Even in the eighteenth century, Adam Smith noted that banks failed and there was a need to regulate their activities (1776/1861, Book II, Chapter II). The history of banking shows that regulation tends to be reactive: regulation is refined following a crisis, and thus, banking regulation has evolved with banking

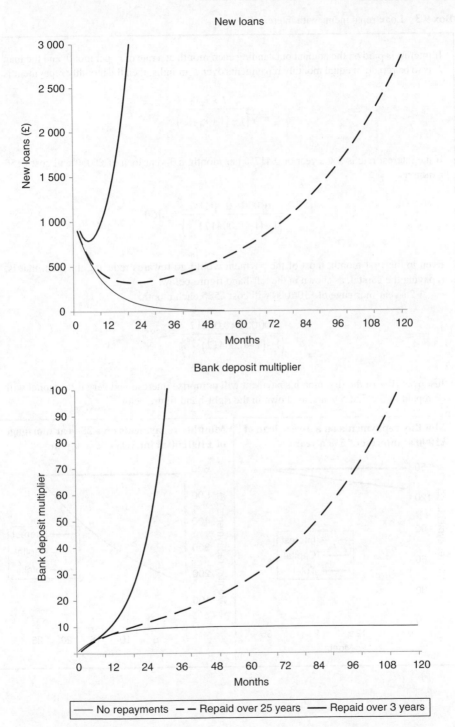

Figure 9.1   Example of the cumulative power of repayments: initial £1000 deposit.

Box 9.3   Loan repayments with interest.

If interest is paid on the amount outstanding each month at a rate of r_m per month and the loan L is to be repaid in equal monthly repayments over T months, then the monthly repayment is

$$\frac{L \times r_m}{\left(1 - \left(1 + r_m\right)^{-T}\right)}$$

If the interest rate is 5% a year or 0.417% per month, a 3-year loan of £5000 will cost £150 a month:

$$\frac{10\,000 \times 0.00417}{\left(1 - \left(1 + 0.00417\right)^{-36}\right)} = £150$$

Even in the first month, most of the payment would go towards reducing the loan, that is, repaying the capital, as shown in the left-hand figure below.

A 25-year mortgage of £100 000 will cost £585 each month:

$$\frac{100\,000 \times 0.00417}{\left(1 - \left(1 + 0.00417\right)^{-300}\right)} = £585$$

Just over 70% of the first month's payment will comprise interest; and very little capital will be repaid in the first 5 years, as shown in the right-hand figure below.

Monthly repayments on a 3-year loan of £5000 at interest of 5% a year

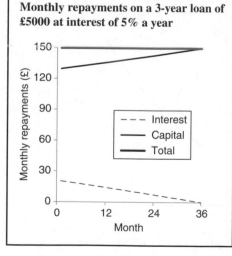

Monthly repayments on a 25-year mortgage of £100 000 at interest of 5% a year

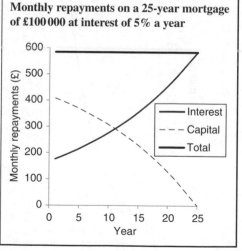

(Ferguson, 2008, p.56). This is illustrated by the very brief history of banking crises and regulation in Box 9.4.

There are basically two types of banking crises: liquidity crises and solvency crises. Regulators have established different approaches to deal with each. In practice, the two types of crises can be closely related. If a bank has insufficient liquidity, it may have to sell assets 'cheap', which in turn makes it insolvent.

A liquidity crisis occurs when a bank cannot meet the immediate needs for payment because it has lent out a high proportion of the money deposited with it and is a direct consequence of the fractional reserve banking system. The regulators address this problem by requiring banks to hold a minimum proportion of their assets in a highly liquid form (i.e. can be quickly converted into money). Traditionally, the reserve ratio was the proportion of liquid assets to deposits (and this is still used in economics textbooks such as Begg *et al.*, 2011, p.424). Liquidity regulation in this form was, however, abolished in the United Kingdom in 1981 at which time the ratio was 10%

Box 9.4   Brief history of banking crises and regulation.

In the nineteenth century, there were successive waves of bank failures in England. For example, in 1825, 'about 50 banks went bankrupt', and there were banking crises in 1836 and 1839, with panics in 1847, 1857 and 1866 (Quinn, 2004, pp.163, 166–7). Various methods of control were tried, such as not allowing bank owners the protection of limited liability so that they stood to lose everything if their bank failed. In the 1870s, the Bank of England adopted the system of providing liquidity in times of panic but at a high price. This, together with the amalgamation of banks to produce larger units, stopped banking panics in England (Quinn, 2004, p.167). That is why the *Financial Times* (2012) claimed that the run on Northern Rock in 2007 was the first run on a British bank in 'over 140 years', that is, since the panic of 1866. There had, however, been crises in the intervening period, such as the Baring crisis in 1890, which resulted the requirement for banks to increase their reserves (Cottrell, 2004, pp.270–279). Of course, there have subsequently been many changes since in detail of the regulation of British banks (see, e.g. Howson, 2004).

In the United States, there was no central bank like the Bank of England, and the Federal Reserve System was not established until 1913 following several financial panics. While by the early twentieth century there were just a handful large banks in Britain, in the United States by 1922, there were some 30000 small banks of which about 10000 failed during the Great Depression (Ferguson, 2008, pp.57, 163). This resulted in the United States being the first country to introduce deposit insurance to protect small savers (Alessandri & Haldane, 2009). Friedman and Schwartz's (1963) classic book, *A Monetary History of the United States: 1867–1960*, gives more detail.

There has been increasing international cooperation to promote financial stability. The Bank for International Settlements (BIS) was established in 1930, with the Bank of England and the US Federal Reserve among the founders, and has taken the lead in the regulation of internationally important banks following the 1970s crises (BIS, 2013a). Since 1988, there have been a succession of international agreements, known as Basel I, II and III, intended to 'strengthen the soundness and stability of the international banking system' (BIS, 2013a). Furthermore, the latest development, so-called bail-in, is designed to 'prevent massive public bail-outs of banks' (EU, 2013).

For more on the development of banking regulation and on the latest banking crisis, see, for example, Begg *et al.* (2011, pp.424, 426–433). And for a global view of financial crises, see Reinhart and Rogoff (2009).

(Howson, 2004, p.161). (In the United States, a reserve ratio of 10% is still used (Board of Governors of the Federal Reserve System, 2013).) Under the latest international system, Basel III, a minimum liquidity coverage ratio (LCR) is imposed. The LCR measures the ratio of 'reliably liquid assets' to 'prospective liquidity outflows during a period of stressed market conditions'. Under EU regulations, banks will have to have a 'minimum LCR ratio of 60% by 1 January 2015 rising to 100% by 1 January 2018' (Bank of England, 2013a, pp.23, 69).

Solvency crises arise because banks' liabilities exceed their assets due to the value of their assets falling. For example, when banks have lent money to people who have used their homes as security for the loans and the value of those homes falls, then the loans are worth less and this may make the bank insolvent. The regulators address this problem by imposing a minimum capital adequacy ratio. In effect, this requires banks to have sufficient capital to make good any likely deficiency. Alessandri and Haldane (2009) reported that 'since the start of the twentieth century, capital ratios have fallen by a factor of around five in the US and UK', from over 10% to under 5%. But the precise definition of this ratio varies over time. The current basic definition is the ratio of share capital to risk-weighted assets: for example, cash is regarded as a risk-free asset, while commercial loans are treated as very risky. Francis and Osborne (2009) found that the risk-weighted capital adequacy ratios for large UK banks varied from 13 to 18% between 1998 and 2006. But they also noted large differences between banks in each year. The Bank of England reported in June 2013 that the aggregate capital adequacy for 'major British banks' was 11% (based on Tier 1 capital as defined under Basel III, i.e. capital that could be used to 'absorb losses without a bank being required to cease trading', such as ordinary share capital (BIS, 2010)). Nevertheless, at the same time, the Bank of England tested the accounts of eight UK banks against the required capital adequacy and found five of the eight failed (Bank of England, 2013b). Averages can hide wide differences between banks.

A simple example

A simple example of a bank balance sheet is shown in Box 9.5. The bank's assets are loans plus liquid assets, while its liabilities are its deposits, shareholders' capital and retained profit. In practice, banks have a much wider range of assets and liabilities than shown here:

- For a simple description, see, for example, Begg *et al.* (2011, Chapters 18 & 19).

- For more technical information, see the Bank of England website (http://www.bankofengland. co.uk) or the BIS website (http://www.bis.org).

- For a more detailed worked example, see the Reserve Bank of New Zealand (2007).

Here, we follow the usual textbook approach and use the reserve ratio defined as

$$\frac{\text{Liquid assets}}{\text{Deposits}}$$

In this example, the reserve ratio is 11.1%.
The capital adequacy ratio is defined as

$$\frac{\text{Capital} + \text{Retained profit}}{\text{Risk weighted assets}}$$

And in this example is 12.5%.

Box 9.5 Simple example of a bank's reserve and capital adequacy ratios.

Balance sheet			
Assets		Liabilities	
Liquid	1 000	Deposits	9 000
Mortgages	2 000	Ordinary capital (from shareholders)	800
Loans	7 000	Retained profit	200
Total	**10 000**	**Total**	**10 000**

Reserve ratio

$$\text{Reserve ratio} = \frac{\text{Liquid assets}}{\text{Deposits}} = \frac{1000}{9000} = 11.1\%$$

Capital adequacy ratio

Liquid assets have no risk attached, and mortgages are risky, but not as risky as loans to individuals or businesses.

Assets		Weight	Risk-weighted assets
Liquid	1 000	0	0
Mortgages	2 000	50%	1 000
Loans	7 000	100%	7 000
Total	**10 000**		**8 000**

$$\text{Capital adequacy ratio} = \frac{\text{Capital} + \text{Retained profit}}{\text{Risk weighted assets}} = \frac{800 + 200}{8000} = 12.5\%$$

What happens if the value of the mortgages on the bank's balance sheet drops by 200 due to mortgage defaults?

Assets		Weight	Risk-weighted assets
Liquid	1 000	0	0
Mortgages	1 800	50%	900
Loans	7 000	100%	7 000
Total	**9 800**		**7 900**

This loss is funded from the retained profit, which falls to zero, so

$$\text{Capital adequacy ratio} = \frac{\text{Capital} + \text{Retained profit}}{\text{Risk weighted assets}} = \frac{800}{7900} = 10.1\%$$

To restore the capital adequacy ratio to 12.5%, the bank could issue more shares to raise 185 more capital so that

$$\text{Capital adequacy ratio} = \frac{\text{Capital} + \text{Retained profit}}{\text{Risk weighted ssets}} = \frac{985}{7900} = 12.5\%$$

What happens in a solvency crisis? Let us assume that it is discovered that the assets of the bank are less than they were believed to be. Maybe borrowers have defaulted. This means that the bank's assets no longer cover its liabilities. To make the balance sheet balance again, some liabilities must be reduced: the bank must either draw on its capital, its retained profit or raid its depositors' funds. This is illustrated in the bottom panel of Box 9.5. (For a full description of such a 'bail-in' process, see, e.g. the arrangements due to be introduced in 2016 in the EU (2013) or the joint paper by the Bank of England and Federal Deposit Insurance Corporation (2012).)

9.2   The banking model

Any simple model of the banking system has to omit a great deal. It must focus on a few selected aspects and make assumptions about the world outside the model. For example, Baradi's agent-based model (2007) focusses on the heterogeneity of banks and households, while Mallet (2011) is concerned with the fractional reserve system and interbank lending.

We too focus on the effect of the fractional reserve system but also on the capital adequacy requirement in order to examine the relationships between the banking sector, bank regulators, savers and borrowers. The aim is to tease out the key processes.

The model has just one bank to represent the banking sector. However, there are 10 000 households. Each household is allocated a monthly budget, based on the method used in Chapter 3, so as to give a Gini distribution of about one third with an average budget of £1000. Households receive this sum every month. Most households have little or no savings as indicated in Box 9.1. To reflect this, it is assumed initially that 100 households are savers with deposits of £10 000. The bank therefore has total initial deposits of £1 million. The remaining 9000 households initially have neither savings nor loans. In addition, there is a regulatory authority that pays interest on liquid assets held as reserve by the bank.

Since the mid-1980s, banks in the United Kingdom have made both mortgage and other types of loans (Watson, 2004). However, the model assumes that the bank makes only one kind of loan at a time: either 25-year mortgages or 3-year consumer loans. By examining these two extremes, we can bracket possible values. The bank decides how much to lend, given its actual reserve and capital adequacy ratios, and the targets set by the regulatory authority (in fact, the modeller). Loans are made to those who do not have loans and, if required, who also meet an affordability test. These loans are used to buy from other households who then put the money they receive back in the bank. The borrowers make monthly repayments of capital and interest to the bank, and the bank can then make new loans and pay interest to the savers. The process is set out in the flow diagram in Figure 9.2.

A basic example

To replicate the theoretical example shown in Box 9.5, we start by assuming a reserve ratio of 10% but no minimum capital adequacy ratio (i.e. a ratio of zero), no affordability test and an interest rate of zero. Loans of £100 000 are made for 25 years. Borrowers therefore repay £333 each month. When borrowers take a loan, they transfer the sum – the £100 000 – to another household selected at random that represents the end of the house-buying chain. This 'seller' household saves the money by depositing it at the bank. The model is run for 120 months, that is, 10 years. Borrowers only take out one loan at a time. This means that the bank's lending may be limited by the number of households in the model.

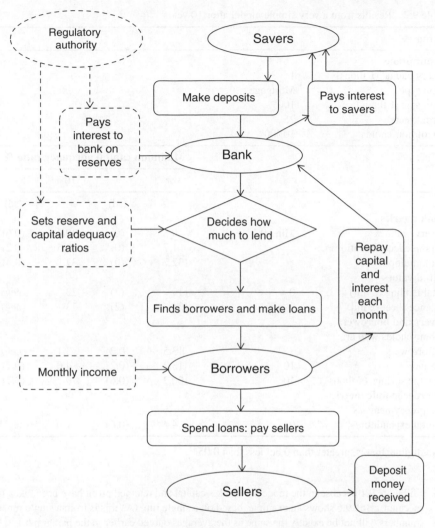

Figure 9.2   Summary of the banking model.

The results are shown in the left column of Table 9.2, taking the average of 10 runs (as there is little stochastic variation in this very simple model). Three sets of metrics are reported after 10 years: for the bank, for households and for the economy as a whole:

- For the bank: the reserve ratio, the capital adequacy ratio, total lending, the value of the balance sheet and the bank deposit multiplier. The reserve ratio is just above the 10% target at 10.8% (sd 0), but the capital adequacy ratio falls to 1.7% (sd 0). Total lending is £119m (sd 1.7). The bank's balance sheet – its assets and liabilities, which by definition are equal – is worth £134m (sd 2). The bank deposit multiplier, the ratio of current deposits to initial deposits, is 132.7 (sd 1.8). (Note that this is slightly higher than implied by the simple example

Table 9.2   Results from a very simple model after 10 years.

10 runs					
Assumptions					
Equity capital (£ thous)	1				
Loan type	Mortgage				
Loan size (£ thous)	100				
Term (years)	25				
No. of households	10 000				
		Minimum capital adequacy ratio %			
		0%		10%	
			(sd)		(sd)
Bank metrics					
Reserve ratio %	Min 10%	10.8	(0)	30.4	(0.6)
Capital adequacy ratio %		1.7	(0)	8.5	(0.2)
Bank multiplier		132.7	(0)	32.2	(0.4)
Initial values					
Total lending (£ mil)	0	119	(2)	23	(neg)
Balance sheet (£ mil)	2	134	(2)	33	(neg)
Savers and borrowers					
% households who are:					
Borrowers		13.5	(0.2)	3.1	(neg)
Savers	10	13.2	(0.2)	4.0	(0.1)
Average savings (£ thous)	10	100.2	(0.6)	79.7	(0.7)
Macroeconomic metric					
Loan repayments as					
% total expenditure	0	4.4	(0.6)	1.0	(neg)*

*Negligible, that is, greater than 0 but less than 0.05.

in Figure 9.1 because in the model the bank's capital and retained profit have been taken into account.) Box 9.6 shows an example, based on a single run. (As this is from a single run, the numbers will not be exactly the same as the averages quoted earlier in the paragraph.)

• For households: the proportion who are borrowers and savers and the average amount of savings. In this model, after 10 years, about 13% of households are borrowers and a similar proportion are savers (defined as households with at least £10 000 of savings). These ratios are below those seen in the United Kingdom because the model is focussing on a single tranche of lending to a limited population and funded by a small group of savers, while the position observed in the United Kingdom has evolved over many such tranches. However, the average saving of the savers has risen from £10 000 to £100 000.

• For the economy as a whole: the proportion of households' budgets which are spent on mortgage repayments. After 10 years, this has risen to 4%. This depends crucially on the absolute number of households in the model but is included here to demonstrate how the model can produce both micro and macro data and to give an indicator of the scale of the borrowing.

Box 9.6   Results: Example of lending and balance sheet, with capital adequacy ratio rules and no interest.

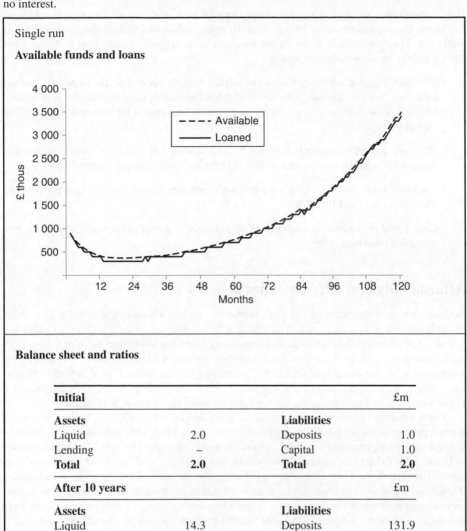

Single run

Available funds and loans

£ thous — *Months*

- - - - Available
——— Loaned

Balance sheet and ratios

Initial			£m
Assets		**Liabilities**	
Liquid	2.0	Deposits	1.0
Lending	–	Capital	1.0
Total	**2.0**	**Total**	**2.0**

After 10 years			£m
Assets		**Liabilities**	
Liquid	14.3	Deposits	131.9
Lending	118.6	Capital	1.0
Total	**132.9**	**Total**	**132.9**

Reserve ratio %	10.8
Capital adequacy ratio %	1.7
Bank deposit multiplier	131.9

Introducing the capital adequacy ratio target

Next, we introduce the capital adequacy ratio target of 10%, but keep all the other assumptions the same. The results, based on 10 runs after 10 years, are shown in the right-hand column of Table 9.2. The introduction of the capital adequacy ratio target has considerably damped the bank's activity by constraining its lending:

- The bank's capital adequacy ratio is on average slightly lower than the target because the bank only monitors the ratio at the end of each lending round, and if it breaches the minimum required, it can take some time to increase it to meet the target as the bank cannot raise more capital in the model.

- The bank deposit multiplier is now only 32.2 (instead of 132.7). But as a result, banks have 'spare cash' and the reserve ratio is 30% (against a minimum requirement of 10%).

- Far fewer households are borrowers or savers, and the average saving of savers is about £80000 (instead of £100000).

- Only 1% of expenditure is on mortgage repayments, a quarter of the share when there was no capital adequacy target.

Affordability and different types of loans

We now introduce the 'affordability test': borrowers are not allowed to take out a loan if the monthly repayment would exceed half their budget. We also introduce short-term loans: £5000 for 3 years. The monthly repayments on these consumer loans are lower than the mortgage repayments: the mortgage is £333 per month and the consumer loan is £139 per month. This means that more households can afford consumer loans than mortgages. The initial £1m of deposits will provide 20 times as many consumer loans than mortgages. To keep things simple, the bank can offer either mortgages or consumer loans, but not both. All other variables are unchanged.

The two different types of lending produce very different results as suggested by the examples of lending patterns in Figure 9.2. The bank can only make loans when it has sufficient funds, there are households wanting loans and the capital adequacy ratio limit permits. The 'spikes' of lending shown in Figure 9.3 are due to the capital adequacy ratio being breached and preventing lending until the correct level is restored. For the bank, the capital adequacy ratio constraint takes effect 3 years earlier if consumer loans are made than if the lending is for mortgages because the risk weights are higher for consumer loans (as explained in Box 9.5). Note, too, that the level of lending is much lower with mortgages than with consumer loans – the vertical axes on the two graphs are very different – because the mortgages take longer to pay off and therefore the money is recycled more slowly.

Figures 9.4 and 9.5 show the processes underlying the examples shown in Figure 9.3. The top row of Figure 9.4 shows that the capital adequacy ratio falls below 10% because, as explained earlier, the bank bases its lending on the capital adequacy ratio at the end of the last month, and once it has fallen, it may not be easily restored. But because lending is constrained, the bank's reserve ratio rises. The bottom row shows that the multiplier on mortgages is 30 after 10 years, while for consumer loans, it is 100. This is because the short-term consumer loans are being repaid much faster: over 3 years instead of 25. Because the repayments are lower, the impact on total consumer expenditure is lower for consumer loans at around 1% compared to 4% for mortgages.

The impact on savers is also quite different. With mortgages, a few households receive very large windfall sums, while for the consumer loans, more households receive much smaller sums: so mortgage lending results in fewer savers with higher average savings than consumer lending. (This is shown in the left column of Figure 9.5.) The total volume of savings is, however, higher with consumer loans. (This is shown on the bottom row of Figure 9.5.) Figure 9.5 provides a nice

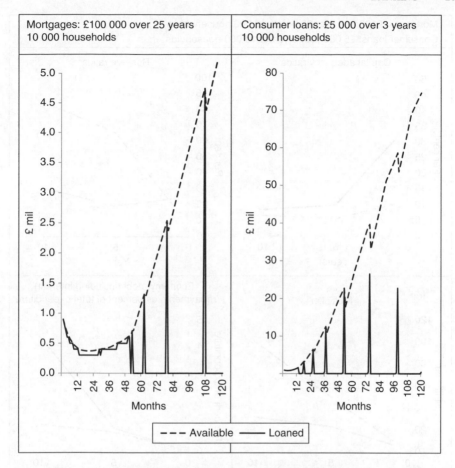

Figure 9.3   Examples of the supply of new loans.

example of how agent-based modelling using heterogeneous agents facilitates disaggregation, allowing the modeller to drill down from the aggregate data on the right to see how it has been generated. For instance, if there were only a single representative agent, the model could say nothing about savers versus non-savers.

Adding interest

So far, we have refrained from modelling interest payments. Charging borrowers interest at 5% increases the monthly costs of a £100 000 mortgage over 25 years from £333 to £585. This means that after 10 years, servicing mortgage repayments averages (over 10 runs) 8% of total expenditure, double the share when no interest is payable. Savers are paid 2% on their deposits, which they allow to accumulate in their accounts at the bank, thereby adding to deposits and in turn boosting lending. The bank receives the same interest on the assets it does not lend out. Thus, after 10 years, the multiplier is much higher: on average, 156, five times greater than if no interest is paid. The bank also makes a profit: the sum of the interest paid by borrowers and the interest earned from its liquid assets, minus what it has to pay to savers. It is assumed that profits are retained by the bank. These results are shown by the 'No shock' lines in Figure 9.6. Different assumptions about how the savers use the interest they receive and how the bank uses its profits would produce different results.

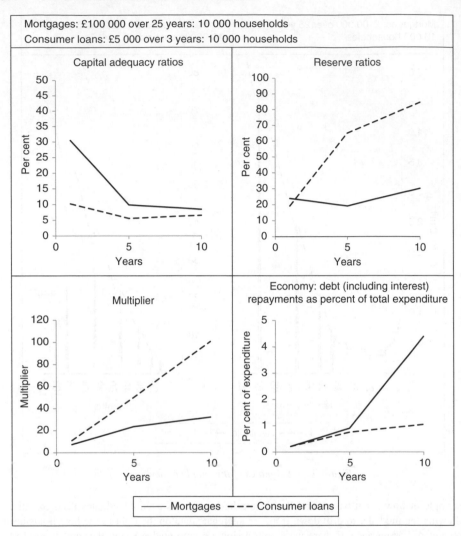

Figure 9.4   Results: mortgages compared to consumer loans: bank metrics and the economy (10 runs).

A shock to the system

To test the resilience of the system to a shock, the model was run with 1% of borrowers defaulting after 30 months. Defaulting is defined as borrowers stopping repaying and the bank writing off the loans. The impact on the bank's metrics at 5 and 10 years are shown by the 'With shock' lines in Figure 9.6. The defaults put the bank into a loss, and because it does not have sufficient resources, lending stops. So instead of the multiplier averaging 156 after 10 years, it is only 22. More importantly, the bank is plunged into increasing losses, as shown by the bottom right-hand graph. Thus, quite a modest shock – 1% defaulters – has had major effects.

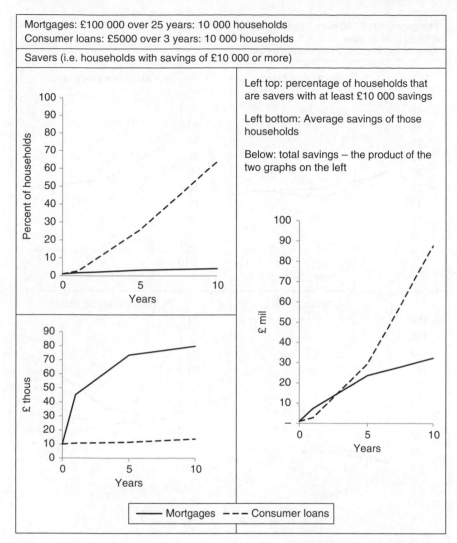

Mortgages: £100 000 over 25 years: 10 000 households
Consumer loans: £5000 over 3 years: 10 000 households

Savers (i.e. households with savings of £10 000 or more)

Left top: percentage of households that are savers with at least £10 000 savings

Left bottom: Average savings of those households

Below: total savings – the product of the two graphs on the left

Figure 9.5   Results: household savings: mortgages and consumer loans compared (10 runs).

Figure 9.7 shows the results if the bank charges 10% for its mortgages and consumer loans and gives savers only 1%. This allows the bank to build up sufficient retained profit to keep it afloat if it makes mortgage loans, but if it makes small loans to consumers, this interest rate is still not sufficient, even 10% being a low rate for consumer loans. (This is because if the bank makes consumer loans, it has a much larger balance sheet; and so a 1% default is a much larger sum.)

Both examples show how a shock to a bank with insufficient capital caused by defaulting puts a stop to lending and plunges the bank into increasing loss. The ratchet effect that leads to rising loans and rising profit when all goes well has now gone into reverse. This illustrates the inherent instability of fractional reserve banking.

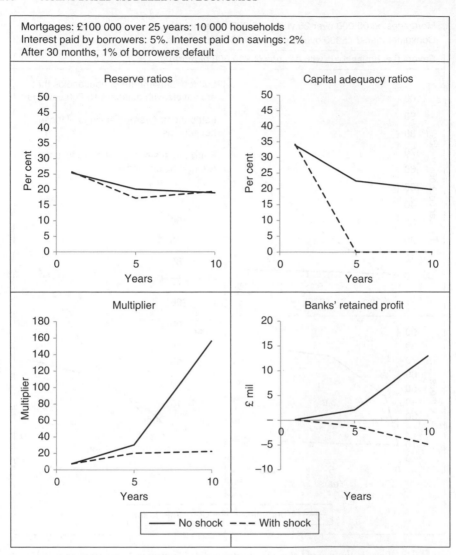

Figure 9.6   Results: a shock to mortgage lending: bank metrics (10 runs).

9.3   Discussion

This chapter has presented a simple agent-based model that captures the essential features of fractional reserve banking. Of the themes of this book – modelling heterogeneity, dynamics and interaction – this chapter has focussed on dynamics but also touched on heterogeneity and interaction.

Because agent-based models can accommodate heterogeneity, we have been able to distinguish between borrowers and savers, unlike models using representative agents. Nobel Prize winner Joseph Stiglitz (2010, p.258) pointed out that '... if all individuals are identical, there can be no borrowing and lending – that would simply be moving money from the left pocket to the

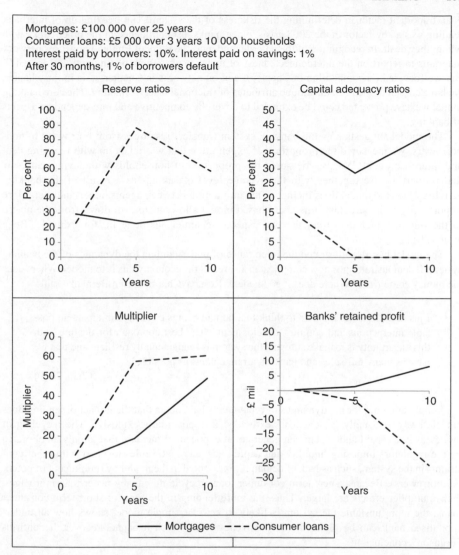

Mortgages: £100 000 over 25 years
Consumer loans: £5 000 over 3 years 10 000 households
Interest paid by borrowers: 10%. Interest paid on savings: 1%
After 30 months, 1% of borrowers default

Figure 9.7   Results: a shock to lending, mortgages and consumer loans: bank metrics (10 runs).

right pocket'. We have also allowed some heterogeneity between borrowers: borrowers have different budgets and so are not always able to afford loans. More could be made of this. For instance, this model has not considered in any detail the responsiveness of savers to different interest rates, only taking into account the fact that higher interest rates reduce the affordability of loans.

We have used a single agent to represent the banking system. The banking system of course comprises many banks, and these banks both compete and rely on one another. They compete to attract savers and borrowers in order to maximise their profits. The more banks can lend – driving down their liquidity and capital adequacy ratios – the greater their profit, but the more vulnerable they are to shocks. Although banks compete, they are also highly interdependent, and this interdependency is an important factor in determining the riskiness of the system. The freezing up of interbank lending was a key factor in the 2008 crisis, when banks lost confidence in the other banks with whom they dealt. In recognition of this interdependency, the Bank of England now uses network diagrams to report on the interconnectedness of major banks (Bank of England, 2013a, p.47). But we focussed on competition in Chapter 6 and on networks in Chapter 4, so in this chapter, we have chosen to focus on the unique attributes of fractional reserve banking. The core banking model we have presented could be extended to cover the competitive and interdependent aspects of banking.

The model suggests how the banking system transfers resources from borrowers to non-borrowers. We measured the proportion of expenditure that was taken up with repaying debt and interest on debt. We also measured the proportion of households with savings and saw that proportion rise together with the average level of savings as a result of the banking activity. Thus, the model does include some interaction between agents, albeit indirect. More importantly, by its structure, this agent-based model allows us to drill down from the macro to the micro, rather than treat the two aspects separately as done in, for example, Begg *et al.* (2011).

The model has also illustrated the importance of understanding the dynamics of the banking system. It demonstrates just how complicated an area of the economy this is to model. Where does the money come from? Where does it go? Federal Reserve Chairman Ben Bernanke said

> I just think it is not realistic to think that human beings can fully anticipate all possible interactions and complex developments. The best approach for dealing with this uncertainty is to make sure that the system is fundamentally resilient and that we have as many fail-safes and back-up arrangements as possible.
>
> (Chan, 2010)

Simply allowing for the dynamics of repayments has shown that the impact of lending does not die away as usually presented in textbooks: it is potentially explosive. The recycling of money as it is repaid and re-lent can generate an exponential increase that is only ameliorated by the regulators imposing liquidity and capital adequacy ratio rules together with other constraints in the system, such as lack of demand (represented in the model by running out of potential borrowers). Because short-term consumer loans recycle the money faster than mortgages, their multiplier effects are larger. Thus, the more lending in the form of short-term consumer loans, the more unstable the system is likely to be. Our simple model shows how an under-capitalised bank can be plunged into insolvency from which it cannot recover. It confirms Ferguson's conclusion:

> ...I have come to understand that few things are harder to predict accurately than the timing and magnitude of financial crises, because the financial system is so genuinely complex and so many of the relationships within it are non-linear, even chaotic.
>
> (Ferguson, 2008, p.14)

We make no apologies for taking some major simplifying assumptions in order to be able to tease out the key dynamic processes and enable the tracking of the long-term impact of a tranche of lending. The model permits an examination of the relationship between bank lending policy, banking regulation, household behaviour and overall macro variables. This chapter has shown that agent-based modelling can be a valuable tool in checking the resilience of the banking system.

Appendix 9.A   How to do it

Banking model

Purpose: The aim of the model is to examine the effect of a £1 million stimulus over several years.
Entities: One agent is the bank, and there are up to 10 000 agents representing households.
Stochastic processes: Distribution of household budgets, which households take loans, which households receive payments and, if the shock to the system is activated, which households default.
Initialisation:

- Set the number of households.

- Set the number of savers. This will determine the size of the bank's initial deposits: each saver has £10 000 deposited.

- Set the bank's capital.

- Set the reserve ratio and capital adequacy targets: these ratios can be zero.

- Choose whether the affordability test used or not.

- Choose whether a shock is required, and if so, its size and timing.

- Set the interest rates for savers and borrowers: these rates can be zero.

- Choose a run name and set the number of months and runs required.

Output:

For the first run, an extensive set of graphics is produced as illustrated in Figure 9.A.1. For months 12, 60 and 120, the following metrics are recorded, averaged over all the runs:

- Bank metrics:

  o Reserve ratio %

  o Capital adequacy ratio %

  o Bank deposit multiplier

  o Bank balance sheet: liabilities and assets

  o Retained profit

  o Total lending

  o New money loaned in month

- Macro: total expenditure by households and total repayments

- Households:

  o Numbers of borrowers, savers and potential borrowers

  o Mean savings of savers

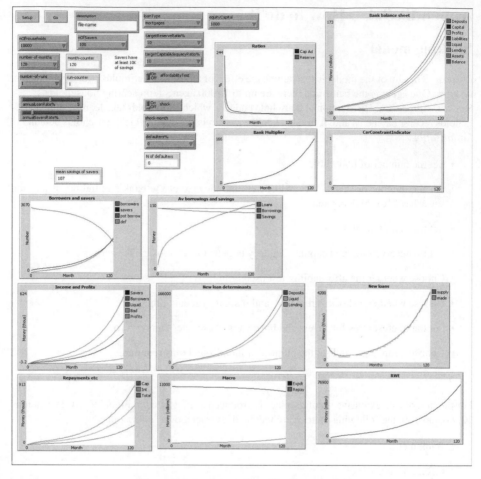

Figure 9.A.1   Screenshot of banking model.

The pseudocode is in Box 9.A.1 and a screenshot in Figure 9.A.1. For the full code, see the website: *Chapter 9 –Banking*.

Things to try

Using sliders and options, explore the effects of:

- Increasing the initial deposits at the bank by increasing the number of savers

- Increasing the bank's equity capital to permit more lending with a given target ratio

- Reducing the target ratios

- Raising borrowers' interest rates on the demand for loans

- Raising savers' interest rates on the supply of loans

- An earlier or larger shock to the system

Box 9.A.1   Pseudocode for banking model.

Create a world sized with wrap-around to ensure the density of households is 1% (e.g. for 1000 households, 315×317).

Define two loan types:

- Mortgage loans are of £100000 over 25 years, risk weight 50%.

- Consumer loans are of £5000 over 3 years, risk weight 100%.

  Calculate the monthly repayments required for each loan type, taking into account any interest payable.

Create agents:

- Households: create required number of agents, representing households, and allocate to each a monthly budget designed to produce a Gini coefficient of about 0.3 and an average budget of £1000 (on the basis of the method used in Chapter 3).

- Bank: create one agent to represent the banking sector.

Select the number the households set by the modeller to be savers. (These savings are the initial deposits of the bank.)
The bank makes loans based on the initial deposits, applying the affordability test if selected. (The affordability test means that only if the repayments are less than half the household's budget can the household take a loan.)

At the start of the second and each following month:
    The bank

- Collects the repayments. (If the shock is switched on, the set percentage of borrowers default in the specified month.)

- Pays interest to savers.

- Collects interest on its liquid assets.

Households who received payment last month deposit the money. (None in first month.)

The bank looks at its reserve and capital adequacy ratios at the end of the previous month and calculates how much it has available to lend. If it has funds to lend, it then makes loans to those randomly selected households that do not have loans (and pass the affordability test if set) until its funds are all lent out.

If the bank cannot lend all the money it has available without breaching the target ratios, it has to keep the funds liquid and will earn the rate paid to savers.

Households receiving loans transfer the loan to another household selected at random.

The reserve and capital adequacy ratios are calculated and other data collected.

  Data are collected for months 12, 60 and 120. Graphs are plotted for the first run, and all data are sent to a csv file.

Advanced – requiring amending the program:

- The model currently assumes that savers allow any interest they receive to accumulate in the bank. What would happen if they did something else, for example, spent the money?

- The model currently assumes that the bank retains its profits. What would happen if some of the profit was distributed to shareholders?

- In 2015, the LCR will be introduced. This requires banks to have sufficient 'cash or assets that can be converted into cash at little or no loss of value in private markets to meet its liquidity needs for a 30 calendar day liquidity stress scenario' (BIS, 2013b). Rework the model to measure the LCR.

- Drawing on the material in Chapter 4, adapt the model to simulate a bank run.

- Drawing on the material in Chapter 6, introduce competing banks.

References

Alessandri, P. & Haldane, A. (2009) *Banking on the state*. Bank of England [Online]. Available at: http://qed. econ.queensu.ca/faculty/milne/870/Bank%20on%20the%20State.pdf [Accessed 6 August 2013].

Bank for International Settlements (1988) *International Convergence of Capital Measurement and Capital Standards*. Basel: Basle Committee on Banking Supervision [Online]. Available at: http://www.bis.org [Accessed 6 August 2013].

Bank for International Settlements (2010) *Group of Governors and Heads of Supervision Announces Higher Global Minimum Capital Standards*. Basel Committee on Banking Supervision Press release 35/2010 [Online]. Available at: http://www.bis.org [Accessed 19 April 2013].

Bank for International Settlements. (2013a) *BIS History – Overview*. [Online]. Available at: http://www.bis. org/about/history.htm [Accessed 13 August 2013].

Bank for International Settlements. (2013b) *Group of Governors and Heads of Supervision endorses revised liquidity standard for banks*. Basel Committee on Banking Supervision Press release 1/2013 [Online]. Available at: http://www.bis.org [Accessed 3 May 2013].

Bank of England (2013a) *Financial Stability Report*. Issue No. 33 (June) [Online]. Available at: http://www. bankofengland.co.uk [Accessed 6 August 2013].

Bank of England (2013b) *News release: Prudential Regulation Authority (PRA) completes capital shortfall exercise with major UK banks and building societies* [Online]. Available at: http://www.bankofengland. co.uk/publications/Pages/news/2013/081.aspx (20 June) [Accessed 3 January 2015].

Bank of England/Federal Deposit Insurance Corporation (2012) *Resolving Globally Active, Systemically Important, Financial Institutions*. [Online]. Available at: http://www.bankofengland.co.uk/publications/ Documents/news/2012/nr156.pdf [Accessed 16 July 2013].

Baradi, M. (2007) *Beyond the static money multiplier: In search of a dynamic theory of money*. Munich Personal RePEc Archive [Online]. Available at: http://mpra.ub.uni-muenchen.de/id/eprint/19287 [Accessed 20 June 2013].

Begg, D., Vernasca, G., Fischer, S. & Dornbusch, R. (2011) *Economics*. Tenth Edition. London: McGraw-Hill Higher Education.

Board of Governors of the Federal Reserve System (2013) *Reserve Requirements*. Washington, DC: The Board [Online] Available at: http://www.federalreserve.gov/monetarypolicy/reservereq.htm [Accessed 9 August 2013].

Chan, S. (2010) Is Ben Bernanke having fun yet? *New York Times*. 15 May 2010 [Online]. Available at: http:// www.nytimes.com/2010/05/16/business/16ben.html?pagewanted=1&_r=0&dbk [Accessed 2 May 2013].

Cottrell, P. (2004) Domestic Finance, 1860–1914. In Floud, R. & Johnson, P., eds, *The Cambridge Economic History of Modern Britain, Vol II, Economic Maturity: 1860–1939*. Cambridge, MA: Cambridge University Press, pp.253–279.

EU (2013) *Commissioner Barnier welcomes trilogue agreement on the framework for bank recovery and resolution*. Press release: MEMO-13-1140 (12 December) [Online]. Available at: http://europa.eu/rapid/press-release_MEMO-13-1140_en.htm [Accessed 3 January 2015].

Ferguson, N. (2008) *The Ascent of Money*. London: Allen Lane.

Financial Times (2012) Northern Rock exposed regulatory failings (12 September) [Online]. Available at: http://www.ft.com/cms/s/0/7bb1ab1a-fc00-11e1-af33-00144feabdc0.html#axzz2bPh90ob8 [Accessed 8 August 2013].

Francis, W. & Osborne, M. (2009) *On the behaviour and determinants of risk-based capital ratios: Revisiting the evidence from UK banking institutions*, Occasional Paper no. 31 Financial Services Authority, London [Online]. Available at: http://www.fsa.gov.uk/pubs/occpapers/op31.pdf [Accessed 3 January 2015].

Friedman, M. & Schwartz, A. (1963) *The Monetary history of the United States: 1867–1960*. Princeton: Princeton University Press.

HM Treasury (2010) *Households without access to bank accounts 2008–2009* [Online]. Available at: http://webarchive.nationalarchives.gov.uk/20130129110402/http://www.hm-treasury.gov.uk/d/stats_briefing_101210.pdf [Accessed 3 January 2015].

Howson, S. (2004) Money and monetary policy since 1945. In Floud R. & Johnson P., eds, *The Cambridge Economic History of Modern Britain, Vol III, Economic Maturity: 1939–2000*. Cambridge, MA: Cambridge University Press, pp.134–166.

Mallett J. (2011) Modeling the Textbook Fractional Reserve Banking System. *Eighth International Conference on Complex Systems*. Boston, MA [Online]. Available at: http://www.researchgate.net/publication/226989260_Modeling_the_Textbook_Fractional_Reserve_Banking_System/file/32bfe511ec46db59eb.pdf [Accessed 20 June 2013].

ONS (2011) *Wealth in Great Britain: Main Results from the Wealth and Assets Survey: 2008/10: Part 1* [Online]. Available at: http://www.ons.gov.uk [Accessed 12 April 2013].

ONS (2012) *Wealth in Great Britain Wave 2, 2008–2010: Chapter 3: Financial Wealth* [Online]. Available at: http://www.ons.gov.uk/ons/rel/was/wealth-in-great-britain-wave-2/2008-2010--part-2-/report--chapter-3--financial-wealth.html [Accessed 3 January 2015].

Quinn, S. (2004) Money, Finance and Capital Markets. In: Floud, R. & Johnson, P., eds., *The Cambridge Economic History of Modern Britain, Vol 1, Industrialisation: 1700–1860*. Cambridge, MA: Cambridge University Press, pp.147–174.

Smith, A. (1776/1861) *Wealth of Nations*. Edinburgh: Adam Charles & Black.

Stiglitz, J.E. (2010) *Freefall: Free Markets and the Sinking of the Global Economy*. London: Penguin Books.

Reinhart, C. & Rogoff, K. (2009) *This Time Is Different: Eight Centuries of Financial Folly*. Princeton: Princeton University Press.

Reserve Bank of New Zealand (2007) *Capital adequacy ratios for banks - simplified explanation and example of calculation*. [Online]. Available at: http://www.rbnz.govt.nz/finstab/banking/regulation/0091769.html [Accessed 19 April 2013].

Watson, K. (2004) The Financial Services Sector Since 1945. In: Floud R. & Johnson P., eds, *The Cambridge Economic History of Modern Britain, Vol III, Economic Maturity: 1939–2000*. Cambridge, MA: Cambridge University Press, pp.167–188.

10

Tragedy of the commons

10.1 Introduction

The term 'tragedy of the commons' was coined in 1968 by Garrett Hardin, a professor of biology at the University of California, Santa Barbara. His famous paper (Hardin, 1968) primarily addressed the problem of human overpopulation and argued that technology could not be relied on to accommodate ever-increasing numbers: social changes were required to limit the population. As one example among several, he described a pasture open to all and argued that, eventually, if each herdsman behaved rationally and pursued his own interest by adding animals to the pasture, the 'tragedy of the commons' would ensue because the pasture could not support an ever-increasing number of animals. Thus, the herdsman pursuing his own private interest did not promote the interest of the community as a whole: Adam Smith's invisible hand (see Box 5.4) was not at work. But this analysis fails to acknowledge that people have found ways of avoiding the 'tragedy of the commons' by cooperating. For instance, Nobel laureate Elinor Ostrom (1990, pp.58–88) described systems that have persisted for hundreds of years for managing alpine pastures in Switzerland, forests in Japan and water for irrigation in Spain, while Straughton (2008) described the management of moorlands in northern England.

Before discussing the issues, we first define exactly what we mean by 'commons'. Formally, a 'common pool resource' (CPR) is 'a natural or man-made resource system that is sufficiently large as to make it costly (but not impossible) to exclude potential beneficiaries from obtaining benefits from its use' (Ostrom, 1990, p.30). In economic terms, a CPR is not a public good because it is a limited resource and use by one person means that it cannot be used by another. Indeed, it is because the CPR is a limited resource that the problem of management arises. In contrast, the use of a public good by one person does not reduce its availability for another, for example, a weather forecast (Ostrom, 1990, pp.31–32).

There are many different types of CPRs, and each has its own distinct characteristics requiring different management arrangements to make best use of it. For example, compared to managing grazing, forestry involves very long time horizons, while the management of fisheries has to

Agent-Based Modelling in Economics, First Edition. Lynne Hamill and Nigel Gilbert.
© 2016 John Wiley & Sons, Ltd. Published 2016 by John Wiley & Sons, Ltd.

Box 10.1   Common land in England.

In England, Parliament has made laws on common land since the thirteenth century (Natural England, 2014; Straughton, 2008, p.10). The Commons Act 2006 brought together in one Act of Parliament all the common land legislation passed in the previous 700 years (Natural England, 2014). The 2006 Act aims to protect common land 'in a sustainable manner delivering benefits for farming, public access and biodiversity' (DEFRA, 2014).

There is a popular misconception that common land belongs to everyone, but that is not the case (Natural England, 2014). In England, common land is privately owned land over which third parties have certain rights (Straughton, 2008, p.9).

There are currently just over 7000 commons in England, together accounting for 3% of the land area; much is poor-quality grazing (Natural England, 2014).

accommodate the movement of fish. Both forestry and fishery are covered in detail in Perman *et al.* (2003: Chapters 17 & 18), which is also a useful introduction to this area of economics.

This chapter focuses on grazing because it is simpler and it is the typical CPR found in England. (See Box 10.1 for background on English common land.) Following Natural England (2014), we call those with the right to use the common 'commoners'.

Economic analysis

Game theory is sometimes applied to the CPR problem, representing it as a prisoner's dilemma game (see Box 10.2). To model the 'tragedy of the commons' in this way, two commoners share a pasture, and instead of jail sentences, the reward matrix shows how benefits vary with the number of animals grazed. In our example, the optimum herd size is 100, and this produces a total profit of £1000. If the optimum size of the herd is exceeded, the total profit declines. In the real world, this would perhaps happen because the cows are in poorer condition. In this example, profit (π) earned by the commoners declines according to the equation

$$\pi = -0.1H^2 + 20H$$

where H equals the number of cows, the total size of the herd: thus, if there are 200 cows, the total profit is zero. This is illustrated in the top part of Box 10.3. If the two commoners share equally and both put half the optimum number of cows on the pasture, they both earn the same income of £500 and the total profit is maximised. However, if one commoner 'defects' by putting 60 cows on the pasture while the other puts only 50, then the herd size rises to 110. Given the profit function above, the total profit falls to £990 or £9 per cow. Nevertheless, the 'defector' gains at the expense of the other, with a total gain of $60 \times £9 = £540$ instead of £500 under the optimum scenario. However, the other commoner receives less than the optimum, only $50 \times £9 = £450$ instead of £500. If both commoners think the other will put 60 cows on the common, both have an incentive to graze 60 cows. The total herd size then rises to 120 and the total gain falls to £960 or £8 per cow. Both commoners therefore receive £480, and both are worse off than in the optimum scenario. If this continues to the extreme and each commoner puts 100 cows on the pasture, the tragedy occurs and both commoners get no income. The reward matrix is shown in the lower part of Box 10.3. The precise figures are not important, but simply illustrate the principle, namely, that the incentives for individuals are such that they bring about an outcome that is undesirable for all.

But setting out the tragedy in this way demonstrates why the prisoner's dilemma is not applicable to this situation. The simple, single prisoner's dilemma game assumes that there is no

Box 10.2   Prisoner's dilemma and the 'tragedy of the commons'.

The scenario is as follows. Two friends are suspected of committing a crime and are taken into police custody. They are put in separate cells, so that they cannot communicate with each other. They are both told:

- If you do not confess, but your friend does, you will get a sentence of 10 years.

- If you confess, you will only get a sentence of 5 years.

- If neither of you confess, we will charge you with a lesser crime, and you will still get a sentence, but only a year.

The reward matrix looks like this with the sentences shown as, for example, (10, 5), meaning that A gets 10 years and B gets 5 years.

Suspect B	Suspect A	
	Confesses	Does not confess
Confesses	(5, 5)	(10, 5)
Does not confess	(5, 10)	(1, 1)

It is in the interests of both not to confess, and then each would receive a sentence of one year. But if A does not confess and B does, then A will receive the maximum sentence. And the same holds for B. Neither knows what the other will do. Consequently, both will probably confess in order to avoid the maximum sentence, and each will get 5 years.

For more information on game theory and the prisoner's dilemma, see, for example, Varian (2010: Chapters 28 & 29) or Begg *et al.* (2011, pp. 206–212).

communication and no cooperation and the commoners have no regard for the future. People do not always act in their short-term interest: they care about the long-term future, be it their own or that of their children. In a stable society in which people expect that they and their families will continue to live and work alongside one another for years or even generations, the kind of behaviour implied by the prisoner's dilemmas is unlikely. The key characteristic of the prisoners' dilemma is that cooperation is forbidden. (For further discussion, see Ostrom, 1990, pp.2–20.) Similarly, in the Cournot–Nash equilibrium problem discussed in Chapter 6, there was no cooperation allowed. Indeed, the Cournot–Nash model presented in Chapter 6 can be adapted to model uncooperative behaviour in this context. However, in this chapter, we focus on cooperation.

However, it is not clear how cooperation emerges. Ostrom (1990) suggests that it is a slow, protracted process. Game theory based on an unlimited number of repeated games may provide a clue. If a prisoner's dilemma game is repeated indefinitely, a 'tit-for-tat' strategy – in which each player copies what the other player did in the previous round – cooperation can emerge. (See, for instance, Varian, 2010, pp.529–530.) Here, we extend the prisoner's dilemma example by increasing the number of commoners to 10. Now, on the basis of the example used earlier, and assuming that the size of the herd is 150, compared to the optimum of 100, then it is clearly beneficial overall if the herd size were to be reduced. But if one of the commoners reduces the number of their cows, the group as a whole will gain but the reducer will lose out. At the other extreme, if all reduce the number of their cows, all benefit too. In this example, it is possible for both the group and all individuals to benefit if just four commoners reduce the number of their cows. This is illustrated in Table 10.1. It demonstrates how cooperation might start. Again, the precise numbers are not important.

Box 10.3   Example of how the 'tragedy of the commons' occurs in prisoners' dilemma format.

Once the optimum size of the herd, 100, is exceeded, the total profit (π) earned by the commoners declines according to the equation $\pi = -0.1H^2 + 20H$ where H equals the total size of the herd. This is illustrated in the left-hand graph. Each commoner's profit is calculated as the total profit divided by the number of cows, illustrated in the right-hand graph.

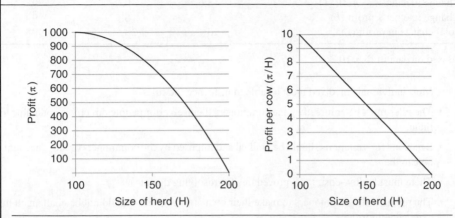

Commoner B's cows		Commoner A's cows		
		50	**60**	**100**
50				
	Size of herd	100	110	150
	Profit per cow (£)	10	9	5
	A's profit (£)	500	540	500
	B's profit (£)	500	450	250
	Total profit (£)	1 000	990	750
60				
	Size of herd	110	120	160
	Profit per cow (£)	9	8	4
	A's profit (£)	450	480	400
	B's profit (£)	540	480	240
	Total profit (£)	990	960	640
100				
	Size of herd	150	160	200
	Profit per cow (£)	5	4	0
	A's profit (£)	250	240	0
	B's profit (£)	500	400	0
	Total profit (£)	750	640	0

Ostrom (1990, p.90) defined seven key conditions for cooperative systems to manage CPRs to endure over long periods, which can be paraphrased as follows:

- Clearly defined boundaries: both users and the extent of the CPR must be well defined.
- Rules of use must reflect local conditions: different rules will be appropriate for different times and places.

Table 10.1   Example of cooperation generating benefits[a].

No. of commoners reducing	1	4	10
No. of commoners unchanged	9	6	0
Change in size of herd	−1	−4	−10
Change in reducers' profit (£)	−3.6	0.6	9
Change in other's profit (£)	1.5	6	9
Total change in profit (£)	10	38	90

[a] Based on data in Box 10.3.

- Most individuals involved must be able to influence the rules.

- The rules must be enforced by the commoners themselves or people directly accountable to them.

- Sanctions for violations should be gradual and imposed by the commoners or those accountable to them.

- There must be low-cost, local procedures for resolving disputes.

- The rights of the commoners to make their own arrangements should not be challenged by external authorities.

The essence of these conditions is cooperation, supported by social constraints, especially those that operate in stable societies.

More recently, after studying a range of systems in very different environments, Liu *et al.* (2007) concluded that 'couplings between human and natural systems vary across space, time, and organizational units. They also exhibit nonlinear dynamics with thresholds, reciprocal feedback loops, time lags, resilience, heterogeneity, and surprises'. These all suggest there is a potential for effective use of ABM.

10.2   Model

Chapman *et al.* (2009) have produced a detailed simulation of the management of moorlands in northern England, but this is too detailed for our purpose. Schindler (2012a & 2012b) has created two models using NetLogo that address the tragedy of the commons on grazing land, but these models are too complicated and, in one case, are based on African herdsmen. Our model is designed to demonstrate the dynamics and interaction as simply as possible taking English common land as its inspiration.

We start by creating a model of a meadow and establishing its 'carrying capacity', which we define as the number of cows that it can support over a given period of time. We then add commoners so that we can examine alternative strategies for sharing the meadow.

The carrying capacity of the meadow

'Carrying capacity' will, of course, vary with the type of animals, the climate and the nature of the soil. For example, the number of sheep that can be supported on sparse grazing on the hills in northern England will be quite different to the number of ponies that can be supported by the same area of land in the New Forest in warmer southern England. Detailed biological models have been built such as Armstrong *et al.*'s (1997) hill grazing management model. But our focus of interest is not on the detailed biological processes but the strategies adopted by commoners; so at this stage, we keep our modelling of biological processes as simple as possible, although we draw very broadly on data for the United Kingdom such as EBLEX (2013).

The rate at which grass grows depends on all sorts of factors and varies during the year. In England, it is faster in the spring and early autumn and less in the summer and barely grows at all in winter. Here, we focus on summer grazing and for simplicity assume that grass grows at the same rate throughout the period. The growth of grass is modelled using a logistic function following Perman *et al.* (2003, p.562). Logistic functions are explained in Box 10.4. For example, if a cow grazes a patch of grass down to 0.25 of its maximum, the grass growth rate is set at 0.2 per week, and a grazed patch is not grazed again until it reaches 0.9 of its maximum, it will take 16 weeks for a grazed patch to recover sufficiently to be grazed again. This is illustrated at the

Box 10.4   Grass growth using a logistic function.

The logistic equation, devised by Verhulst in 1838 to describe the growth of populations, can be used to produce a simple non-linear model in which the change depends on the level in the previous period and the growth rate (Strogatz, 1994, pp. 9–10 & 22–23).

If G_t is the amount of grass at time t and g the rate at which grass grows each week, then the amount of grass in the next week is given by

$$G_{t+1} = G_t + G_t(1 - G_t)g$$

where $0 < G_t \leq 1$ and $g \leq 1$.

For example, if G_t equals 0.25 and g is set at 0.2, then after 1 week, G_{t+1} will be 0.2875:

$$G_{t+1} = 0.25 + (0.25 \times 0.75 \times 0.2) = 0.2875$$

If, however, the grass has nearly reached its maximum, the absolute level of growth will be much lower. For example, if G_t equals 0.95 and g is set at 0.2, then after 1 week, G_{t+1} will be 0.9595:

$$G_{t+1} = 0.95 + (0.95 \times 0.05 \times 0.2) = 0.9595$$

Example of grass growing at rate of 0.2 per week. If it is grazed down to 0.25, it will recover to 0.9 after 16 weeks.

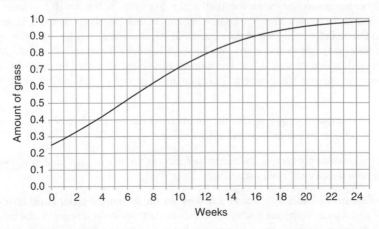

bottom of Box 10.4. These parameter values have been chosen to ensure that the carrying capacity is a reasonably small number of cows in order to reduce the time taken by each run.

The model meadow comprises 9999 patches. Initially, each patch has 1 unit of grass. The modeller sets the initial number of cows, and these cows are distributed randomly. Each cow then eats 0.75 units of grass and the next week moves on to the nearest unoccupied patch with sufficient grass, defined at 0.9 units. (Cows are not allowed to eat all the grass on a patch as it will not then regrow!) If a cow cannot find a suitable patch, it dies.

If the cows eat the grass faster than it grows, the pasture available will decline. As the rate at which grass grows is fixed, if there are too many cows, the pasture will be overgrazed and the cattle will starve. The model runs for 25 weeks to represent a summer of grazing. To establish the basic characteristics of the model, we start by assuming that the grass does not grow. With 400 cows, each consuming 1 patch of grass a week, then the meadow will support all the cows for 25 weeks. The model produces this result.

Allowing the grass to grow a little each week transforms this scenario. Using a growth rate of 0.2 (as illustrated in Box 10.4), as many as 600 cows will survive the summer season although very little grass is then left by the end, suggesting that this level of use will not be sustainable in the long run. However, if there are more than 700 cows, they cannot survive the summer: the grass runs out after 16 weeks. This is shown in Figure 10.1.

More information on this model – the *Carrying capacity model* – is in Appendix 10.A.

Managing the meadow

Having established the characteristics of the model meadow, in particular its carrying capacity, we now introduce commoners to manage the cattle.

Instead of modelling just one summer's grazing, the meadow management model covers many years. Of course, in reality, the rate of growth of the grass and thus the carrying capacity would vary from year to year. But in order to be able to draw out the key dynamics, it is assumed that the grass grows at the same rate in all years. As before, the cows graze for 25 weeks. They are then removed and the grass has the opportunity to recover a little: it is assumed that there are only 5 weeks of growth, reflecting the fact that grass in England grows only a little over winter. (See, e.g. EBLEX, 2013.)

There are 10 commoners and at the start of the run the number of cows – set at 300 in our examples – is divided equally between them. At the beginning of each year, the commoners decide whether to increase or reduce the number the cows they will graze that summer. In the examples used in the introduction, the commoners made their decisions on the basis of a loss function. In the model, the grazing of the meadow in effect replaces this loss function in that it determines how many cows survive and thus how much money the commoners make. We also saw in the introduction how, if a few commoners responded to a loss by cutting back, the situation could be improved for everyone. Based on this, a pair of simple heuristic decision rules is used:

- If all the commoner's cows survive the summer, the commoner increases their herd by an upward factor, to reflect an incentive to take more.

- If all the cows do not survive, the commoner reduces the size of their herd by a downward factor, to reflect a dislike of losses.

Each commoner is randomly allocated a downward and an upward factor based on a normal distribution with a mean set by the modeller and the standard deviation set equal to the mean. The upward and downward factors cannot be negative but can be zero and are arbitrarily constrained to be less than one in order to avoid any commoner making very large increases or being left with

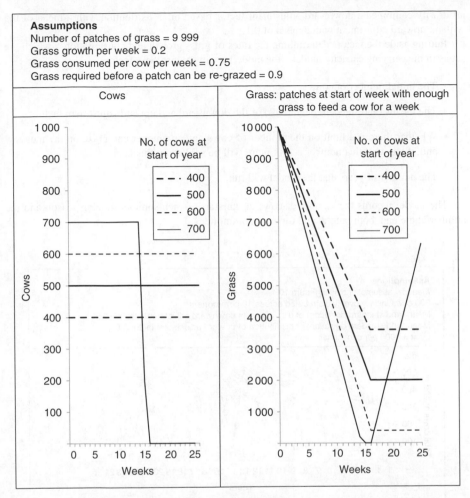

Figure 10.1   Cows supported and grass available when the grass grows. (The standard deviations are not shown to keep the diagrams clear).

no cows. (A commoner always has at least one cow at the start of the summer.) So a commoner with a downward adjustment factor of zero will never react to losses, while the one with an upward adjustment factor of zero will never increase the number of their cows. It is implicit in the rules that the commoners can make these adjustments, either by selling unwanted stock or by buying more, so a commoner is always able to replace any lost cows.

These adjustment factors can be interpreted in terms of risk aversion and cooperativeness:

- A high downward adjustment factor could be interpreted as risk aversion, trying to protect against future losses, or as cooperativeness.

- A high upward adjustment factor could be interpreted as greed, while a low upward adjustment factor could again represent risk aversion.

Kahneman and Tversky (1979) suggested that people feel losses more than they relish gains. This implies that risk aversion typically outweighs greed. Translated into our model, it means that upward adjustment factors should be lower than downward adjustment factors. So we have arbitrarily combined a downward adjustment factor based on a distribution with a mean of 0.5 with an upward adjustment with a mean of 0.1.

Putting aside the factors determining the rates of grass growth and consumption – which are set as in the carrying capacity model – the modeller can set just these factors:

- The initial number of cows

- The means (and standard deviations) of the downward and upward adjustment factors

- Whether there is a limit on the number of cows any commoner can graze on the meadow and, if so, what that number is (but more will be said about this later)

- The number of years that the model will run.

The model records the number of cows at the start of each summer grazing season and the number at the end, both in total and for each commoner.

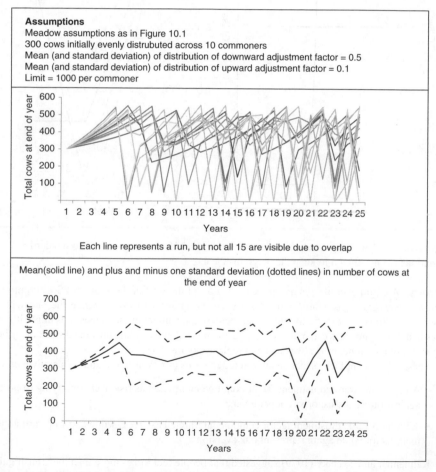

Figure 10.2   Meadow management model results: limit of 1000 cows per commoner. 15 runs over 25 years.

The aim is to establish how best to create sustainable stability. Four indicators are used:

- The average number of cows at the end of each year: the more the better.

- The survival rate: the percentage of cows that survive the summer. The higher this number, the better and ideally the survival rate should be 100%.

- The proportion of years in which some cows die, that is, the survival rate is less than 100%. The lower this number, the better: ideally, it should be zero.

- Whether there is any variation in the number of cows at the end of year during the last 10 years: the less variation, the better and ideally there should be none, indicating that the system is stable.

Furthermore, comparing the first three indicators calculated over all 25 years with the same indicators calculated over just the last 10 years shows whether the system is becoming more sustainable and stable over time. It is important to consider these four indicators together. For example, it would not be an efficient use of the resources provided by the meadow if there were on average only 100 cows grazing even if the survival rate was then always 100% and the number of cows on the common was constant as we know that the meadow can support significantly more.

To explore the dynamics of this simple model, we start by setting the limit for each commoner at 1000, which in effect means there is no limit as this level is way above the total carrying capacity of the meadow. Each commoner starts with 30 cows. The model is run 15 times for 25 years. Figure 10.2 shows the number of cows at the end of each year: it is highly volatile. For example, after 5 years, the number of cows at the end of any given year often ranges from zero to over 500 from one run to another. Furthermore, although the commoners all start with the same number of cows, by the end of the 25th year, most of the cows being grazed tend to belong to just one or two commoners. When there are any cows left at all, on average, one commoner owns 58% (sd 18). How this concentration arises is shown in Box 10.5 which uses actual examples from one of these runs.

What then might bring more stability to this system? A rule found in both England (Straughton, 2008, p.119) and Switzerland (Ostrom, 1990, pp.61–65) is that commoners are allowed to put on the common land pasture the same number of animals that they can support over winter. In practice, this means those with larger farms will be able to put more animals on the common because they have more land with which to produce forage (such as hay) to feed to the animals during the winter months when there is no grass available. This prevents commoners buying in animals to graze on the commons over the summer to sell on before winter. For simplicity, we have assumed that the limit for each commoner is set at the same level and leave it as an exercise for readers with programming skills to explore the impact of an unequal distribution. This limit could be enforced by some well-informed public official, or it could evolve over time as Ostrom's work suggests.

We know that the carrying capacity of the meadow is less than 700 cows. However, even if the limit were set at 100 per commoner, thus potentially allowing up to 1000 cows in total, there is still a significant improvement in all four indicators compared to when there is in effect no limit. The first two columns of Table 10.2 show that with a limit of 100 per commoner, the meadow supports more cows than when there is no limit: on average, 414 with a survival rate of 95% instead of 370 with a survival rate of 85%. Also, with this limit, the indicators over the last 10 years are better than for the period as a whole, while this is not the case for when there is no limit. Furthermore, the extreme inequality in the distribution of cows across the commoners is reduced. With a limit of 100 cows per commoner, after 25 years on average, the commoner with the most cows on the meadow has 22% (sd 3) of the total.

Reducing the limits increases the benefits. Arguably, a limit of 60 cows per commoner produces the best results, with an average of 476 cows being grazed with a survival rate of 99.7%. With a limit of 60 cows per commoner, there is only a slight increase in inequality over 25 years, and on average, 7 of the 10 commoners have the maximum number of cows permitted. But the

Box 10.5   Examples of commoners' experiences.

A's downward adjustment factor=0.5 and upward adjustment factor=0.1
B's downward adjustment factor=0.5 and upward adjustment factor=0.2
Both commoners start with 30 cows, as do all the other commoners.

In year 1, all A's cows survive, and so in year 2, A grazes 30×1.1=33 cows. All B's survive too, but B increases the number of cows in year 2 to 30×1.2=36.

This continues until year 11, by which time at the start of the year A puts 72 cows on the common and B 177. In total, the 10 commoners put 573 cows on the common. This overloads the common, and only 330 survive, including 42 belonging to A and 98 belonging to B. Following the adjustment rule, the next year, both graze only half as many as at the start of the previous year: A grazes 36 (72×0.5) and B 89 (177×0.5).

All is well until year 19. At the start of that year, A puts 66 cows on the meadow and B 313. In total, the 10 commoners put 598 cows on the common. The meadow cannot support this number and all but are 86 lost. Just 11 of A's cows and 50 of B's survive. The next year, year 20, A puts out 33 and B 157, being half of the number with which they started the previous year.

Each year, all the other commoners put more cows on the common until in year 25 there is another crash. By the end of year 25, there are just 182 cows on the common, of which A has 17 and B has 118.

Short bars mean that the number of cows at the end of the year was the same as at the start. Long bars mean that the number of cows dropped during the year, that is, less than 100% survived.

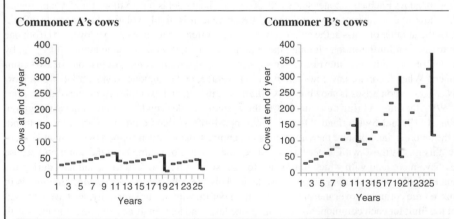

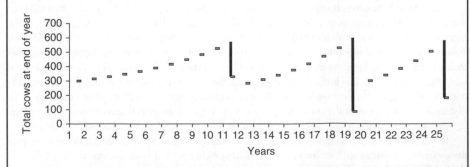

Table 10.2   Effect of imposing limits on the number of cows each commoner can graze on the meadow.

Limits	1000	100	90	80	70	60	50
Over 25 years							
Number of cows at end of year	370	414	414	410	443	476	425
(*Standard deviation*)	(25)	(23)	(31)	(20)	(26)	(27)	(29)
Per cent of cows surviving the summer	85.3	95.4	95.8	96.9	98.8	99.7	100.0
Per cent of years in which survival rate is less than 100%	22	11	11	8	4	2	0
Over the last 10 years							
Number of cows at end of year	361	446	440	439	490	506	443
(*Standard deviation*)	(45)	(28)	(41)	(30)	(35)	(36)	(33)
Per cent of cows surviving the summer	37.0	96.8	96.6	97.6	99.8	99.7	100.0
Per cent of years in which survival rate is less than 100%	32	13	13	7	1	2	0
Probability of achieving stability[a]	0	0	0	40	87	80	100

[a] Per cent of runs in which the number of cows was constant.

risk of occasional 'crashes' remains as indicated by the figures shown in Table 10.2 and shown in the top panel of Figure 10.3. To avoid any crashes, it would be necessary to impose a limit of 50, as shown in the last column of Table 10.2 and the bottom panel of Figure 10.3. But to achieve this stability means that there would on average be fewer cows grazed.

More information on this model – the *Meadow management model* – is in Appendix 10.A.

10.3   Discussion

To investigate the tragedy of the commons, we created a simple world, comprising two types of agents – commoners and cows – and an environment, and experimented with it. By keeping the model as simple as possible, with the minimum number of variables, we have been able to obtain a clear understanding of the processes involved by experimentation: by holding everything else the same and changing just one variable at a time. Despite its simplicity, the model can generate a wide variety of outcomes due to the fact that there are so many dynamic processes interacting, which is perhaps why it can be so difficult to reach sustainable stability.

The commoners are not assumed to optimise, but use only two heuristic behavioural rules. The only information they require is what happened to their cows during the last summer. So there are no additional monitoring costs involved. Nor is there any assumption that they possess full information of the past, let alone of the future.

This model has shown how the tragedy of the commons can be avoided using a simple rule that is actually observed in the real world. The key is having a limit on how many animals each commoner is allowed to graze. That is hardly a surprising result. Of more interest is the finding that even though the optimal limit might not be known, an approximation will still produce useful benefits (as shown in Table 10.2). Furthermore, because the system is grown from the action of individual agents, it is possible to drill down to see what happens. The model shows that if there is no limit set on the number of cows a commoner can graze, the distribution of cows between the commoners can become very unequal over the years. Even a simple limit of 100 significantly reduces this inequality. A simple rule has, in effect, brought some order to the highly unstable – maybe chaotic – system.

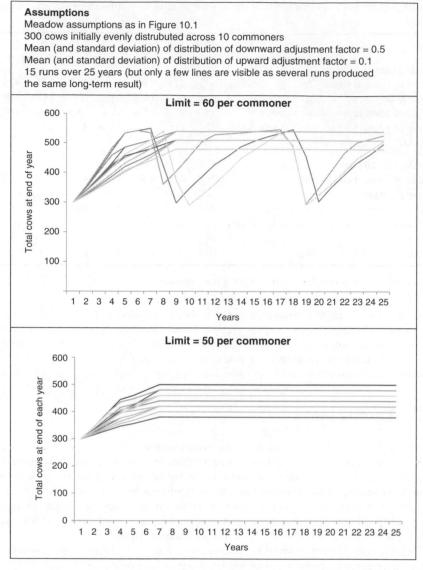

Figure 10.3   The number of cows at the end of each year with a limit of 60 or 50 per commoner.

This basic model could be explored by using different parameter values; and it could be extended in many other ways. For example, with very little reprogramming, the commoners could be given other decision rules. One of the advantages of ABM is that it is possible to test the effect of different behavioural rules. For instance, instead of using limits on the number of cows each commoner can graze, we could say that at the start of each year, the commoners inspect the grass on the meadow. If there is less than a certain amount – we have arbitrarily chosen 4000 grazing patches – then each commoner puts less stock out to graze in the coming summer. How many each commoner puts on depends on how many they grazed the previous year and their downward adjustment factor. If there is plenty of grass, the commoners increase their stock by their upward adjustment factors. This time,

Box 10.6   Cooperative action when little grazing is available.

Assumptions

Meadow assumptions as in Figure 10.1

500 cows initially evenly distributed across 10 commoners

Mean (and standard deviation) of distribution of downward adjustment factor = 0.1, triggered by less than 4000 grazing patches at the start of year

Mean (and standard deviation) of distribution of upward adjustment factor = 0.1

10 runs over 25 years

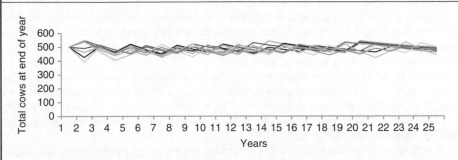

Each line represents a run: but not all 10 are visible due to overlap.

Mean (solid line) and plus and minus one standard deviation (dotted lines) in number of cows at the end of the year

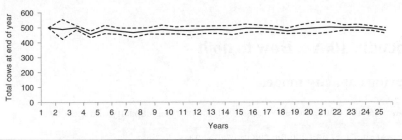

Over 25 years	
Number of cows at end of year	486
(*Standard deviation*)	(*28*)
Per cent of cows surviving the summer	99.5
Per cent of years in which survival rate is less than 100%	2

Over the last 10 years	
Number of cows at end of year	492
(*Standard deviation*)	(*11*)
Per cent of cows surviving the summer	100.0
Per cent of years in which survival rate is less than 100%	0
Probability of achieving stability[a]	0

[a] Per cent of runs in which the number of cows was constant.

we start each commoner with 50 cows and assume that both adjustment factors are distributed with a mean (and standard deviation) of 0.1. So, for example, if a commoner grazed 60 last year and there are less than 4000 grazing patches available at the start of this year and his downward adjustment factor is 0.1, then he will graze 54; but if there are 4000 or more grazing patches, he will increase his stock by 10% to 66%. At the macro level, although complete stability is not achieved, a large number of cows are supported, and there is a very high survival rate as shown in Box 10.6. But at the micro level, after 25 years, there is much more diversity between commoners in the sizes of their grazing herds than if there was simply a limit of 50 or 60 cows per commoner set. In this example, after 25 years, one commoner has on average 31% (sd 8) of the cows on the meadow.

Other scenarios are suggested in the 'Things to try' sections. Alternatively, readers may like to explore *Sugarscape*, a well-known agent-based model in which agents move across a landscape consuming its resources (Epstein & Axtell, 1996). Parts of the *Sugarscape* model are available in the NetLogo Library (Li & Wilensky, 2009).

Our model does not explain how cooperation is attained. While case studies have shown what factors contribute to long-term cooperative solutions, how such solutions have emerged is not clear. Exploring this, perhaps using variations of the repeated prisoner's dilemma game, may prove interesting. (There are examples of a multi-person iterated prisoner dilemma game in the NetLogo Library (Wilensky, 2002).)

Returning to the themes of the book – interaction, heterogeneity and dynamics, this chapter has demonstrated the importance of combining all three. The commoners interact with their environment and, indirectly, with each other over time, and they are heterogeneous in that they react to changes in different ways. Agent-based modelling facilitates the modelling of this complex dynamic system in a way that other methods simply cannot.

Appendix 10.A   How to do it

Carrying capacity model

Purpose: The aim of the model is to establish the carrying capacity of a meadow.

Entities: Agents are cows and the patches carry grass.
Stochastic processes: Distribution of cows over the meadow.
Initialisation:

- The initial number of cows

- How much each cow eats each week

- The weekly rate at which grass grows

- The minimum amount of grass on a patch required to feed a cow for a week

- The number of runs required

Outputs: Data on the amount of grass and the number of cows is collected and sent to a csv file.

The pseudocode is in Box 10.A.1 and a screenshot in Figure 10.A.1. For the full code, see the website: *Chapter 10 – Carrying Capacity Model*.

Box 10.A.1   Pseudocode for the carrying capacity model.

Create a world $101 \times 99 = 9999$ patches with no wrap-around.
Put grass with the maximum value of 1 on all the patches.
Create cows and distribute them over the meadow.

Weekly cycle

  The cows eat the grass on their patch.

  The grass then grows, according to a logistic function.

  Each cow moves to the nearest patch with sufficient grass to support it for a week.

  If a cow cannot find a patch with enough grass, the cow dies.

  Repeat this process for 25 weeks.

Data collection

  Ongoing counters record the number of runs performed, the number of weeks passed, the number of cows and the number of grass patches that can support a cow.

  Record at the start and end of each week the number of cows and the number of patches with enough grass to support a cow for a week.

  Record at the end of each run the distribution of patches by amount of grass at the start and end of the summer.

  Calculate the averages and standard deviations for the number of cows and number of grazing patches over all the runs.

  Display resulting data and send to a csv file.

Things to try using the carrying capacity model

Use the sliders to investigate:

- What happens if the cows eat more each week

- What happens if the grass grows more slowly

- What happens if the minimum amount of grass on a patch required to feed a cow is less

Advanced – requiring amending the program:

- What happens if the grass grows faster in the spring?

- What happens if the cows have different grazing habits, such as only being able to seek grazing within a limited distance?

- What happens if the cows have calves?

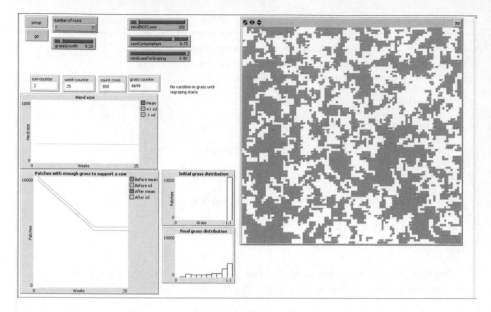

Figure 10.A.1   Screenshot of the carrying capacity model.

Meadow management model

Purpose: The aim of the model is to illustrate how a common area of grazing can be managed.
Entities: The patches carry grass and there are two types of agents: cows and commoners.
Stochastic processes:

- Distribution of cows over the meadow

- Each commoner's adjustment factors

- Allocation of cows to commoners

Initialisation:
The meadow

- How much each cow eats every week

- The weekly rate at which grass grows

- The minimum amount of grass on a patch required to feed a cow

The commoners

- The initial number of cows

- The mean (and standard deviation) of the adjustment factors

- The number of years

Box 10.A.2 Pseudocode for the meadow management model

Reproduce the carrying capacity model but with a larger world to accommodate the commoners in an area outside the meadow recording the results for just one run at a time (as because of the volatility it is not appropriate to average the results over several runs).

Create 10 commoners and locate in an area outside the meadow.
Allocate to each commoner:

- One tenth of the initial number of cows

- A downward adjustment factor based on a random normal distribution with a mean set by the modeller (and a standard deviation to equal the mean)

- An upward adjustment factor based on a random normal distribution with a mean set by the modeller (and a standard deviation to equal the mean)

- Ensure both the adjustment factors lie between 0 and 0.9, inclusive.

Annual cycle

- Cows graze as in the carrying capacity model.

- At the end of each year, all the cows die.

- The grass grows a little over the winter.

- Each commoner decides how many cows to put on the meadow for the summer based on their experience of the previous year and their adjustment factors.

- Repeat the process for the number of years chosen by the modeller.

Data collection

Record the number of cows grazed by each commoner at the start of each summer and how many survive until the end.

Record at the start and end of each year the number of cows and the number of patches with enough grass to support a cow for a week.

Outputs: Data on the amount of grass and the number of cows in total and belonging to each commoner is collected and sent to a csv file.

The pseudocode is in Box 10.A.2 and a screenshot in Figure 10.A.2. For the full code, see the website: *Chapter 10 – Meadow Management Model*.

Things to try using the meadow management model

Use the sliders to investigate the effect changing:

- What is the effect of changing the initial number of cows? It has been assumed that the initial number of cows is below the carrying capacity of the meadow. What happens if the initially number of cows put out to graze is above the sustainable level, say, 700?

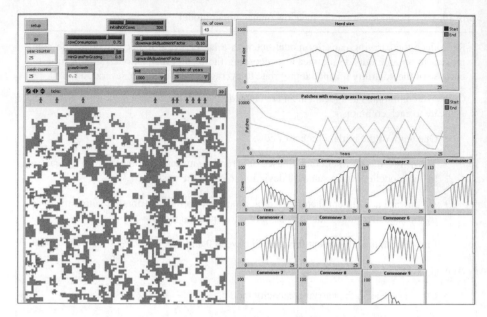

Figure 10.A.2   Screenshot of the meadow management model.

- What is the effect of using different mean (and standard deviation) of the adjustment factors?

- Under what circumstances is there more likely to be stability if the model is run for 50 instead of 25 years?

Advanced – requiring amending the program:

- Devise other decision rules: for example, in making their decision as to how many cows to graze, commoners might consider what happened to other commoners, perhaps their immediate neighbours, as well as themselves in the last year.

- It is very unlikely that all commoners have the same capacity to overwinter animals, and we suspect that in many cases, the distribution will roughly follow a power law with an exponent of about −1, that is, with one farmer having significantly more capacity than all the rest. (For a discussion of power law distributions, see Box 7.5.) Instead of distributing the cows evenly between the 10 commoners, give one 50% of the cows, two 12.5% each, three 5% each and the remaining four 2.5% each. (Hint: See how employees were distributed between firms in the *Guildford labour market model* in Chapter 7.)

- Explore how the limits might be reached through direct cooperation between commoners, drawing on Ostrom's seven key conditions for successful management of a CPR.

References

Armstrong, H.M., Gordon, I.J., Grant, S.A.. Hutchings, N.J., Milne, J.A. & Sibbald, A.R. (1997) A model of the grazing of hill vegetation by the sheep in the UK. I. The prediction of – vegetation biomass. A model of the grazing of hill vegetation by sheep in the UK. II. The prediction of offtake by sheep. *Journal of Applied Ecology*, 34, pp.166–207.

Begg, D., Vernasca, G., Fischer, S. & Dornbusch, R. (2011) *Economics*. Tenth Edition. London: McGraw-Hill Higher Education.

Chapman, D.S., Termansen, M., Quinn, C.H., Jin, N., Bonn, A., Cornell, S.J., Fraser, E.D.G., Hubacek, K., Kunin, W. E. & Reed, M.S. (2009) Modelling the coupled dynamics of moorland management and upland vegetation. *Journal of Applied Ecology*, 46, pp.278–288 [Online]. Available at: http://onlinelibrary.wiley.com/doi/10.1111/j.1365-2664.2009.01618.x/full [Accessed 29 September 2014].

DEFRA (2014) *Common land: management, protection and registering to use*. [Online]. Available at: https://www.gov.uk/common-land-management-protection-and-registering-to-use [Accessed 29 September 2014].

EBLEX (2013) *Planning Grazing Strategies for Better Returns*. Agriculture and Horticulture Development Board, Kenilworth [Online]. Available at: http://www.eblex.org.uk [Accessed 11 September 2014].

Epstein, J. & Axtell, R. (1996) *Growing Artificial Societies: Social Science from the Bottom Up*. Washington, DC: Brookings Institution Press.

Hardin, G. (1968) The Tragedy of the Commons. *Science*, 162, pp.243–1248.

Kahneman D. & Tversky, A. (1979) Prospect theory: An analysis of decision under risk. *Econometrica*, 47(2), pp.263–292.

Li, J. and Wilensky, U. (2009). *NetLogo Sugarscape 1 Immediate Growback model*. http://ccl.northwestern.edu/netlogo/models/Sugarscape1ImmediateGrowback and *NetLogo Sugarscape 2 Constant Growback model* Center for Connected Learning and Computer-Based Modeling, Northwestern University, Evanston, IL [Online]. Available at: http://ccl.northwestern.edu/netlogo/models/Sugarscape2ConstantGrowback. [Accessed 10 August 2014].

Liu, J., Dietz, T., Carpenter, S., Alberti, M., Carl Folke, C., Moran, E., Pell, A., Deadman, P., Kratz, T., Lubchenco, J., Ostrom, E., Ouyang, Z., Provencher, W., Redman, C., Schneider, S. & Taylor, W. (2007); Complexity of coupled human and natural systems. *Science*, 317, pp.1513–1516.

Natural England (2014) *Common Land* [Online]. Available at: http://www.naturalengland.org.uk/ourwork/landscape/protection/historiccultural/commonland/ [Accessed 10 August 2014].

Ostrom, E. (1990) *Governing the Commons*. Cambridge, MA: Cambridge University Press.

Perman, R. Ma, Y., McGilvray, J. & Common, M. (2003) *Natural Resource and Environmental Economics*. Harlow: Pearson.

Schindler, J. (2012a) Rethinking the tragedy of the commons: The integration of socio-psychological dispositions. *Journal of Artificial Societies and Social Simulation*, 15(1), 4 [Online]. Available at: http://jasss.soc.surrey.ac.uk/15/1/4.html [Accessed 5 August 2014].

Schindler, J. (2012b) A simple agent-based model of the tragedy of the commons. In: Troitzsch, K., Möhring, M. & Lotzmann, U., eds, *Proceedings 26th European Conference on Modelling and Simulation*. Dudweiler: European Council for Modelling and Simulation [Online]. Available at: http://www.openabm.org/files/models/3051/v1/doc/Article-Conf-Proceedings.pdf [Accessed 5 August 2014].

Straughton, E.A. (2008) *Common Grazing in the Northern English Uplands, 1800–1965*. Lewiston, New York: Edwin Mellon Press.

Strogatz, S. (1994) *Nonlinear Dynamics and Chaos*. Cambridge, MA: Westview.

Varian, H. (2010) *Intermediate Microeconomics*. Princeton: Princeton University Press.

Wilensky, U. (2002) *NetLogo PD N-Person Iterated model*. Center for Connected Learning and Computer-Based Modeling, Northwestern University, Evanston, IL [Online]. Available at: http://ccl.northwestern.edu/netlogo/models/PDN-PersonIterated [Accessed 3 January 2015].

11

Summary and conclusions

11.1 Introduction

We start this final chapter by summarising the models produced. We then go on to discuss the usefulness of agent-based models and the pros and the cons of using ABM in economics. We finally leave the reader with a list of further reading and resources.

11.2 The models

We have presented 19 models in this book. These include modules which are inputs to other models, models to illustrate theory, models for policy and a model of a real-world event. Some models have just two agents, but most have 1 000 and the largest has 10 001. In many models, the agents represent individuals or households. But in some, they represent institutions: firms or countries. In one case, they even represent non-human actors, namely, cows. These basic features are summarised in Table 11.1. The common characteristic is that all are parsimonious in that they make the minimum number of assumptions required to produce the desired result, following Doran and Palmer's (1995) advice:

> A standard modelling principle is that the level and complexity of a model should be chosen so that it answers the questions and embodies the theoretical elements we are interested in, but is otherwise as simple as possible.

We started in Chapter 3 with a model of the distribution of household income that matches the distribution observed in the United Kingdom. This introduced heterogeneity and established a micro–macro link in that it can be seen how each household contributes to the overall pattern observed. Next, we used this distribution alongside neoclassical utility theory to model consumer

Agent-Based Modelling in Economics, First Edition. Lynne Hamill and Nigel Gilbert.
© 2016 John Wiley & Sons, Ltd. Published 2016 by John Wiley & Sons, Ltd.

demand. But we then went on to show that for practical purposes, consumer demand can be modelled using budget constraints and price elasticities.

In Chapter 4, we introduced dynamics and interaction by allowing consumers to influence one another. We presented a simple way to model social networks, based on the idea of social circles. We then used this to explore the potential impact of positive feedback on consumer demand using threshold models. We showed how agent-based modelling is particularly suitable for threshold models because it can deal with both local influence and the influence of society as a whole. We then combined these two models, with other procedures, to examine the adoption of fixed-line phones in the United Kingdom between 1951 and 2001. That model showed that economic factors – prices and incomes – are not sufficient to explain the pattern observed: social interaction is essential. Overall, this chapter demonstrated that ABM offers a very powerful approach to the modelling of positive feedback because it can also allow for both heterogeneity and interaction.

In Chapter 5, we moved on to interaction in a market through barter. We started with the neo-classical framework of the Edgeworth Box and used ABM to explore its dynamics. First, we assumed the existence of a Walrasian auctioneer, but then we relaxed this assumption and allowed the agents to negotiate with one another directly. We then extended this to model a simple trading system involving 200 agents and two products. The model allowed us to explore various trading arrangements, and we showed that a simple stochastic peer-to-peer trading mechanism can produce a large increase in welfare, even if total utility is not actually maximised.

In Chapter 6, we introduced firms, starting with a model of a Cournot–Nash equilibrium. We introduced a simple dynamic system in which each firm based its output on what it believed the other firm produced in the last period. With ABM, it is easy to explore the dynamics and to allow for incomplete information. We show how even small errors in firms' knowledge can result in oscillations in output. We then added consumers. We started with the neoclassical perfect competition scenario to establish a baseline and then relaxed its assumptions, so that prices were simply a markup on costs and the shops adjust their supply, altering both their short- and long-term costs. Consumer demand was based on willingness to pay. Shops that did not compete successfully went out of business. This simple model produced the result that the greater competition, the higher are sales. Next, we adapted this model for digital products and services, such as selling software, music and games. Here, the diminishing returns to scale assumed in neoclassical economics does not hold. For simplicity, we ignored capacity constraints altogether. The model illustrated why firms selling such products should initially price high and then drop to increase quantity.

In Chapter 7, we turned to the labour market. The labour market is dynamic and there is great diversity among the participants, both workers and employers. We started by creating a model of the wage distribution, similar, but not the same, as the distribution of household income modelled in Chapter 3. We then produced a simple model of job search and explored the implications of our assumptions. Both modules were then incorporated into a model of a labour market based on our home town of Guildford. We were able to show how the large flows between different employment statuses observed in the UK labour market are consistent with stability at the macro level and how the greater is wage flexibility, the lower is the rate of unemployment, the lower the proportion of unemployed who are long-term unemployed and the greater the probability of moving from unemployment into work.

Chapter 8 examined the demand and supply of foreign currency. We focussed on the determination of exchange rates under different policy regimes. One agent represented a country and another, the rest of the world. The modeller could assign different characteristics to the country agent and choose the policy environment, either a floating or a fixed exchange rate. The model was used to explore different scenarios and highlighted the contrast between the dynamic systems of countries with floating exchange rates, like the United Kingdom and the United States, and those in the Eurozone.

Next, Chapter 9 examined the banking system, focussing on the dynamics of the fractional reserve system. Our model showed how potentially explosive this system is, which is not evident

Table 11.1 Summary of models.

Models	Type of model	No. of agents	Type of agents	Heterogeneity	Dynamics	Interaction	Macro–micro
					Key features		
Chapter 3							
Distribution of household budgets	Module	1000	Households	✓			✓
Utility function-based demand	Theoretical	1000	Households	✓			✓
Practical demand model	Policy	1000	Households	✓			✓
Chapter 4							
Social circles	Module	1000	Individuals/households	✓	✓	✓	✓
Threshold	Module	1000	Individuals/households	✓	✓	✓	✓
Phone adoption	Case study	1000	Households	✓	✓	✓	✓
Chapter 5							
Edgeworth Box game	Theoretical	2	Individuals	✓			
Edgeworth Box random	Theoretical	2	Individuals	✓			
Red Cross parcels	Theoretical	200	Individuals	✓			
Chapter 6							
Cournot–Nash	Theoretical	2	Firms	✓	✓	✓	
Shops	Theoretical	1000	Firms and consumers	✓	✓	✓	
Digital world	Theoretical	1000	Firms and consumers	✓	✓	✓	
Chapter 7							
Wage distribution	Module	1000	Individuals	✓	✓		
Job search	Module	1100	Firms and individuals	✓	✓	✓	✓
Guildford labour market	Policy	1100	Firms and individuals	✓		✓	✓
Chapter 8							
International trade	Policy	2	Countries		✓		✓
Chapter 9							
Banking	Policy	10 001	Firm and individuals	✓	✓	✓	
Chapter 10							
Carrying capacity	Module	100–2000	Cows		✓	✓	
Meadow management	Policy	110–1010	Individuals and cows	✓	✓	✓	✓

in the standard textbook presentation, and demonstrated the importance of liquidity and capital adequacy rules for the stability of the banking system. The model distinguished between borrowers and savers and was therefore able to allow for the fact that only a minority are savers (unlike representative agent models) and to suggest the effect of the banking system on the distribution of savings and loans. It also brought together in one model the micro and the macro, usually treated separately in economic textbooks.

Finally, Chapter 10 illustrated how ABM can be used to model the interaction between humans and the environment. Taking the tragedy of the commons as its theme, the first model created an environment (a meadow) and allowed the modeller to assess how many grazing animals (cows) it could support. People were then added and different management systems of this common pool resource explored. The model was able to generate a wide variety of outcomes because there are so many dynamic processes interacting, which is perhaps why it can be so difficult to reach sustainable stability. Furthermore, the commoners are not assumed to optimise, but use only two heuristic behavioural rules, which nevertheless still produce useful benefits. Also, because the system is grown from the action of individual agents, it is possible to drill down from the top level to see how it was created by individual actions.

Table 11.1 summarises the 19 models. It divides them into four types:

- Modules: models can stand alone but which are later incorporated into larger models.

- Theoretical: models designed to implement economic theory.

- Policy: practical models that could be used to address policy questions.

- Case study: a model designed to reproduce an observed event.

11.3   What makes a good model?

We have mentioned in Chapter 2 and elsewhere the importance of verification, that is, of ensuring that the program is doing what the modeller intended. This is clearly essential. But a bigger and more difficult question is: what makes a model a good one? This assessment is called validation. As Windrum *et al.* (2007) noted, the validation of agent-based models in economics is not straightforward.

Putting aside the questions that apply to the validation of all modelling, such as the quality of the data used to validate the model, agent-based modelling produces special problems because of the stochastic processes involved and its modelling of complex, in the sense of non-linear, systems. For instance, simply counting the number of times the model reproduces the observed phenomenon may not be a good indicator of the model's quality. It may be that under the circumstances described by the model, the observed outcome is unlikely, but is nevertheless what actually happened. The problem is that we do not, and can never, know which is the case: the model is wrong or the actual situation is rare, although we may be able to assess probabilities. That is why sensitivity analysis, important in all modelling, is arguably more so in agent-based modelling.

For real-world models like that of phone adoption, which we presented in Chapter 4, we followed a standard approach in simulation modelling: to see whether the model can reproduce the observed macro data. Goodness of fit can be measured using standard statistical measures. But a good fit is not sufficient to make a good model. As Morgan (2012, pp.330–334) pointed out, just because the simulated data 'mimics' the real world does not mean that the process generating the data in the model is equivalent to the process operating in the real world. But Morgan was not discussing agent-based models. Epstein, commenting on the issue in relation to ABM, argued that 'generative sufficiency is a necessary but not sufficient condition for explanation' and that, to be judged a good model, it must also make sense at the micro level (Epstein, 2006, p.53). In other words, the model as a whole must tell a convincing 'story'. Thus, in the phone adoption model, we used both the goodness-of-fit criterion and the plausibility of the underlying assumptions, such as households influencing one another. The model of the Guildford labour market in Chapter 7 illustrates Epstein's point well in that the overall macro level could be easily replicated by a much simpler model but the value of the model lies in reproducing the underlying micro activity and showing that it does generate the observed macro phenomenon.

However, for abstract models, there is no real-world data with which to compare the output. That is true of many of the models presented in this book. But the models allowed us to investigate theories, so as to:

- Move away from the textbook focus on comparative statics to dynamic processes: for example, the dynamics of the Cournot–Nash model in Chapters 6 suggested a source of economic instability, as did the potentially explosive dynamics in the banking system identified in Chapter 9.

- Investigate non-equilibrium positions as in the labour market model in Chapter 7.

- Discard assumptions about actors optimising in favour of various types of bounded rationality using heuristics, for example, in Chapter 10.

Whether an abstract agent-based model is of value depends on its contribution to our understanding of the economic system.

To sum up, the aim of validation is to assess the quality of the model. One approach is to measure the extent to which the observed macroeconomic data can be explained by micro level interactions. But that alone is not sufficient. To be good, an agent-based model must also make sense at the micro level, both in the characteristics of the agents and the manner in which they interact. Doing such assessments in a consistent and coherent way remains a challenge. For more on the general issues of the validation of agent-based models, see Gilbert (2007, pp.64–76) and with special reference to agent-based economic models, Windrum et al. (2007).

11.4   Pros and cons of ABM

We have demonstrated the ease with which ABM can handle heterogeneity, dynamics and interaction, and we have shown how it can be used to bridge the gap between micro and macro. We have also shown that ABM can be used to model systems without assuming that agents – be they people or institutions – are optimising or that the system reaches an equilibrium. This is in stark contrast to the economic mathematical models that are based on optimisation or equilibrium or both (Morgan, 2012, pp.394–396). To make the mathematics tractable, it has been necessary to rely on a set of highly unrealistic assumptions which have been widely criticised by the complexity and 'post-Walrasian' economists mentioned in Chapter 1 and by many others. With ABM, we can move away from this restrictive, traditional approach. Repeatedly, we have shown that useful models can be built without these assumptions. Rather than optimising with full information, the agents follow rules of thumb based on limited information. For example, in the practical demand model in Chapter 3, households managed their budget rather than maximised their utility, and in Chapter 5, shops did not maximise profits but followed simple pricing rules.

ABM certainly has potential to improve our understanding of economics, but there are many issues still to be addressed and ABM is not without its critics. Some of the criticisms result from a failure to understand simulation (Waldherr & Wijermans, 2013). This implies that ABM practitioners have to explain better and be more transparent, by, for instance, making their code available.

An example of the sort of criticism made by traditional economists is when they ask 'where are the equations?' As shown in this book, it is possible to express some of the key processes in equations. Mathematics is used in ABM but usually not to solve sets of equations in order to optimise or find an equilibrium. A possibly related criticism is that ABMs have too many variables (Waldherr & Wijermans, 2013). Yet surely one of the advantages of ABM is that it exposes the assumptions that have to be made in formulating any kind of model. Is it really better that these are left unidentified?

However, there is a real and major problem with the use of ABM in economics and that is the lack of standardisation as noted, for example, by Windrum *et al.* (2007). Once modellers move away from optimisation, they are faced with an enormous choice of alternative behavioural rules. There are no standards and each modeller uses their own, often probably without thoroughly exploring the implications of their assumptions. For example, Balke and Gilbert (2014) identified 14 types of decision-making processes used in ABM. Much more work of this kind is needed. The lack of standardisation is recognised within the ABM community: for example, Heath *et al.* (2009) called for 'standard techniques, practices, philosophies and methodologies' and Squazzoni (2010) called to move on from the current 'hand-crafted' approach to use instead 'standard practices, methods and scientific communication'. This situation is perhaps inevitable given that ABM is relatively new. The time and effort devoted to Agent-Based Computational Economics (ACE) has to date been very small. (See Farmer, 2014, for an estimate.) In contrast, neoclassical economics has been the focus of economists for 100 years or more; and dynamic stochastic general equilibrium (DSGE) models have been developed over some 40 years. The ACE community needs to develop suites of modules that are based on widely agreed assumptions and accepted behavioural rules which can be plugged together to build models.

Not only do models need to be standardised but also better data is needed. For example, for some policy work, we need demographic modules that reflect reality. The phone adoption model in Chapter 4 showed just how difficult modelling the real world is and how it required an enormous amount of detail about demographic dynamics. This need is becoming recognised and is starting to be addressed, for example, by France's *Agence Nationale de la Recherché (2014)*. Its project *Gen** is developing tools and methods to generate realistic synthetic populations for agent-based social simulation. More work of this kind is needed. There is a related issue: lack of data. As Keynes' theories and the development of macroeconomic models in the 1930s gave rise to identifying the need for new types of data, so ABM requires new data. Often, modellers do not know how economic agents will behave and have to resort to stochastic processes. Behavioural economics will help to fill this gap.

Practitioners of ABM are keen to use their skills in the policy context. We touched on this when we modelled the labour market in Chapter 7. However, policy analysts will only adopt ABM if it provides something better than they already have. For example, in the early 1980s, micro-simulation was adopted because it provided a much better way of examining the impact of changes in tax and benefits than the method then used, applying changes to hypothetical families. ABM needs to demonstrate that it can offer more than existing models. We have shown that it does have this potential, but that much work needs to be done for that potential to be realised. We hope that this book provides the incentive to develop further the use of ABM in economics.

References

Agence Nationale de la Recherché (2014) *Gen** [Online] Available at: http://www.irit.fr/genstar/ [Accessed 30 December 2014].

Balke, T. & Gilbert, N. (2014) How do agents make decisions? A survey. *Journal of Artificial Societies and Social Simulation*, 17(4), p.13 [Online] Available at: http://jasss.soc.surrey.ac.uk/17/4/13.html [Accessed 30 December 2014].

Doran, J. & Palmer, M. (1995) The EOS Project. In: Gilbert, N. & Conte, R., eds, *Artificial Societies*. London: UCL Press, pp.103–125.

Epstein, J.M. (2006) *Generative Social Science*. Princeton: Princeton University Press.

Farmer, D. (2014) *Slides presented to ESRC Conference on Diversity in Macroeconomics*, University of Essex, Wivenhoe Park. [Online] Available at: http://www.acefinmod.com/docs/ESRC/Session%202/ essexMacro2.pdf [Accessed 30 December 2014].

Gilbert, N. (2007) *Agent-Based Models*. London: Sage.

Heath, B. Hill, R. & Ciarallo, F. (2009) A survey of agent-based modeling practices (January 1998 to July 2008). *Journal of Artificial Societies and Social Simulation*, 12(4), p.9 [Online] Available at: http://jasss. soc.surrey.ac.uk/12/4/9.html [Accessed 30 December 2014].

Squazzoni, F. (2010) The impact of agent-based models in the social sciences after 15 years of incursions. *History of Economic Ideas*, xviii, pp.197–233.

Waldherr, A. & Wijermans, N. (2013) Communicating social simulation models to sceptical minds. *Journal of Artificial Societies and Social Simulation*, 16(4), p.13 [Online] Available at: http://jasss.soc.surrey.ac. uk/16/4/13.html [Accessed 30 December 2014].

Windrum, P., Fagiolo, G. & Moneta, A. (2007) Empirical validation of agent-based models: Alternatives and prospects. *Journal of Artificial Societies and Social Simulation*, 10(2) [Online] Available at: http://jasss. soc.surrey.ac.uk/10/2/8.html. [Accessed 5 January 2015].

Further reading and resources

Economics

Arthur, W.B. (2014) *Complexity and the Economy*. New York: Oxford University Press.

Boero, R., Morini, M., Sonnessa, M. & Terna, P. (2015) *Agent-based Models of the Economy*. London: Palgrave Macmillan.

Colander, D. (2006) *Post Walrasian Macroeconomics*. Cambridge, MA: Cambridge University Press.

Gilbert, N. (2007) *Agent-Based Models*. London: Sage.

Helbing, D. & Kirman, A. (2013) Rethinking economics using complexity theory. *Real-World Economics Review*, 64, 2 July 2013, pp.23–52 [Online] Available at: http://www.paecon.net/PAEReview/issue64/ HelbingKirman64.pdf [Accessed 3 January 2015].

Morgan, M.S. (2012) *The World in the model*. Cambridge: Cambridge University Press.

Tesfatsion, L. & Judd, K.L. (2006) *Handbook of Computational Economics. Volume 2*. Amsterdam: North-Holland.

Agent-based modelling (ABM)

Epstein, J.M. (2014) *Agent_Zero: Toward Neurocognitive Foundations for Generative Social Science*. Princeton: Princeton University Press.

Epstein, J.M. & Axtell, R. (1996) *Growing Artificial Societies. Social Science from the Bottom Up*. Cambridge, MA: MIT Press.

Gilbert, N. & Troitzsch, K. (2005) *Simulation for the Social Scientist*. Oxford: Oxford University Press.

Grimm, V., Berger, U., DeAngelis, D.L., Polhill, J.G., Giske, J. & Railsback, S.F. (2010) The ODD protocol: A review and first update. *Ecological Modelling*, 221, pp.2760–2768.

Railsback, S.F. & Grimm, V. (2011) *Agent-Based and Individual-Based Modeling: A Practical Introduction*. Princeton: Princeton University Press.

Wilensky, U. & Rand, W. (2015) *An Introduction to Agent-Based Modeling: Modeling Natural, Social and Engineered Complex Systems with NetLogo*. Cambridge, MA: MIT Press.

Online resources

Agent-Based Computational Economics http://www2.econ.iastate.edu/tesfatsi/ace.htm [Accessed 3 February 2015].

Journal of Artificial Societies and Social Simulation http://jasss.soc.surrey.ac.uk/JASSS.html [Accessed 3 February 2015].

NetLogo. https://ccl.northwestern.edu/netlogo [Accessed 3 February 2015].

Open ABM: tutorials, model library and forums run by Network for Computational Modeling for SocioEcological Science (CoMSES Net) http://www.openabm.org/ [Accessed 3 February 2015].

Mailing lists and forums

NetLogo Users Group email list. https://groups.yahoo.com/neo/groups/netlogo-users/info [Accessed 3 February 2015].

SIMSOC mailing list. https://www.jiscmail.ac.uk/cgi-bin/webadmin?A0=simsoc [Accessed 3 February 2015].

StackOverflow community. http://stackoverflow.com/questions/tagged/netlogo [Accessed 3 February 2015].

Organisations

Artificial Economics Conferences http://www.irit.fr/AE2014/ [Accessed 31 January 2015].

Computational Social Science Society of the Americas (CSSSA) https://computationalsocialscience.org/ [Accessed 8 January 2015].

European Social Simulation Association (ESSA) http://www.essa.eu.org/ [Accessed 8 January 2015].

Pan-Asian Association for Agent-based Approach in Social Systems Sciences (PAAA) [Accessed 8 January 2015].

Index